PowerShell Fundamentals

A practical foundation in PowerShell commands, modules, data, objects, operators, and control flow

Chris Dent

<packt>

PowerShell Fundamentals

Portfolio Director: Kartikey Pandey
Relationship Lead: Aaron Tanna
Project Manager: Sonam Pandey
Content Engineer: Sayali Pingale
Technical Editor: Aysha Nadeem
Indexer: Tejal Soni
Presentation Designer: Vijay Kamble
Growth Lead: Meghal Patel

First published: September 2026

Production reference: 1250826

Published by Packt Publishing Ltd.
Grosvenor House
11 St Paul's Square
Birmingham
B3 1RB, UK.

ISBN 978-1-80876-139-3
www.packtpub.com

Contributors

About the author

Chris Dent is an automation specialist with a deep interest in the PowerShell language. He is often found answering questions about PowerShell in UK and virtual PowerShell user groups. Chris has been developing in PowerShell since 2007 and has released several modules over the years.

I would like to thank my wife, Emily, and my children, Lizzy and Thomas, for their continued support.

About the reviewer

Mike Roberts is a PowerShell ninja, both in his profession and on his blog, where he teaches it: `https://gngr.ninja`. Through his blog he hopes to educate and inspire others by demonstrating what different technologies are capable of.

I am eternally grateful for the support of my friends and family. Thank you!

Table of Contents

Chapter 3: Variables, Arrays, and Hashtables 77

Chapter 6: Conditional Statements and Loops 255

Preface

PowerShell is an object-oriented scripting language aimed at systems administrators that was invented by Jeffrey Snover. PowerShell was first conceived as far back as 2002 and entered mainstream use in 2006. Exchange 2007 was one of the first major systems to adopt it as an administration language.

PowerShell has come a long way over the years. PowerShell 7 smooths over a lot of the rough edges in the original releases of the cross-platform PowerShell Core (PowerShell 6).

Like any good scripting language, PowerShell is the glue that ties automated processes together. It is a vital part of the Microsoft ecosystem and is great in heterogeneous environments.

Who this book is for

This book is for PowerShell developers, system administrators, and script authors, new and old, who wish to explore the capabilities and possibilities of the language.

What this book covers

Chapter 1, Introduction to PowerShell, introduces you to editors, the help system, command naming, and more.

Chapter 2, Modules, explores finding, installing, and using modules in PowerShell. Snap-ins are not part of PowerShell 7 but are briefly explored as a legacy feature of PowerShell 5.

Chapter 3, Variables, Arrays, and Hashtables, covers important topics in PowerShell. The chapter explores the use of variables, as well as the capabilities of collections.

Chapter 4, Working with Objects in PowerShell, looks at the concept of objects in PowerShell and the generic commands available for selecting, filtering, and manipulating values.

Chapter 5, Operators, explores the large variety of operators available in PowerShell.

Chapter 6, Conditional Statements and Loops, covers the tools used to make decisions in scripts in PowerShell. This chapter explores keywords like If and the different loop styles available.

To get the most out of this book

Some familiarity with operating systems would be beneficial.

Visual Studio Code (`https://code.visualstudio.com/`) is used a few times in the book and is a useful tool to have available throughout.

Download the color images

Your purchase includes a color, DRM-free PDF copy of this book, ideal for viewing color images, screenshots, and diagrams. Refer to the *Free benefits with your book section* at the end of the *Preface* to unlock your PDF copy.

Conventions used

There are a number of text conventions used throughout this book.

CodeInText: Indicates code words in text, environment variables, class and method names, filenames, extensions, paths, commands, and user input. For example: "By default, `Save-Help` (and `Update-Help`) will not download help content more often than once every 24 hours."

A block of code is set as follows:

```
Get-Process |
    Select-Object Name, ID -First 1
```

When we wish to draw your attention to a particular part of a code block, the relevant lines or items are set in bold:

```
Get-Process |
    Select-Object Name, ID
```

Any command-line input or output is written as follows:

```
PS> Get-Process | Select-Object Name, ID -First 1

Name    Id
----    --
Pwsh  5068
```

Bold: Indicates a new term, an important word, or words that you see on the screen. For example: "Select **System info** from the **Administration** panel."

Note

Warnings or important notes appear like this.

Tip

Tips and practical recommendations appear like this

Free benefits with your book

This book comes with free benefits to support your learning. Activate them now for instant access (see the "*How to Unlock*" section for instructions).

Here's a quick overview of what you can instantly unlock with your purchase:

How to Unlock

Scan the QR code (or go to `packtpub.com/unlock`). Search for this book by name, confirm the edition, and then follow the steps on the page.

UNLOCK NOW

Note: Keep your invoice handy. Purchases made directly from Packt don't require one

Share your thoughts

Once you've read *PowerShell Fundamentals,* we'd love to hear your thoughts! Scan the QR code below to go straight to the Amazon review page for this book and share your feedback.

`https://packt.link/r/1808761391`

Your review is important to us and the tech community and will help us make sure we're delivering excellent quality content.

Stay ahead in AI-Powered networking – join 16,000+ subscribers

AI is changing how networks are designed, managed, automated, and secured. The AI Networking newsletter delivers focused, practical insights to help networking professionals keep pace with this shift.

Each issue explores topics such as:

- AI-assisted network automation and troubleshooting
- Agentic workflows for network operations
- MCP, network copilots, and emerging AI tools
- Guardrails for safe and reliable automation
- Real-world approaches to building AI-ready networks

Whether you're a network engineer, infrastructure professional, automation specialist, or technology leader, AI Networking helps you understand what is changing (and how to apply it) without the noise.

Scan the QR code to join for free and get weekly insights straight to your inbox:

`Https://theainetworkengineer.substack.com/`

Get in touch

Feedback from our readers is always welcome.

General feedback: If you have questions about any aspect of this book or have any general feedback, please email us at `customercare@packt.com` and mention the book's title in the subject of your message.

Errata: Although we have taken every care to ensure the accuracy of our content, mistakes do happen. If you have found a mistake in this book, we would be grateful if you reported this to us. Please visit `http://www.packt.com/submit-errata`, click **Submit Errata**, and fill in the form.

Piracy: If you come across any illegal copies of our works in any form on the internet, we would be grateful if you would provide us with the location address or website name. Please contact us at `copyright@packt.com` with a link to the material.

If you are interested in becoming an author: If there is a topic that you have expertise in and you are interested in either writing or contributing to a book, please visit `http://authors.packt.com/`.

1

Introduction to PowerShell

PowerShell is a shell scripting language from Microsoft originally released for Windows in 2006. PowerShell was written to appeal to systems administrators and presents a great deal of its functionality as commands such as `Get-ChildItem`, `Get-Content`, `New-Item`, and so on.

Microsoft Exchange was one of the first systems to embrace PowerShell with the release of Exchange 2007.

Active Directory tools followed a few years later along with tools to manage on-premises virtualization platforms from VMware and Microsoft Hyper-V.

More recently, PowerShell is offered as a management tool for cloud platforms like Azure and AWS. In addition to modules which can be used to interact with either service, Azure and AWS both offer in-browser shells to directly manage services.

Windows PowerShell, or Desktop Edition, includes the original version through to 5.1, which is the final release of the Windows-specific shell. Windows PowerShell versions are based on .NET Framework.

In 2018 the first version of PowerShell Core Edition was released with PowerShell 6. The move from .NET Framework to .NET Core allows the latest versions of PowerShell to run on Linux and macOS, as well as Windows.

Since then, PowerShell 7 has been released and continues to receive new features and updates. The core edition of PowerShell has seen a move through .NET Core 3.1 to .NET 10 with PowerShell 7.6.

The other significant difference between Windows PowerShell and PowerShell is that PowerShell 6 and above are open source. The project is on GitHub and is open to public contributors: `https://github.com/powershell/powershell`.

A significant number of community contributors have been making changes, making commands more usable and useful, adding new features, and fixing bugs. For example, the `Invoke-WebRequest` and `Invoke-RestMethod` were completely overhauled in PowerShell 6, greatly improving how they perform while retaining much in the way of backward compatibility.

Several core commands were removed while these changes were being made. For example, the `Get-WmiObject` and `New-WebServiceProxy` commands have been removed. The reasons for this vary; in some cases, the commands are fundamentally incompatible with .NET Core. In a few cases, the commands were under restricted licensing agreements and could not be made open source. These differences are highlighted in this book, and alternatives are demonstrated where possible.

Despite all this change, PowerShell still maintains strong backward compatibility with very few breaking changes between the two editions. Operators and language keywords remain the same, and most changes are new features instead of changes to existing ones. Exceptions to this tend to be edge cases like parameter changes to `Get-Content` when reading byte content. These differences in behavior are highlighted throughout this book. Lessons learned using Windows PowerShell can be applied to PowerShell 7, and they will continue to be applicable to future versions of PowerShell.

While exploring the fundamentals of the language, this first section of the book attempts to cover as many of the building blocks as possible.

This chapter explores a diverse set of topics:

- What is PowerShell?
- The command line
- PowerShell editors
- Getting help
- Command naming and discovery
- About profile scripts
- Parameters, values, and parameter sets
- Introduction to providers
- Introduction to splatting
- Parser modes
- Experimental features

> **Note**
>
> **Technical requirements**
>
> This chapter makes use of the following on the Windows platform: PowerShell 7

At the start of this chapter, PowerShell was described as a shell scripting language. But this is perhaps not a complete description.

> **Note**
>
> **Download the PDF version of this book**
>
> Your purchase includes a DRM-free PDF copy of this book, the code bundle, and a range of exclusive benefits. To unlock everything, follow the *Free benefits with your book* section in the *Preface*.

What is PowerShell?

PowerShell is a mixture of a command-line interface, a functional programming language, and an object-oriented programming language. PowerShell is based on Microsoft .NET, which gives it a level of open flexibility that was not available in Microsoft's scripting languages (such as VBScript or batch) before this.

PowerShell has been written to be highly discoverable. It has substantial built-in help which is accessible within the console via the `Get-Help` command. PowerShell has commands such as `Get-Member` to allow a user to discover the details of any objects it returns.

PowerShell 7 can be installed alongside Windows PowerShell. Windows PowerShell is installed in `Windows\System32` by the Windows Management Framework packages, and it cannot be moved elsewhere. PowerShell Core and 7 are both installed in the `Program Files` folder and do not share any of the files used by Windows PowerShell. Preview versions of PowerShell can be installed alongside the full releases and have separate folder structures.

Command line customization is a popular subject, and several tools are available to help.

Installing PowerShell

PowerShell 7 is not installed with the operating system by default. It can be installed in a variety of ways. Perhaps the easiest is to use `winget`:

```
winget install --id Microsoft.PowerShell
```

PowerShell is also available on the Microsoft Store, and via third-party package managers including Chocolatey (`https://chocolatey.org/`) and Scoop (`https://scoop.sh/`).

PowerShell may also be downloaded directly from GitHub, which includes preview versions and release candidates: `https://github.com/PowerShell/PowerShell/releases`.

When installing PowerShell, the 64-bit version should be preferred. Up until PowerShell 7.6, an MSI installer is offered. Releases from 7.7 onwards will offer an MSIX installer instead.

The PowerShell team provides documentation for installing PowerShell on all supported platforms: `https://learn.microsoft.com/en-us/powershell/scripting/install/install-powershell?view=powershell-7.6`.

Once PowerShell is installed, execution policy is a common hurdle.

About execution policy

Execution policy is a feature of PowerShell used to control how (if at all) scripts can run on a system or for a user.

For example, if a script is created and then runs, one of two errors may be shown, the first when execution policy is `AllSigned`:

```
PS> Set-Content -Path .\test.ps1 -Value 'Write-Host "Hello world"'
PS> .\test.ps1
.\test.ps1: File C:\dev\test.ps1 cannot be loaded. The file C:\dev\test.ps1 is not
digitally signed. You cannot run this script on the current system. For more
information about running scripts and setting execution policy, see
about_Execution_Policies at https://go.microsoft.com/fwlink/?LinkID=135170.
```

Or the second when execution policy is `Restricted`:

```
.\test.ps1: File C:\dev\test.ps1 cannot be loaded because running scripts is
disabled on this system. For more information, see about_Execution_Policies at
https://go.microsoft.com/fwlink/?LinkID=135170.
```

The current policy may be seen using `Get-ExecutionPolicy`:

```
PS> Get-ExecutionPolicy
Restricted
```

Execution policy may be applied in several scopes; it may be organizationally set, or just a default value. The `List` parameter can be used to show the source of the policy:

```
PS> Get-ExecutionPolicy -List

        Scope ExecutionPolicy
        ----- ---------------
MachinePolicy       Undefined
   UserPolicy       Undefined
      Process      Restricted
  CurrentUser       Undefined
 LocalMachine    RemoteSigned
```

In the example above, the policy is set for the current process only; it was set to demonstrate this problem.

The `about_Execution_Policies` help file is also available online: `https://learn.microsoft.com/powershell/module/microsoft.powershell.core/about/about_execution_policies`. It shows the default and briefly explains each policy.

As described in the first part of the long description, execution policy is not a security system. There are many ways to bypass policy, even if it is using the strictest setting.

If desirable, and assuming appropriate permissions, the policy may be permanently changed for the current user (or `LocalMachine`) using the following command:

```
Set-ExecutionPolicy RemoteSigned -Scope CurrentUser
```

Execution policy must be permissive to run the `PSReadLine` module, which improves the command line experience.

The command line

PowerShell 7 comes with a module called PSReadLine. A module is a collection of related commands. Modules are explored in greater detail in *Chapter 2, Modules*.

`PSReadLine` provides command-line syntax highlighting, preserves history between sessions, and offers completion services when writing commands.

`PSReadLine` can be configured to offer command completion based on previously typed commands. This is a useful feature when using similar commands in the console and one which can save searching history for the right command. By default, PSReadLine 2.4.5 uses a history and a command prediction plugin. The plugin may be explicitly enabled using the `Set-PSReadLineOption` command.

```
Set-PSReadLineOption -PredictionSource HistoryAndPlugin
```

Once enabled, PSReadLine will offer suggestions based on typed content which may be completed using *Tab* as shown in *Figure 1.1*.

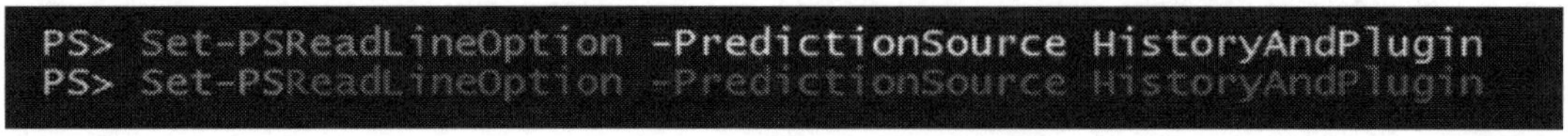

Figure 1.1: PSReadLine Predictive completion

By default, Tab can be used to complete any command or parameter, and a variety of arguments for parameters. In addition to tab completion, PSReadLine allows the use of control and space to provide menu style completion. For example, entering the following partial command:

```
Get-ChildItem -
```

Then pressing control and space (immediately after the hyphen) will show a menu which can be navigated using the cursor keys as shown in *Figure 1.2*:

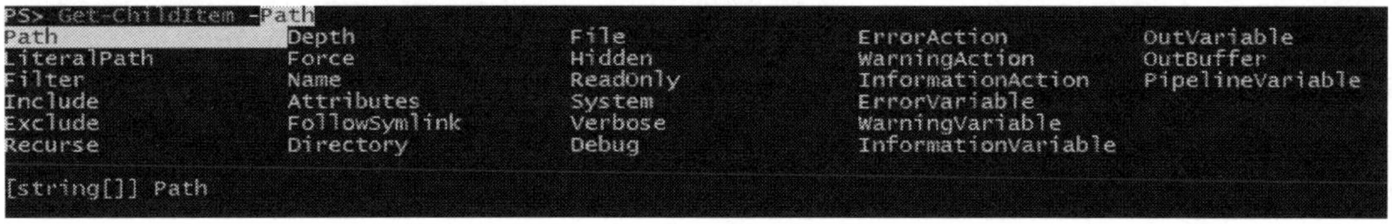

Figure 1.2: PSReadLine List completion

In PowerShell, the prompt displayed is controlled by a function named prompt. A very simple prompt can be set as shown below:

```
function prompt {
    "$env:USERNAME $pwd PS>"
}
```

On Mac and Linux, `$env:USERNAME` would be swapped for `$env:USER`.

The default prompt can be restored by restarting PowerShell. A profile script is required to make changes on console restart. See `about_profiles` for more information:

```
Get-Help about_profiles
```

Several modules and tools exist to help customize prompts in PowerShell:

- PowerLine: `https://github.com/Jaykul/PowerLine`
- oh-my-posh: `https://ohmyposh.dev/`
- Starship: `https://starship.rs/`

PowerShell is a complex language; a good editor can save time finding the right syntax to use in a script.

PowerShell editors

While PowerShell scripts can be written using the Notepad application alone, it is rarely desirable. Using an editor that was designed to work with PowerShell can save a lot of time.

Editors with explicit support for PowerShell, such as Visual Studio Code (VS Code with the PowerShell extension) and the PowerShell Studio editor offer automatic completion (IntelliSense). IntelliSense reduces the amount of cross-referencing help content required while writing code. Finding a comfortable editor early on is a good way to ease into PowerShell; memorizing commands and parameters is not necessary.

In addition to VS Code and PowerShell Studio, Windows PowerShell comes with PowerShell ISE. PowerShell ISE has not been updated for PowerShell 6 and higher and will only function correctly for Windows PowerShell Desktop Edition.

PowerShell Studio is not free but includes graphical user interface development features.

VS Code is a highly recommended editor for PowerShell as it is free and supports a wide variety of different languages. VS Code is an open-source editor that was published by Microsoft and can be downloaded from `http://code.visualstudio.com`. VS Code tends to be the editor of choice for many in the PowerShell community.

The functionality of VS Code can be enhanced by using extensions from the marketplace: `https://marketplace.visualstudio.com/VSCode`. The Extension installer is part of the VS Code user interface, and the types of available extensions are shown in *Figure 1.3*:

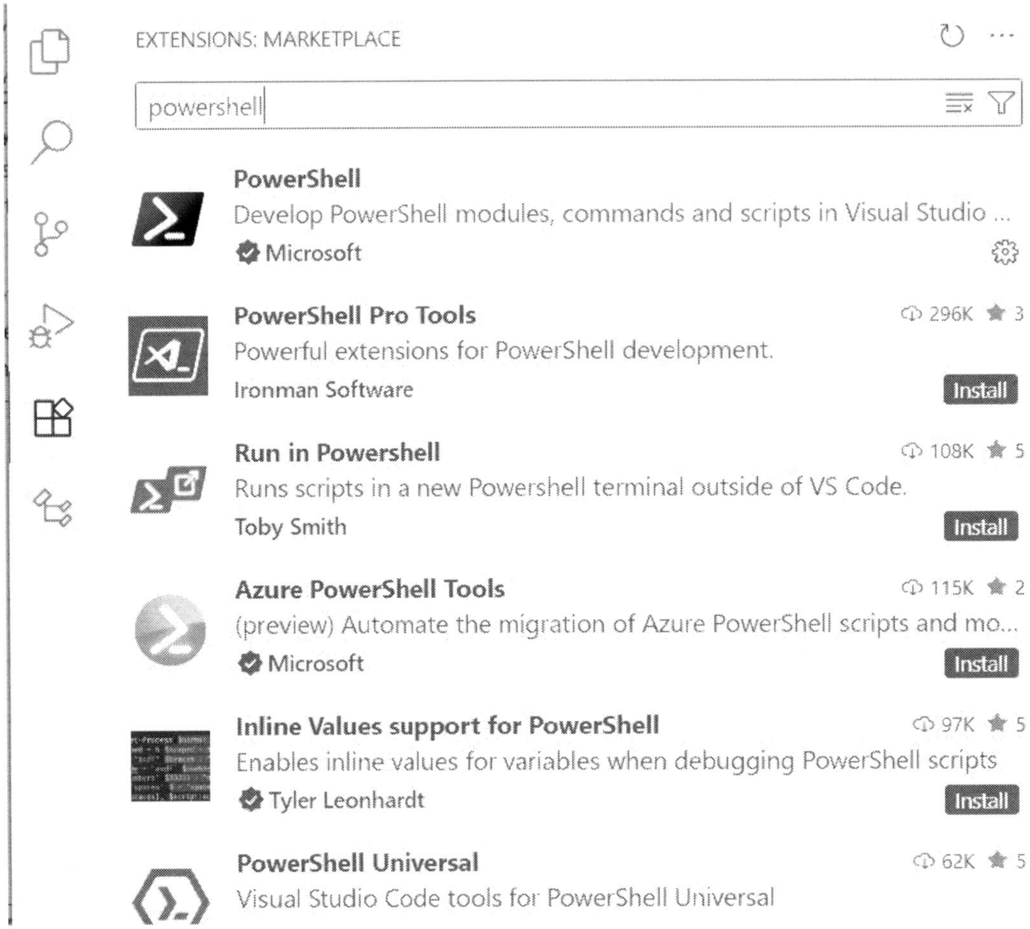

Figure 1.3: PowerShell extensions in VS Code

The icons available on the left-hand side change depending on the extensions installed. A new installation of VS Code will show fewer icons than *Figure 1.3*.

The PowerShell Extension should be installed. Other popular extensions might include:

- Blockman
- Error Lens
- Live Share
- Prettify JSON

Paid-for extensions, such as PowerShell Pro Tools, offer us the ability to design user interfaces in VS Code.

The integrated console in VS Code can be used with all installed versions of PowerShell. The following screenshot shows how to change the version of PowerShell used when editing a script. Note the clickable version in the bottom-right corner:

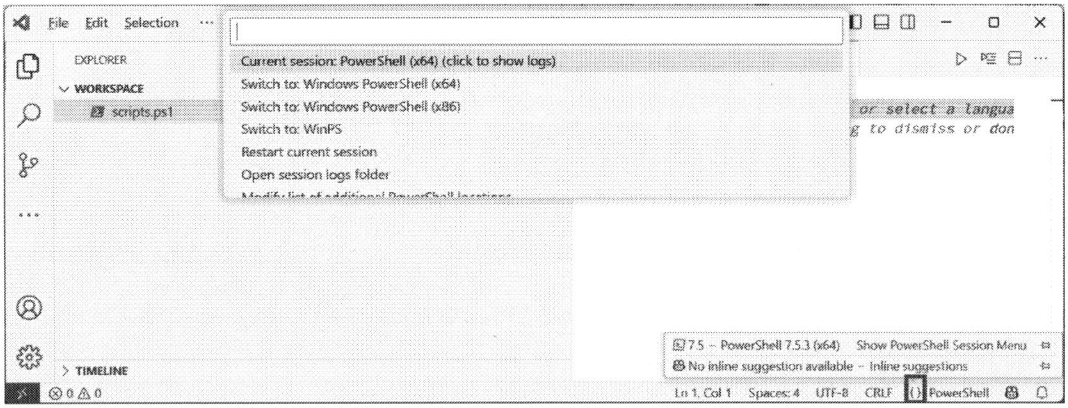

Figure 1.4: Choosing a PowerShell version

The IntelliSense version provided by the editor will list and hint at the possible commands and parameters available. Help content is available to fill in the details.

About AI

AI has become increasingly popular over the last few years and is widely used for programming. Visual Studio Code includes Microsoft Copilot, one of the many options available at this point.

Several forks of VS Code are available, such as Cursor, with other integrated AI options. These forks tend to integrate AI in much the same way as Copilot, offering both suggestions when typing and an agent to chat with for more extensive checks and changes.

In addition to editor tools, AI can be added to the Windows Terminal, for instance by making use of AIShell: `https://learn.microsoft.com/en-us/powershell/utility-modules/aishell/overview?view=ps-modules`

The PowerShell gallery includes several modules which offer AI capabilities. A search for the tag can be used to find these: `https://www.powershellgallery.com/packages?q=Tags%3A%22ai%22`

The use of AI-enabled editors and AI modules is beyond the scope of this book. They are rapidly changing products and services and while they can certainly be used to great effect, they are a separate tool as opposed to being part of the PowerShell language.

Getting help

PowerShell includes a built-in help system accessible using the `Get-Help` command. Help content in PowerShell is often rich and detailed, frequently including multiple examples. Gaining confidence using the built-in help system is an important part of working with PowerShell. Script authors and PowerShell developers can easily write their own help content when working with functions, scripts, and script modules.

Updatable help

The concept of updatable help was added in Windows PowerShell 3. It allows users to obtain the most recent versions of their help documentation outside of PowerShell on a web service. Help content can be downloaded and installed using the `Update-Help` command in PowerShell.

> Note
>
> **Which modules support updatable help?**
>
> The command below shows a list of modules that support updatable help:
>
> ```
> Get-Module -ListAvailable | Where-Object HelpInfoURI
> ```

Help for the core components of PowerShell is not part of the PowerShell 7 installation package. Content must be downloaded before it can be viewed.

The first time `Get-Help` runs, PowerShell prompts to update help.

Computers with no internet access or computers behind a restrictive proxy server may not be able to download help content directly. The `Save-Help` command can be used in this scenario, which is discussed later in this section, to work around the problem.

If PowerShell is unable to download help, it can only show a small amount of information about a command; for example, without downloading help, the content for the `Out-Null` command is minimal, as shown here:

```
PS> Get-Help Out-Null
NAME
    Out-Null

SYNTAX
    Out-Null [-InputObject <psobject>] [<CommonParameters>]
```

```
ALIASES
    None

REMARKS
    Get-Help cannot find the Help files for this cmdlet on this computer.
    It is displaying only partial help.
        -- To download and install Help files for the module that
           includes this cmdlet, use Update-Help.
        -- To view the Help topic for this cmdlet online, type:
           "Get-Help Out-Null -Online" or go to
           http://go.microsoft.com/fwlink/?LinkID=113366.
```

The help content in the preceding example is automatically generated by PowerShell. PowerShell inspects the command to determine which parameters are available.

Updatable help as a `help` file can be viewed using the following command:

```
Get-Help about_Updatable_Help
```

Updatable help is not entirely free from issues. Internet resources change as content moves around over time, which may invalidate `HelpInfoUri`, the URL stored within the module and used to retrieve help files.

The Get-Help command

When `Get-Help` is used without parameters, it shows introductory help about the help system. This content is taken from the default help file (`Get-Help default`); a snippet of this is as follows:

```
PS> Get-Help
TOPIC
 PowerShell Help System

SHORT DESCRIPTION
 Displays help about PowerShell cmdlets and concepts.

LONG DESCRIPTION
 PowerShell Help describes Windows PowerShell cmdlets, functions,
```

> **Note**
>
> **Help content can be long**
>
> The help content, in most cases, does not fit on a single screen. The `help` command differs from `Get-Help` in that it pauses (waiting for a key to be pressed) after each page; for example:
>
> ```
> help default
> ```

The previous command is equivalent to running `Get-Help` and piping it into the `more` command:

```
Get-Help default | more
```

Alternatively, `Get-Help` can be asked to show a window:

```
Get-Help default -ShowWindow
```

The available help content may be listed using either of the following two commands:

```
Get-Help *
Get-Help -Category All
```

Help for a subject can be viewed as follows:

```
Get-Help -Name <Topic>
```

For example, help for the `Get-Variable` command may be shown:

```
Get-Help Get-Variable
```

If a help document includes an online version link, it may be opened in a browser with the `-Online` parameter:

```
Get-Help Get-Command -Online
```

The URL used for online help can be viewed using `Get-Command`:

```
Get-Command Get-Command | Select-Object HelpUri
```

The help content is broken down into several sections: name, synopsis, syntax, description, related links, and remarks.

Name simply includes the name of the command. Synopsis is a short description of the functionality provided by the command, often no more than one sentence. Description often provides much greater detail than synopsis. Related links and remarks are optional fields, which may include links to related content.

Syntax is covered in the following section in more detail as it is the most complex part of the help document. A good understanding of the syntax allows quick evaluation of how to use a command, often removing the need to do more than skim help content.

Syntax

The syntax section lists each of the possible combinations of parameters a command accepts; each of these is known as a parameter set.

A command that has more than one parameter set is shown by this example for the `Get-Process` command:

```
SYNTAX
    Get-Process [[-Name] <System.String[]>] [-FileVersionInfo] [-Module]
[<CommonParameters>]

    Get-Process [-FileVersionInfo] -Id <System.Int32[]> [-Module]
[<CommonParameters>]
```

The syntax elements written in square brackets are optional; for example, syntax help for `Get-Process` shows that all its parameters are optional, as the following code shows:

```
SYNTAX
    Get-Process [[-Name] <System.String[]>] [-FileVersionInfo] [-Module]
[<CommonParameters>]
```

As the `Name` parameter is optional, `Get-Process` may be run without any parameters. The command may also be run by specifying a value only and no parameter name. Alternatively, the parameter name can be included as well as the value.

Each of the following examples is a valid use of `Get-Process`:

```
Get-Process
Get-Process pwsh
Get-Process -Name pwsh
```

> Note
>
> **Get-Command can show syntax**
>
> `Get-Command` may be used to view the syntax for a command. For example, running the following command will show the same output as seen in the *Syntax* section of `Get-Help`:
>
> ```
> Get-Command Get-Variable -Syntax
> ```

The different parameter types and how they are used are explored later in this chapter.

Examples

The Examples section of help provides working examples of how a command may be used. Help often includes more than one example.

In some cases, a command is sufficiently complex that it requires a detailed example to accompany parameter descriptions; in others, the command is simple, and a good example may serve in lieu of reading the help documentation.

> Note
>
> **PowerShell users can update help**
>
> Help documentation for built-in commands is open source. If a cmdlet is missing helpful examples, they can be added.
>
> A link to the PowerShell-Docs repository is available at the bottom of the online help page. It should send a user to the en-US version in the GitHub repository: `https://github.com/MicrosoftDocs/PowerShell-Docs`

Examples for a command can be requested by specifying the `Examples` parameter for `Get-Help`, as shown in the following example:

```
Get-Help Get-Process -Examples
```

The help information for most cmdlets usually includes several examples of its use, especially if the command has more than one parameter set.

Parameter

Parameters in PowerShell are used to supply named arguments to PowerShell commands.

Help with specific parameters can be requested as follows:

```
Get-Help Get-Command -Parameter <ParameterName>
```

The `Parameter` parameter allows for the quick retrieval of specific help for a single parameter; for example, help for the `Path` parameter of the `Import-Csv` command may be viewed:

```
PS> Get-Help Import-Csv -Parameter Path

-Path [<String[]>]
    Specifies the path to the CSV file to import. You can also
    pipe a path to `Import-Csv`.

    Required? false
    Position? 1
    Default value None
    Accept pipeline input? true (ByValue)
    Accept wildcard characters? false
```

This avoids needing to scroll through a potentially large help file to see how to use just one parameter.

The preceding content describes the parameter, whether the parameter is mandatory (`Required`), its position, default value, pipeline behavior, and support for wildcards.

Detailed and Full switches

The `Detailed` switch parameter (a parameter that does not require an argument) asks `Get-Help` to return the most help content.

The default sections returned by help are Name, Synopsis, Syntax, Description, Related Links, and Remarks.

When `Detailed` is requested, Parameters and Examples are added. Related Links is excluded.

The `Detailed` parameter is used as follows:

```
Get-Help Get-Process -Detailed
```

The `Full` switch parameter includes all the default sections, as well as Parameters, Inputs, Outputs, Notes, and Examples.

The following code shows the sections detailing the input and output types for `Get-Process` from the full help document; content before those sections has been removed from this example:

```
PS> Get-Help Get-Process -Full
... <content removed> ...
INPUTS
    System.Diagnostics.Process
        You can pipe a process object to Get-Process.
OUTPUTS
    System.Diagnostics.Process
        By default, this cmdlet returns a
        System.Diagnostics.Process object.

    System.Diagnotics.FileVersionInfo
        If you use the FileVersionInfo parameter, this cmdlet
        returns a FileVersionInfo object.

    System.Diagnostics.ProcessModule
        If you use the Module parameter, without the
        FileVersionInfo parameter, this cmdlet returns a
        ProcessModule object.
```

`INPUTS` is typically used to describe the value types that can be piped to a command. Pipelines are introduced in *Chapter 4, Working with Objects in PowerShell.*

In addition to the extra sections, the `Full` switch parameter includes metadata in the parameter section, the same parameter metadata seen when using `Get-Help Get-Process -Parameter Name`.

Help content in PowerShell is extensive and a valuable resource to have on any system running PowerShell.

Save-Help

The `Save-Help` command can be used with modules that support updatable help. It allows help content for installed modules to be saved to disk.

Help for a module can be downloaded using the following command. The destination folder must exist before running the command:

```
New-Item -Path C:\PSHelp -ItemType Directory
Save-Help -Module Microsoft.PowerShell.Management -DestinationPath C:\PSHelp
```

By default, `Save-Help` attempts to download help content for the current UI culture; that is, the current user interface language. The `Get-UICulture` command can be used to view the current culture, as the following example shows:

```
PS> Get-UICulture

LCID             Name             DisplayName
----             ----             -----------
2057             en-GB            English (United Kingdom)
```

If help content is not available for that culture, `Save-Help` will not do anything and will not raise an error. For UI cultures other than `en-US`, the `C:\PSHelp` folder will likely be empty.

`Save-Help` can be instructed to download help in a specific language by using the `UICulture` parameter:

```
Save-Help -Module Microsoft.PowerShell.Management -DestinationPath C:\PSHelp -
UICulture en-US
```

If help content is available, it is downloaded as shown in the `C:\PSHelp` folder here:

Figure 1.5: Downloaded help content for en-US

By default, Save-Help (and Update-Help) will not download help content more often than once every 24 hours as a rate-limiting control. This can be seen using the Verbose switch parameter:

```
PS> Save-Help -Module Microsoft.PowerShell.Management -DestinationPath C:\PSHelp -
UICulture en-US -Verbose
VERBOSE: Help was not saved for the module Microsoft.PowerShell.Management,
because the Save-Help command was run on this computer within the last 24 hours.
```

The Verbose switch parameter is used to make any verbose messages the command author has included visible in the console.

If help content is available for other cultures, and that content is downloaded immediately after en-US, then the Force parameter must be added:

```
Save-Help -Module Microsoft.PowerShell.Management -DestinationPath C:\PSHelp -
UICulture pl-PL -Force
```

However, as help content for the Microsoft.PowerShell.Management module is only available in en-US, the preceding command displays an error message describing which cultures help is available for.

Help content for all modules supporting updatable help can be saved as follows:

```
Save-Help -DestinationPath C:\PSHelp -UICulture en-US
```

Saved help content can be copied to another computer and imported using Update-Help. This technique is useful for computers that do not have internet access as it means help content can be made available.

Update-Help

The Update-Help command performs two tasks:

- Update help files on the local computer from the internet.
- Update help files on the local computer from previously saved help files.

To update help from the internet for all modules that support updatable help, run the Update-Help cmdlet with no parameters:

```
Update-Help
```

The `Update-Help` command includes a `Scope` parameter which may be used to make help content available without needing administrative access.

```
Update-Help -Scope CurrentUser
```

When the `Scope` parameter is set to `CurrentUser`, help content is downloaded to and read from (by `Get-Help`) `$home\Documents\PowerShell\help`. This path may be affected by folder redirection of the Documents folder, such as with services like OneDrive.

The `Scope` parameter is not available in Windows PowerShell and administrative rights are required to update help content.

For UI cultures other than `en-US`, the `UICulture` parameter may be required:

```
Update-Help -UICulture en-US
```

Like `Save-Help`, `Update-Help` will not download help for a module more than once every 24 hours by default. This can be overridden by using the `Force` parameter:

```
Update-Help -Name Microsoft.PowerShell.Management -Force -UICulture en-US
```

Help content that was saved using `Save-Help` can be imported from a folder using the `SourcePath` parameter:

```
Update-Help -SourcePath C:\PSHelp
```

If the folder does not contain content for the current UI culture (shown with `Get-UICulture`), an error message will be displayed:

```
PS> Update-Help -Module Microsoft.PowerShell.Management -SourcePath C:\PSHelp
Update-Help: Failed to update Help for the module(s)
'Microsoft.PowerShell.Management' with UI culture(s) {en-GB} : Unable to retrieve
the HelpInfo XML file for UI culture en-GB. Make sure the HelpInfoUri property in
the module manifest is valid or check your network connection and then try the
command again..
```

The `UICulture` parameter can be used again to update help content from the folder:

```
Update-Help -Module Microsoft.PowerShell.Management -SourcePath C:\PSHelp -
UICulture en-US
```

Help content is not limited to help for specific commands. PowerShell includes many topical help documents.

About_* help files

About_* documents describe features of the language or concepts that apply to more than one command. These items do not fit into help for individual commands.

The list of help files can be viewed by running Get-Help with the category set to HelpFile, as demonstrated in the following code:

```
Get-Help -Category HelpFile
```

Alternatively, wildcards can be used with the Name parameter of Get-Help:

```
Get-Help -Name About_*
```

These help files cover a huge variety of topics ranging from aliases to modules, to WMI. A number of these are shown here. The list will vary, depending on the modules installed on the computer running the command:

```
Name                         Category  Module  Synopsis
----                         --------  ------  --------
default                      HelpFile          SHORT DESCRIPTION
about_PSReadLine             HelpFile
about_Configuration          HelpFile          The Configuratio...
about_Aliases                HelpFile
about_Alias_Provider         HelpFile
about_Arithmetic_Operators   HelpFile
about_Arrays                 HelpFile
about_Assignment_Operators   HelpFile
about_Automatic_Variables    HelpFile
about_Break                  HelpFile
```

Using help content is an important part of working with PowerShell. Memorizing content is not necessary where instructions and reference material are easily accessible.

Get-Help may lead to finding a command to help achieve a task; however, it is often quicker to search using Get-Command.

Command naming and discovery

Commands in PowerShell are formed around verb and noun pairs in the form verb-noun.

This feature is useful when finding commands; it allows educated guesses about the names of commands so that there is little need to memorize long lists of commands. Commands use verbs to describe intent, and nouns to describe the target.

Verbs

The list of verbs is maintained by Microsoft. Verbs are words such as `Add`, `Get`, `Set`, and `New`. This formal approach to naming commands greatly assists in discovery.

The list of verbs can be seen in PowerShell using the following command:

```
Get-Verb
```

Verbs are grouped around different areas, such as data, life cycle, and security. Complementary actions such as encryption and decryption tend to use verbs in the same group; for example, the verb `Protect` may be used to encrypt something and the verb `Unprotect` may be used to decrypt something.

More commonly, `Get` and `Set`, or `New` and `Remove` commands may also be seen as complementary.

> Note
>
> **Verb descriptions**
>
> A detailed list of verbs, along with their use cases, is available on MSDN:
>
> `https://learn.microsoft.com/en-us/powershell/scripting/developer/cmdlet/approved-verbs-for-windows-powershell-commands?view=powershell-7.3&viewFallbackFrom=powershell-7`
>
> It is possible, although not recommended, to use verbs other than those in the approved list. If a command with an unapproved verb is written and included in a module, a warning message will be displayed every time the module is imported.

Verbs are paired with nouns which describe the target of a command.

Nouns

A noun provides a very short description of the object the command is expecting to act on. The noun part may be a single word, as is the case with `Get-Process`, `New-Item`, or `Get-Help`, or more than one word, as seen with `Get-ChildItem`, `Invoke-WebRequest`, or `Send-MailMessage`.

Command names often include a prefix on the noun. The Microsoft AD module uses the `AD` prefix. The Microsoft Graph modules are prefixed with `Mg`. Commands for managing the network components of the Windows operating system are prefixed with `Net`.

Modules are explored in *Chapter 2, Modules*. As mentioned above, the commands used to manage the networking components of Windows use the `Net` prefix on every noun. This, in turn, allows use of wildcards to search for commands.

Finding commands

The verb-noun pairing strives to make it easier to find commands without resorting to search engines.

For example, if the goal was to list firewall rules, the following command may be used to show the `Get` commands that might affect the firewall:

```
PS> Get-Command Get-*Firewall*

CommandType Name                                 Version Source
----------- ----                                 ------- ------
Function    Get-NetFirewallAddressFilter         2.0.0.0 NetSecurity
Function    Get-NetFirewallApplicationFilter     2.0.0.0 NetSecurity
Function    Get-NetFirewallInterfaceFilter       2.0.0.0 NetSecurity
Function    Get-NetFirewallInterfaceTypeFilter 2.0.0.0 NetSecurity
Function    Get-NetFirewallPortFilter            2.0.0.0 NetSecurity
Function    Get-NetFirewallProfile               2.0.0.0 NetSecurity
Function    Get-NetFirewallRule                  2.0.0.0 NetSecurity
Function    Get-NetFirewallSecurityFilter        2.0.0.0 NetSecurity
Function    Get-NetFirewallServiceFilter         2.0.0.0 NetSecurity
Function    Get-NetFirewallSetting               2.0.0.0 NetSecurity
```

A wildcard might be used for the verb, or the specific parameters for `Verb` and `Noun` might be used with `Get-Command`:

```
Get-Command -Verb Get, Set -Noun *Firewall*
```

The `Get-Help` command may also be used to find the list of commands above:

```
Get-Help Get-*Firewall*
```

As `Get-Help` also searches for help content, it is slower to use to search than `Get-Command`.

The list of commands returned may vary, depending on the modules installed on the computer.

From the preceding list, `Get-NetFirewallRule` closely matches the requirement (to see a list of firewall rules) and should be explored. Notice how each of the commands in the list above maintains the same prefix. This is a common naming practice in PowerShell.

Once a potential command has been found, `Get-Help` can be used to assess whether the command is suitable.

Aliases

An alias in PowerShell is an alternate name for a command. A command may have more than one alias. Unlike languages like Bash, an alias cannot include parameters.

The list of aliases can be viewed by using `Get-Alias`. The first few aliases are shown in the following example:

```
PS> Get-Alias

CommandType Name
----------- ----
Alias       % -> ForEach-Object
Alias       ? -> Where-Object
Alias       ac -> Add-Content
Alias       cat -> Get-Content
Alias       cd -> Set-Location
```

`Get-Alias` may be used to find the command behind an alias:

```
Get-Alias dir
```

The aliases available change depending on the operating system. For example, PowerShell on Linux omits aliases such as `ac` (`Add-Content`), `ls` (`Get-ChildItem`), and `cat` (`Get-Content`).

`Get-Alias` may also be used to find the aliases for any command:

```
PS> Get-Alias -Definition Get-ChildItem

CommandType     Name                        Version    Source
-----------     ----                        -------    ------
Alias           dir -> Get-ChildItem
Alias           gci -> Get-ChildItem
Alias           ls -> Get-ChildItem
```

Examples of aliases that are frequently used in examples on the internet include the following:

- `%` for `ForEach-Object`
- `?` for `Where-Object`
- `cd` for `Set-Location`
- `gc` or `cat` for `Get-Content`
- `ls` or `dir` for `Get-ChildItem`
- `iwr` for `Invoke-WebRequest`
- `irm` for `Invoke-RestMethod`
- `iex` for `Invoke-Expression`

An alias does not change how a command is used. There is no difference in the result of the following two commands:

```
cd $env:TEMP
Set-Location $env:TEMP
```

New aliases are created with the `New-Alias` command. For example, an alias named `grep` for the `Select-String` command can be created as follows:

```
New-Alias grep -Value Select-String
```

Aliases can be removed using the `Remove-Alias` command, including default aliases such as `ls`:

```
Remove-Alias grep
```

Aliases may also be removed using `Remove-Item` as an alternative to `Remove-Alias`:

```
Remove-Item alias:\grep
```

Aliases created in one session are not remembered when a new PowerShell session is started.

More information is available about aliases in the help file `about_Aliases`. The help file is viewed using the following command:

```
Get-Help about_Aliases
```

As mentioned above, aliases do not persist between PowerShell sessions (when the console is restarted). Profile scripts can be used to make an alias (or any other preferences) available when PowerShell is restarted.

About profile scripts

Aliases do not persist between PowerShell sessions. A profile script is often used for user-specific preferences like this.

Profiles are where most user-specific shell customization takes place, from changing prompts and default settings, to loading modules, to creating aliases. As the profile script runs every time PowerShell starts, adding slow loading modules to a profile can increase the time it takes to start PowerShell, in some cases adding several seconds to each startup.

Shell customization with profile scripts is an enormously involved and highly personal topic; this section provides a brief introduction to the topic only.

PowerShell has four different profile paths: two are user specific, and two are machine specific. The profile paths are also dependent on the host; one user and one machine path are specific to the terminal which started PowerShell.

The profile paths are described by the built-in variable `$profile`. The "`Select-Object *`" command is used to show all the possible values in the example below.

```
PS> $profile | Select-Object *

AllUsersAllHosts       : C:\Program Files\PowerShell\7\profile.ps1
AllUsersCurrentHost    : C:\Program
Files\PowerShell\7\Microsoft.PowerShell_profile.ps1
CurrentUserAllHosts    : C:\Users\user\Documents\PowerShell\profile.ps1
CurrentUserCurrentHost : C:
\Users\user\Documents\PowerShell\Microsoft.PowerShell_profile.ps1
```

If the same command is run in the VS Code integrated terminal, the two host-specific paths will differ:

```
PS> $profile | Select-Object *

AllUsersAllHosts       : C:\Program Files\PowerShell\7\profile.ps1
AllUsersCurrentHost    : C:\Program
Files\PowerShell\7\Microsoft.VSCode_profile.ps1
CurrentUserAllHosts    : C:\Users\user\Documents\PowerShell\profile.ps1
CurrentUserCurrentHost : C:
\Users\user\Documents\PowerShell\Microsoft.VSCode_profile.ps1
```

PowerShell will run each of the profile scripts where the script exists. If the script does not exist, the path is ignored.

Starting PowerShell with the `-NoProfile` switch avoids loading profile script files, a useful parameter for any scheduled scripts, or for testing to see if the profile is causing a problem.

The paths used above may not exist at all; to create a profile script, create the directory first, if necessary, then save the script file using one of the names and paths above.

The `about` document for profiles explores this topic further, if `Update-Help` has been successfully run at least once:

```
Get-Help about_profiles
```

A variety of different tools are available to customize look and feel which are typically started from a profile script. Customization of the prompt is a common activity:

- PowerLine: `https://github.com/Jaykul/PowerLine`
- oh-my-posh: `https://ohmyposh.dev/`
- Starship: `https://starship.rs/`

The Windows Terminal customized prompts article makes use of oh-my-posh in an example setup: `https://learn.microsoft.com/en-us/windows/terminal/tutorials/custom-prompt-setup`

Finally, for users with multiple computers the chezmoi tool might be used to ensure all computers use the same configuration: `https://www.chezmoi.io/`

Commands (and aliases) use parameters to pass arguments into a command.

Parameters, values, and parameter sets

As seen while looking at syntax in `Get-Help`, commands accept a mixture of parameters. The following sections show how these parameters are described in help and how to use them.

Parameters

When viewing help for a command, several different conventions are used to describe when a parameter is required and how it should be used. These conventions include:

- Optional parameters, where parameter names and arguments are enclosed in a single pair of square brackets.
- Optional positional parameters, the same as an optional parameter but with the parameter name also enclosed in square brackets.
- Mandatory parameters, where the parameter name and argument are not bracketed.
- Mandatory positional parameters, where the parameter name is in square brackets, but the argument is not.

The following sections show each of these conventions in greater detail.

Optional parameters

Optional parameters are surrounded by square brackets. If a parameter is used, a value (or argument) must be supplied. A fragment of the syntax for Get-Help is shown below; it shows that a `Category` parameter is available, and that the parameter is optional.

```
SYNTAX
    Get-Help ... [-Category <string[]>] ...
```

If a value for the `Category` parameter is to be used, the name of the parameter must also be specified. This is shown in the following example:

```
Get-Help -Category HelpFile
```

The command above filters help documents to help files, the "about" documents.

Optional positional parameters

An optional positional parameter is surrounded by square brackets, like an optional parameter. In addition, the parameter name itself is enclosed in square brackets. This indicates that the parameter is optional and that if it is used, the parameter and value can be supplied, or just the value without the parameter name.

It is not uncommon to see an optional positional parameter as the first parameter:

```
SYNTAX
    Get-Process [[-Name] <string[]>] ...
```

In this example, either of the following may be used:

```
Get-Process -Name pwsh
Get-Process pwsh
```

The output from the two commands is identical. This includes the parameter name, which, even when it is optional, is less ambiguous and therefore a recommended practice.

Mandatory parameters

A mandatory parameter must always be supplied and is written as follows:

```
SYNTAX
    Get-ADUser -Filter <string> ...
```

In this case, the `Filter` parameter name must be used, and it must be given a value. For example, to supply a `Filter` for the command, the `Filter` parameter must be explicitly written:

```
Get-ADUser -Filter 'sAMAccountName -eq "SomeName"'
```

The `Get-ADUser` command has a second parameter set that uses a different parameter name with a positional value.

Mandatory positional parameters

Mandatory parameters must always be supplied, but in some cases, it is possible to supply the value without using the parameter name. The parameter the value applies to is based on position.

Parameters that are mandatory and accept values based on position are written with the parameter name only in square brackets, as shown here:

```
SYNTAX
    Get-ADUser [-Identity] <ADUser> ...
```

In this case, the `Identity` parameter name is optional, but the value is not. This command may be used as described by either of the following examples:

```
Get-ADUser -Identity useridentity
Get-ADUser useridentity
```

In both cases, the supplied value fills the `Identity` parameter.

The `Add-Content` command has a parameter set that uses more than one mandatory positional parameter. The first part of the syntax for the parameter set is shown here:

```
Add-Content [-Path] <string[]> [-Value] <object[]>
```

In this case, the command may be called using any of the following:

```
Add-Content -Path c:\temp\file.txt -Value 'Hello world'
Add-Content -Value 'Hello world' -Path c:\temp\file.txt
Add-Content 'Hello world' -Path c:\temp\file.txt
Add-Content c:\temp\file.txt -Value 'Hello world'
Add-Content c:\temp\file.txt 'Hello world'
```

The first of these is easiest to read as both parameters are explicitly named and tends to be the better style to use.

Each of the parameters so far has required an argument, a value. PowerShell also allows parameters that do not require arguments.

Switch parameters

A switch parameter does not require an argument. If the switch is present, the value is equivalent to true, while if the switch parameter is absent, it is equivalent to false.

As with the other types of parameters, optional use is denoted by using square brackets around the parameter.

Switch parameters are typically used to toggle a behavior on. For example, `Recurse` is a switch parameter for `Get-ChildItem`:

```
SYNTAX
    Get-ChildItem ... [-Recurse] ...
```

Using the switch instructs `Get-ChildItem` to recurse when listing the content of a directory, as shown here:

```
Get-ChildItem c:\windows -Recurse
```

It is possible to supply a value for a switch parameter from a variable. This might be desirable when writing a script where the presence of a switch parameter is based on another variable. As switch parameters do not normally expect a value, a syntax change is required:

```
# Code which determines if Recurse is required
$recurse = $false
Get-ChildItem c:\windows -Recurse:$recurse
```

In some cases, a switch parameter will default to present, and it may be desirable to stop the parameter applying. The most common example is the `Confirm` parameter, which will be explored later in this chapter.

Parameter values

The syntax blocks explored in the preceding sections show the type that is expected when providing a value for a parameter. A type is a .NET concept; it describes what an object is, how it behaves, and what it can do.

The `Get-CimInstance` command expects a string as the argument for the `ClassName` parameter. This is shown in the snippet taken from the syntax block:

```
Get-CimInstance [-ClassName] <String>
```

A string is a sequence of characters. For example, the string `Win32_Service` can be used as follows:

```
Get-CimInstance -ClassName Win32_Service
```

`ClassName` must always be a single value. If more than one value is supplied, an error will be displayed:

```
PS> Get-CimInstance -ClassName Win32_Service, Win32_Process
Get-CimInstance: Cannot convert 'System.Object[]' to the type 'System.String'
required by parameter 'ClassName'. Specified method is not supported.
```

Parameters that accept more than one value use [ ] after the Type name. This indicates that the type is an array. The Name parameter for the Get-Service command is shown here:

```
Get-Service [[-Name] <String[]>]
```

In this case, the parameter type is an array of strings. An array may consist of one or more strings separated by a comma:

```
PS> Get-Service -Name WinDefend, WlanSvc

Status   Name               DisplayName
------   ----               -----------
Running  WinDefend          Windows Defender Antivirus Service
Running  WlanSvc            WLAN AutoConfig
```

PowerShell will attempt to coerce any value supplied into the required type. A single string can be used as an argument for the parameter. PowerShell will convert the single value into an array of strings with one element. For example:

```
Get-Service -Name WinDefend
```

Each of the commands used in this section will allow the value to be entered without the parameter name. For example, for Get-Service, the Name parameter can be omitted:

```
Get-Service WinDefend
Get-Service WinDefend, WlanSvc
```

When using positional parameters, PowerShell can use the type to determine which parameter (and which parameter set) should be used.

Parameter sets

In PowerShell, a parameter set is a set of parameters that may be used together when running a command.

Many of the commands in PowerShell have more than one parameter set. This was seen when looking at the Syntax section when using Get-Help.

For example, the Stop-Process command has three parameter sets:

```
SYNTAX
    Stop-Process [-Id] <Int32[]> [-Confirm] [-Force] [-PassThru] [-WhatIf]
```

```
[<CommonParameters>]

    Stop-Process [-InputObject] <Process[]> [-Confirm] [-Force] [-PassThru] [-
WhatIf] [<CommonParameters>]

    Stop-Process [-Confirm] [-Force] -Name <String[]> [-PassThru] [-WhatIf]
[<CommonParameters>]
```

PowerShell will attempt to find a matching parameter set based on the parameters and values it is given.

The parameter sets for `Stop-Process` have two different sets that will accept a value by position:

```
Stop-Process [-Id] <Int32[]>
Stop-Process [-InputObject] <Process[]>
```

The first expects an ID as an integer. The second expects a `Process` object, an object returned by the `Get-Process` command.

The variable `$PID` is an automatic variable that holds the process ID (an integer) of the current PowerShell console. Running the following command will stop the PowerShell process. The first parameter set for `Stop-Process` is chosen because an integer value is used:

```
Stop-Process $PID
```

The second parameter set expects a value for `InputObject`. Again, this may be supplied as a positional parameter (or via the pipeline). In this case, PowerShell distinguishes based on its type. The following snippet contains the three possible approaches available when using the `InputObject` parameter:

```
$process = Start-Process notepad -PassThru
Stop-Process -InputObject $process
Stop-Process $process
$process | Stop-Process
```

Note

Pipeline input

`Get-Help` shows which parameters accept pipeline input in the help for each parameter. This may be viewed using either of the following commands:

```
Get-Help Stop-Process -Parameter *
Get-Help Stop-Process -Full
```

Examples are likely to show how to use the parameters with a pipeline.

If `Get-Help` is incomplete, `Get-Command` can be used to explore parameters:

```
(Get-Command Stop-Process).Parameters.InputObject.Attributes
```

If parameters from different parameter sets are used at the same time, the following error message is shown:

```
PS> Get-Process -Id $PID -Name pwsh
Get-Process: Parameter set cannot be resolved using the specified named
parameters. One or more parameters issued cannot be used together or an
insufficient number of parameters were provided.
```

ID and Name are both used to identify a process; they are not intended to be used at the same time.

Well-designed commands in PowerShell will have a default parameter set that allows a command to ask for missing parameters if no parameters are used and at least one is required.

A minority of commands are not so well-designed. For example, the commands in the Dism module on Windows are known to show an error if they are run without parameters.

```
PS> Get-WindowsCapability
Get-WindowsCapability: Parameter set cannot be resolved using the specified named
parameters. One or more parameters issued cannot be used together or an
insufficient number of parameters were provided.
```

The most common use of this command is to work with capabilities in the current Windows image (rather than another mounted image). The `Online` parameter is required in this case:

```
Get-WindowsCapability -Online
```

It is not particularly easy to see this from the syntax block in help for this command; the parameters for the command are listed in alphabetical order rather than showing mandatory parameters first. Careful reading will show that either `Online` or `Path` is required, but this can certainly be called out as poor design and documentation.

Each of the parameter sets here also shows that the command supports common parameters.

Common parameters

Common parameters are used to control some of the standardized functionality PowerShell provides, such as verbose output and actions to take when errors occur.

When looking at the syntax, most commands will end with a `CommonParameters` item:

```
SYNTAX
    Get-Process ... [<CommonParameters>]
```

The following is a list of common parameters:

- `Debug`
- `ErrorAction`
- `ErrorVariable`
- `InformationAction`
- `InformationVariable`
- `OutBuffer`
- `OutVariable`
- `PipelineVariable`
- `Verbose`
- `WarningAction`
- `WarningVariable`

Each is described in the `about_CommonParameters` document:

```
Get-Help about_CommonParameters
```

The help document is also available online: `https://learn.microsoft.com/en-us/powershell/module/microsoft.powershell.core/about/about_commonparameters`.

For example, `Stop-Process` does not explicitly state that it has a `Verbose` switch parameter, but since `Verbose` is a common parameter, it may be used. This can be seen if `notepad` is started and immediately stopped:

```
PS> Start-Process notepad -Verbose -PassThru | Stop-Process -Verbose
VERBOSE: Performing the operation "Stop-Process" on target "notepad (5592)".
```

> Note
>
> **Not so verbose**
>
> Just because a command supports common parameters does not mean it uses them. For example, `Get-Process` supports the `Verbose` parameter, yet it does not write any verbose output when `Verbose` is specified.

In addition to common parameters, PowerShell also offers specialized parameters for commands that make changes.

Confirm and WhatIf

`Confirm` and `WhatIf` can be used with commands that make changes to files, variables, data, and so on. These parameters are often used with commands that use the verbs `New`, `Set`, or `Remove`, but the parameters are not limited to specific verbs.

`Confirm` and `WhatIf` have associated preference variables that are used to customize default behavior in PowerShell. Preference variables have an `about` file, which may be viewed using the following command:

```
Get-Help about_Preference_Variables
```

The `Confirm` switch parameter is used to control automatic prompting for high-impact operations by default.

Confirm and ConfirmPreference

The `Confirm` switch parameter and the `ConfirmPreference` variable can be used to decide if a command should prompt. The decision to prompt is based on a comparison of `ConfirmPreference` with `ConfirmImpact` when set by a command author.

ConfirmPreference has four possible values:

- High: Prompts when command impact is High (default)
- Medium: Prompts when command impact is Medium or High
- Low: Prompts when command impact is Low, Medium, or High
- None: Never prompts

ConfirmImpact uses the same four values.

In Windows PowerShell, the default value for ConfirmImpact is Medium.

In PowerShell 7, the default value for ConfirmImpact is None. If the command uses SupportsShouldProcess, then the default is Medium.

Note

Finding commands with a specific impact

The following snippet returns a list of all commands that state they have a high impact:

```
Get-Command -CommandType Cmdlet, Function | Where-Object {
    $metadata = [System.Management.Automation.CommandMetadata]$_
    $metadata.ConfirmImpact -eq 'High'
}
```

If the Confirm parameter is explicitly provided, the value of ConfirmPreference within the scope of the command is set to Low, which will trigger any confirmation prompts.

The Confirm switch parameter therefore causes a command to prompt before an action is taken; for example, the Confirm switch parameter forces Remove-Item to prompt when a file is to be removed:

```
PS> Set-Location $env:TEMP
PS> New-Item FileName.txt -Force
PS> Remove-Item FileName.txt -Confirm

Confirm
Are you sure you want to perform this action?
Performing the operation "Remove File" on target "C:
\Users\whoami\AppData\Local\Temp\FileName.txt".
[Y] Yes [A] Yes to All [N] No [L] No to All [S] Suspend [?] Help (default is "Y"):
```

In the previous example, a confirmation prompt was explicitly requested. In a similar manner, confirmation prompts may be suppressed. For example, the value of the `Confirm` parameter may be explicitly set to `false`:

```
Set-Location $env:TEMP
New-Item FileName.txt -Force
Remove-Item FileName.txt -Confirm:$false
```

The ability to provide a value for the `Confirm` parameter is useful for commands that prompt by default; for example, `Clear-RecycleBin` prompts by default:

```
PS> Clear-RecycleBin

Confirm
Are you sure you want to perform this action?
Performing the operation "Clear-RecycleBin" on target " All of the contents of the
Recycle Bin".
[Y] Yes [A] Yes to All [N] No [L] No to All [S] Suspend [?] Help (default is "Y"):
```

Setting the `Confirm` parameter to `false` for `Clear-RecycleBin` bypasses the prompt and immediately empties the recycle bin:

```
Clear-RecycleBin -Confirm:$false
```

If the `Confirm` parameter is not set, whether a prompt is shown is determined by PowerShell. The value of the `ConfirmPreference` variable is compared with `ConfirmImpact` on a command.

Note

There is more than one way to prompt

There are two ways of requesting confirmation in PowerShell. These are `ShouldProcess` and `ShouldContinue`.

`ShouldProcess` is affected by the `Confirm` parameter and `ConfirmPreference` variable.

`ShouldContinue` is a forced prompt and is unaffected by the `Confirm` parameter and `ConfirmPreference` variable.

For example, `Remove-Item` will always prompt when attempting to delete a directory that is not empty without supplying the `Recurse` parameter.

It is not possible to easily discover commands using forced prompts. Reviewing documentation and testing is vital.

By default, the value of `ConfirmPreference` is `High`. This means that prompts will be raised when `ConfirmImpact` for a command is `High`. The default value for `ConfirmPreference` may be viewed as follows:

```
PS> $ConfirmPreference
High
```

Note

Finding ConfirmImpact

In scripts and functions, the `ConfirmImpact` setting is part of the `CmdletBinding` attribute:

```
[CmdletBinding(ConfirmImpact = 'High')]
```

If `CmdletBinding` or `ConfirmImpact` is not present, the impact is `Medium` in Windows PowerShell and `None` in PowerShell 7.

The impact of a function or cmdlet may be viewed using the `ConfirmImpact` property of a command's metadata:

```
[System.Management.Automation.CommandMetadata](Get-Command Remove-
Item)
```

A new value for `ConfirmPreference` may be set by assigning it in the console; for example, it can be set to `Low`. When the preference variable is set to `Low`, prompts may be raised by all commands where `ConfirmImpact` is `Low`, `Medium`, or `High`.

```
$ConfirmPreference = 'Low'
```

Note

ConfirmPreference and the Confirm parameter

When `ConfirmPreference` is set to None to suppress confirmation prompts, confirmation may still be explicitly requested using the `Confirm` parameter; for example:

```
$ConfirmPreference = 'None'
New-Item NewFile.txt -Confirm
```

Support for confirmation also provides support for `WhatIf`.

WhatIf and WhatIfPreference

`WhatIf` is typically used when testing a command. If implemented correctly by a command author, `WhatIf` should allow a state-changing command to be run without it making the change.

Note

WhatIf is not always implemented as expected

`WhatIf` support for a command is defined by a command author; if the author does not correctly handle the preference, an undesirable change may be made.

The `Set-ADAccountPassword` command had a bug for a while where `WhatIf` was ignored.

Even if a command supports `WhatIf`, test on small sets of data before using the parameter to verify a large change.

The `WhatIf` parameter has an associated preference variable, `WhatIfPreference`, which may be set to either `true` or `false`. The default value is `false`.

The `WhatIf` parameter replaces the confirmation prompt with a simple statement describing the action the command would have taken. Using `Remove-Item` as an example again, a message will be displayed, and the file will not be deleted:

```
PS> Set-Location $env:TEMP
PS> New-Item FileName.txt -Force
PS> Remove-Item FileName.txt -WhatIf
```

```
What if: Performing the operation "Remove File" on target "C:
\Users\whoami\AppData\Local\Temp\FileName.txt".
```

`WhatIf` can be explicitly set on a per-command basis by supplying a value in the same manner as the `Confirm` parameter. For example, `WhatIf` might be explicitly set to `false`:

```
'Some message' | Out-File $env:TEMP\test.txt -WhatIf:$false
```

Setting `WhatIf` in the manner used here might, for instance, be useful if a log file should be written even if other state-changing commands are ignored.

If the preference variable is set to `true`, all commands that support `WhatIf` act as if the parameter is set explicitly. A new value may be set for the variable, as shown in the following code:

```
$WhatIfPreference = $true
```

The `WhatIf` parameter and `$WhatIfPreference` preference variable take precedence over the `Confirm` parameter. For example, the `WhatIf` dialog is shown when running the following `New-Item`, but the `Confirm` prompt is not:

```
PS> $WhatIfPreference = $true
PS> New-Item NewFile.txt -Confirm
What if: Performing the operation "Create File" on target "Destination: C:
\Users\whoami\AppData\Local\Temp\NewFile.txt".
```

Restarting the console will restore preference variables to their default values.

The behavior of `Confirm` and `WhatIf` is prescribed by PowerShell. Parameters such as `Force` and `PassThru` are commonly used in PowerShell but have less well-defined behavior.

Force parameter

The `Force` parameter is not one of the common parameters with behavior defined by PowerShell itself, but the parameter is frequently used.

Force has no fixed usage; the effect of using Force is a choice a command author must make. Help documentation should state the effect of using Force with a command. For example, the use of Force with Remove-Item is available:

```
Get-Help Remove-Item -Parameter Force
```

With the Force parameter, New-Item overwrites any existing file with the same path. When used with Remove-Item, the Force parameter allows the removal of files with Hidden or System attributes.

The error that is generated when attempting to delete a Hidden file is shown by running the following code:

```
Set-Location $env:TEMP
New-Item FileName.txt -Force
Set-ItemProperty FileName.txt -Name Attributes -Value Hidden
Remove-Item FileName.txt
```

When Remove-Item is run, the following error will be displayed:

```
Remove-Item: You do not have sufficient access rights to perform this operation or
the item is hidden, system, or read only.
RemoveFileSystemItemUnAuthorizedAccess,Microsoft.PowerShell.Commands.RemoveItemCom
mand
```

Adding the Force parameter allows the operation to continue:

```
Remove-Item FileName.txt -Force
```

The Force parameter may be worth exploring if a command is prompting, and the prompts cannot be suppressed using the Confirm parameter or the ConfirmPreference variable.

PassThru parameter

The PassThru parameter, like Force, is frequently used, but the behavior of the parameter is not defined by PowerShell. However, PassThru tends to have predictable behavior.

The PassThru parameter is typically used with commands that do not normally generate output and is used to force the command to return the object it was working with.

For example, the `Start-Process` command does not normally return any output. If `PassThru` is used, it will return the process it created:

```
PS> Start-Process notepad -PassThru

 NPM(K)    PM(M)      WS(M)     CPU(s)      Id  SI ProcessName
 ------    -----      -----     ------      --  -- -----------
      9     1.98       6.70       0.05   22636   1 notepad
```

The `PassThru` parameter is therefore useful if more work is to be done with the object after the first command has finished.

For example, `PassThru` might be used with `Set-Service`, which ordinarily does not return output, allowing a service to be started immediately after another change:

```
Get-Service Audiosrv |
    Set-Service -StartupType Automatic -PassThru |
    Start-Service
```

Parameters in PowerShell are a complex topic but are a vital part of working with the language.

Introduction to providers

A provider in PowerShell is a specialized interface to a service or dataset that presents items to the end user in the same style as a filesystem.

All operating systems include the following providers:

- **Alias**: PowerShell aliases
- **Environment**: Environment variables (for the process)
- **FileSystem**: Files and folders
- **Function**: Any functions in the session
- **Variable**: Any variables in the session

Windows operating systems also include Windows-specific providers:

- **Registry**: All loaded registry hives
- **Certificate**: The `LocalMachine` and `CurrentUser` certificate stores
- **WSMan**: Windows remoting configuration

Several modules, such as the `ActiveDirectory` and `WebAdministration` modules, add service-specific providers when imported.

A longer description of `Providers` can be seen by viewing the `about` file:

```
Get-Help about_Providers
```

The available providers can be viewed in the current PowerShell session by running `Get-PSProvider`, as shown in the following example:

```
PS> Get-PSProvider

Name          Capabilities                        Drives
----          ------------                        ------
Registry      ShouldProcess, Transactions         {HKLM, HKCU}
Alias         ShouldProcess                       {Alias}
Environment   ShouldProcess                       {Env}
FileSystem    Filter, ShouldProcess, Credentials {C, D}
Function      ShouldProcess                       {Function}
Variable      ShouldProcess                       {Variable}
Certificate   ShouldProcess                       {Cert}
WSMan         Credentials                         {WSMan}
```

Each of the previous providers has a help file associated with it. In PowerShell, the help files are named `about_<ProviderName>_Provider`; for example:

```
Get-Help -Name about_Certificate_Provider
```

A list of all help files for providers in PowerShell 7 can be seen by running the following command:

```
Get-Help -Name About_*_Provider
```

In Windows PowerShell, the help files have a special category and are accessed by name, for example:

```
Get-Help -Name Certificate -Category Provider
```

Or the provider help files can be listed by category:

```
Get-Help -Category Provider
```

The provider-specific help documents describe the additional parameters added to `*-Item` and `*-ChildItem`, as well as `Test-Path`, `Get-Content`, `Set-Content`, `Add-Content`, `Get-Acl`, `Set-Acl`, and so on.

Provider-specific parameters, when added to the preceding commands, allow provider-specific values for filtering, making changes to existing items, and creating new items.

PowerShell offers tab completion for parameters when the `Path` parameter has been defined. For example, entering the following partial command, then pressing tab, will cycle through the parameters available to the Certificate provider:

```
Get-ChildItem -Path cert:\LocalMachine\Root -
```

For example, pressing Tab several times after the hyphen is entered offers up the `CodeSigningCert` parameter.

The items within a provider can be accessed by following the name of a provider with two colons. For example, the content of the variable provider can be shown as follows:

```
Get-ChildItem variable::
```

The same approach can be used to view the top-level items available in the Registry provider on Windows:

```
Get-ChildItem registry::
```

Child items can be accessed by adding a name; for example, a variable:

```
Get-Item variable::true
```

The preceding command is equivalent to running `Get-Variable true`.

The `FileSystem` provider returns an error when attempting to access `FileSystem::` without specifying a path. A child item must be specified, for example:

```
Get-ChildItem FileSystem::C:\Windows
```

While it is possible to access providers directly using the preceding notation, several of the providers are given names and are presented in the same manner as a Windows disk drive.

Drives and providers

Drives are labels used to access data from providers by name. Drives are automatically made available for `FileSystem` based on the drive letters used for mounted partitions in Windows.

The output from `Get-PSProvider` in the previous section shows that each provider has one or more drives associated with it.

Alternatively, the list of drives can be seen using `Get-PSDrive`, as shown in the following example:

```
PS> Get-PSDrive

Name      Used (GB) Free (GB) Provider      Root
----      --------- --------- --------      ----
Alias                         Alias
C             89.13    111.64 FileSystem    C:\
Cert                          Certificate   \
D              0.45     21.86 FileSystem    D:\
Env                           Environment
Function                      Function
HKCU                          Registry      HKEY_CURRENT_USER
HKLM                          Registry      HKEY_LOCAL_MACHINE
Variable                      Variable
WSMan                         WSMan
```

The `Alias`, `Variable`, and `WSMan` providers shown above also have their own dedicated commands. For aliases and variables, the dedicated commands offer more flexibility than the provider. For WSMan it offers a different way of configuring PS Remoting (which uses WSMan) as well as more specialized commands.

As providers present data in a similar manner to a filesystem, accessing a provider is like working with a disk drive. This example shows how `Get-ChildItem` changes when exploring the `Cert` drive. The first few certificates are shown:

```
PS C:\> Set-Location Cert:\LocalMachine\Root
PS Cert:\LocalMachine\Root> Get-ChildItem

 Directory: Microsoft.PowerShell.Security\Certificate::LocalMachine\Root

Thumbprint                                Subject
----------                                -------
```

```
CDD4EEAE6000AC7F40C3802C171E30148030C072     CN=Microsoft Root Certif...
BE36A4562FB2EE05DBB3D32323ADF445084ED656     CN=Thawte Timestamping C...
A43489159A520F0D93D032CCAF37E7FE20A8B419     CN=Microsoft Root Author...
```

By default, drives are available for the current user, `HKEY_CURRENT_USER` (`HKCU`), and local machine, `HKEY_LOCAL_MACHINE` (`HKLM`), registry hives.

A new drive named `HKCC` might be created for `HKEY_CURRENT_CONFIG` with the following command:

```
New-PSDrive HKCC -PSProvider Registry -Root HKEY_CURRENT_CONFIG
```

After running the preceding command, a new drive may be used to view the content of the hive, as demonstrated by the following example:

```
PS C:\> Get-ChildItem HKCC:

    Hive: HKEY_CURRENT_CONFIG

Name                           Property
----                           --------
Software
System
```

Note

Functions for drive letters

On Windows, running `C:` or `D:` in the PowerShell console changes to a new drive letter. This is possible because `C:` is a function that calls the `Set-Location` command. This can be seen by looking at the definition of one of the functions:

```
(Get-Command C:).Definition
```

Every letter of the alphabet (A to Z) has a predefined function (`Get-Command *:`).

`Set-Location` must be explicitly used to change to any other drive, for example:

```
Set-Location HKCU:
```

Providers are an important part of PowerShell, especially the file system provider.

Introduction to splatting

Splatting is a way of defining the parameters of a command before calling it. This is an important and often underrated technique that the PowerShell team added to PowerShell 2.

Splatting is often used to solve three potential problems in a script:

- Long lines caused by commands that need many parameters
- Conditional use of parameters
- Repetition of parameters across several commands

Individual parameters are written in a hashtable (`@{}`), and then the `@` symbol is used to tell PowerShell that the content of the hashtable should be read as parameters.

This example supplies the `Name` parameter for the `Get-Process` command and is normally written as `Get-Process -Name explorer`:

```
$getProcess = @{
    Name = 'explorer'
}
Get-Process @getProcess
```

In this example, `getProcess` is used as the name of the variable for the hashtable. The name is arbitrary; any variable name can be used.

Splatting can be used with cmdlets, functions, and scripts. Splatting can be used when the call operator is present, for example:

```
$getProcess = @{
    Name = 'explorer'
}
& 'Get-Process' @getProcess
```

The ability to use splatting with the call operator is useful if the command name itself is held in a variable.

The uses of splatting are explored in the following sections.

Splatting to avoid long lines

The benefit of splatting is most obvious when working with commands that expect a larger number of parameters.

This first example uses the module `ScheduledTasks` to create a basic task that runs once a day at midnight:

```
$taskAction = New-ScheduledTaskAction -Execute pwsh.exe -Argument 'Write-Host
"hello world"'
$taskTrigger = New-ScheduledTaskTrigger -Daily -At '00:00:00'
Register-ScheduledTask -TaskName 'TaskName' -Action $taskAction -Trigger
$taskTrigger -RunLevel 'Limited' -Description 'This line is too long to read'
```

Each of the commands is spread out over multiple lines; it is hard to see where one ends and the next begins.

Commands can also be spread out using a tick, the escape character in PowerShell, as shown here:

```
$taskAction = New-ScheduledTaskAction `
    -Execute pwsh.exe `
    -Argument 'Write-Host "hello world"'
$taskTrigger = New-ScheduledTaskTrigger `
    -Daily `
    -At '00:00:00'
Register-ScheduledTask `
    -TaskName 'TaskName' `
    -Action $taskAction `
    -Trigger $taskTrigger `
    -RunLevel 'Limited' `
    -Description 'This line is too long to read'
```

This approach is relatively common, but it is fragile. It is easy to miss a tick at the end of a line, or to accidentally add a space after a tick character. Both break continuation, and the command executes but with an incomplete set of parameters; afterward, an error may be displayed, or a prompt may be shown, depending on the parameter (or parameters) it missed.

This problem is shown in the following screenshot, where a space character has been accidentally included after a tick following the `Daily` switch parameter:

```
PS> New-ScheduledTaskTrigger  -Daily

cmdlet New-ScheduledTaskTrigger at command pipeline position 1
Supply values for the following parameters:
At:
```

Figure 1.6: Space after the escape character

Splatting provides a neater, generally easier to read, and more robust alternative. The following example shows one possible way to tackle these commands when using splatting:

```
$newTaskAction = @{
    Execute = 'pwsh.exe'
    Argument = 'Write-Host "hello world"'
}
$newTaskTrigger = @{
    Daily = $true
    At    = '00:00:00'
}
$registerTask = @{
    TaskName    = 'TaskName'
    Action      = New-ScheduledTaskAction @newTaskAction
    Trigger     = New-ScheduledTaskTrigger @newTaskTrigger
    RunLevel    = 'Limited'
    Description = 'Splatting is easy to read'
}
Register-ScheduledTask @registerTask
```

Switch parameters may be treated as if they are Boolean when splatting.

The `Daily` parameter that was defined in the previous example is a switch parameter.

The same approach applies to `Confirm`, `Force`, `WhatIf`, `Verbose`, and so on.

Conditional use of parameters

Conditional use of parameters is one of the most important ways in which splatting can help.

If a command must be run and the parameters for a command can change based on user input or other circumstances, then it may be tempting to repeat the entire command. For example, a `Credential` parameter might be conditionally used.

The command may be repeated entirely based on there being a value for the `Credential` variable:

```
if ($Credential) {
    Get-ADUser 'Enabled -eq $true' -Credential $Credential
} else {
    Get-ADUser 'Enabled -eq $true'
}
```

The disadvantage of this approach is that any change to the command must be repeated in the second version.

Alternatively, a splatting variable may be used, and the `Credential` parameter added only when it is needed:

```
$params = @{}
if ($Credential) {
    $params['Credential'] = $Credential
}
Get-ADUser 'Enabled -eq $true' @params
```

Using splatting in this manner ensures only one version of the command must be maintained, reducing the risk of introducing a bug when making changes.

Splatting to avoid repetition

Splatting may be used to avoid repetition when a parameter must be optionally passed on to several different commands. It is possible to splat more than one set of parameters.

In this example, the `ComputerName` and `Credential` parameters are used by two different commands:

```
# Parameters used to authenticate remote connections
$remoteParams = @{
    Credential   = Get-Credential
    ComputerName = $env:COMPUTERNAME
}
# Parameters which are specific to Test-WSMan
$testWSMan = @{
    Authentication = 'Default'
    ErrorAction    = 'SilentlyContinue'
}
```

```
# By default, do not pass any extra parameters to New-CimSession
$newCimSession = @{}
if (-not (Test-WSMan @testWSMan @remoteParams)) {
    # If WSMan fails, use DCOM (RPC over TCP) to connect
    $newCimSession['SessionOption'] = New-CimSessionOption -Protocol Dcom
}
# Parameters to pass to Get-CimInstance
$getCimInstance = @{
    ClassName  = 'Win32_Service'
    CimSession = New-CimSession @newCimSession @remoteParams
}
Get-CimInstance @getCimInstance
```

This example takes advantage of several features:

- It is possible to splat no parameters using an empty hashtable (@{}) when all the parameters are conditionally added.
- It is possible to test conditions and dynamically add parameters at runtime (if needed).
- It is possible to splat more than one set of parameters into a command.

As the preceding example shows, it is possible to dynamically choose the parameters that are passed to a command without having to write the command in full more than once in a script.

Splatting and positional parameters

It is possible, although rare and inadvisable in production scripts, to splat positional parameters; that is, to splat a parameter without stating a parameter name.

This can be seen with the `Rename-Item` command, which has two positional parameters: `Path` and `NewName`. `Rename-Item` may be run as follows:

```
Rename-Item oldname.txt newname.txt
```

An array to splat these positional parameters looks as follows:

```
$renameItem = 'oldname.txt', 'newname.txt'
Rename-Item @renameItem
```

A splatting variable with positional parameters may be used with executable files (`.exe` files), although it is often difficult to see any difference between splatting and using a normal variable. For example, both of the following commands execute in the same way:

```
$argumentList = '/t', 2
timeout.exe $argumentList
timeout.exe @argumentList
```

Splatting is a powerful technique and can be used to make code more readable by reducing line length or repetition.

When using splatting, string values in the hashtable must be quoted. Conversely, when using a parameter directly, it is often unnecessary. The parser is responsible for deciding how statements and expressions should be interpreted.

Parser modes

The parser in PowerShell is responsible for taking what is typed into the console, or what is written in a script, and turning it into something PowerShell can execute. The parser has two different modes that explain, for instance, why strings assigned to variables must be quoted, but strings as arguments for parameters only need quoting if the string contains a space.

The parser modes are different modes:

- Argument mode
- Expression mode

Mode switching allows PowerShell to correctly interpret arguments without needing values to be quoted. In the following example, the argument for the `Name` parameter only needs quoting if the name contains spaces:

```
Get-Process -Name pwsh
```

The parser is running in Argument mode at the point the `pwsh` value is used and therefore literal text is treated as a value, not something to be executed.

This means that, in the following example, the second command is interpreted as a string and not executed:

```
Set-Content -Path commands.txt -Value 'Get-ChildItem', 'Get-Item'
Get-Command -Name Get-Content commands.txt
```

The second command in the preceding code therefore does not do anything.

To execute the `Get-Content` command, the argument must be enclosed in parentheses:

```
Set-Content -Path commands.txt -Value 'Get-ChildItem', 'Get-Item'
Get-Command -Name (Get-Content commands.txt)
```

The code in parentheses is executed, and the parser is in Expression mode.

Another example of this can be seen when using an enumeration value. An enumeration is a list of constants described by a .NET type.

```
PS> Get-Date [DayOfWeek]::Monday
Get-Date: Cannot bind parameter 'Date'. Cannot convert value "[DayOfWeek]::Monday"
to type "System.DateTime". Error: "String '[DayOfWeek]::Monday' was not recognized
as a valid DateTime."
```

If the value for the argument is placed in parentheses, it will run first and expand the value. Once the value is expanded, `Get-Date` will be able to work with it:

```
Get-Date ([DayOfWeek]::Monday)
```

The help document, `about_parsing`, explores this topic in greater detail.

Experimental features

PowerShell 7 uses experimental features to make some new functionality available, which is not yet considered to be a mainstream feature. Features may be added to a later release of PowerShell, or discarded if they are not successful.

Three commands are available for working with experimental features:

- `Enable-ExperimentalFeature`
- `Disable-ExperimentalFeature`
- `Get-ExperimentalFeature`

`Get-ExperimentalFeature` can be used to view the available features. The list of features changes, depending on the version of PowerShell. The following list has been taken from PowerShell 7.6.4.

```
PS> Get-ExperimentalFeature

Name                                Enabled Source   Description
----                                ------- ------   -----------
```

```
PSLoadAssemblyFromNativeCode      False PSEngine Expose an API…
PSProfileDSCResource              False PSEngine DSC v3 resour…
PSSerializeJSONLongEnumAsNumber   False PSEngine Serialize enu…
```

In addition to the output shown here, each feature has a description. `Format-Table` can be used to view these descriptions:

```
Get-ExperimentalFeature | Format-Table Name, Description -Wrap
```

The use of these commands is described in the `About_Experimental_Features` help file.

If an experimental feature is enabled, PowerShell must be restarted for us to use the feature. For example, `PSRedirectToVariable` can be enabled:

```
Enable-ExperimentalFeature -Name PSRedirectToVariable
```

Once enabled, the redirect operator can be used to add content to a variable by making use of the variable drive. Viewing the content of the variable will show each of the running pwsh processes (if any are running), like the example below:

```
PS> Get-Process pwsh > Variable:Processes
PS> $Processes

NPM(K)    PM(M)      WS(M)     CPU(s)      Id  SI ProcessName
------    -----      -----     ------      --  -- -----------
   114   101.57     198.95       2.75  100828   6 pwsh
    79   101.60     174.26       1.44  101068   6 pwsh
   100   115.97     205.00       4.14  107488   6 pwsh
```

If the feature is no longer wanted, it can be disabled again:

```
Disable-ExperimentalFeature -Name PSRedirectToVariable
```

In the past, several experimental features have become permanent features in PowerShell.

Summary

This chapter contained several foundational topics for PowerShell, starting with picking an editor, using help content, and command discovery.

More recently, a choice about how AI might be used has become important. When used, AI might be used to check code for errors and bugs, to write tests and documentation, and to generate code based on an idea.

The ability to use the help system and discover commands is vital, regardless of skill level. The availability of help content in the shell allows new commands to be quickly incorporated and used.

Naming plays an important role in PowerShell. Strict use of a reasonably small set of verbs greatly enhances discovery, and reasonable assumptions can be made about a command before reaching for help content. PowerShell tends to use longer and more descriptive command names compared with other scripting languages.

Once a command has been found, it is important to understand how to use the help content and the parameters a command offers to use it effectively.

Providers allow access to data in a similar manner to using a filesystem. Providers play an important role in PowerShell and are explored again later in this book when exploring the filesystem and registry.

Splatting was introduced and will be used repeatedly throughout this book. In the context of this book, it is primarily used to reduce line length. Splatting is an incredibly useful technique when scripting. The ability to conditionally use parameters without repeating code reduces complexity and the chance of introducing bugs.

The parser was introduced to explain command syntax, when values must be quoted, and when parentheses are required. The parser is complex and the examples in `about_parsing` should be reviewed.

Finally, PowerShell 6 introduced the idea of experimental features. This continues into PowerShell 7. Features can be toggled on (or off again) before they become mainstream.

Chapter 2, Modules, moves on to exploring modules and snap-ins, allowing PowerShell users to go beyond the base set of commands and include content published by others.

2

Modules

Modules are packaged collections of commands that may be loaded inside PowerShell, allowing PowerShell to interact with new systems and services. Modules come from a wide variety of different sources, including those installed with PowerShell or the operating system, those installed via product installers, those downloaded from the PowerShell Gallery, and so on.

PowerShell itself is installed with a small number of modules, including `ThreadJob` and `PSReadLine`.

Some modules can be installed by adding Windows features or enabling capabilities. For example, the `ActiveDirectory` and `GroupPolicy` modules can be installed in this way.

Several applications include modules as part of their installers; for example, both the Microsoft **Local Administrator Password Solution** (**LAPS**) and the newer Windows LAPS include a PowerShell module which may be used to manage the component.

The Windows platform itself includes many modules, for example, the `NetFirewall` module. Most of these have been included since Windows 8 was released.

Modules can be installed from the PowerShell Gallery or another registered repository. The PowerShell Gallery can include updated versions of pre-installed modules.

The PowerShell Gallery is therefore a valuable source of modules published by Microsoft, VMware, Amazon Web Services, and many others.

Finally, many modules are just files and directories in the file system. Modules can often be copied between computers.

Snap-ins were included in PowerShell 1 and largely replaced by modules with the release of PowerShell 2. PowerShell 7 does not support snap-ins; snap-ins are limited to Windows PowerShell.

The chapter covers the following topics:

- Introducing modules
- Finding and installing modules
- PowerShell repositories
- About snap-ins

Modules are a vital part of PowerShell, allowing authors to share sets of commands.

Introducing modules

Modules were introduced with the release of PowerShell version 2.0. A module is a packaged set of commands (binary commands, functions, and aliases) that includes any required supporting content; modules often include help content.

Modules tend to target a specific system or focus on a small set of related operations. For example, the `Microsoft.PowerShell.Archive` module contains a small number of commands for interacting with ZIP files.

Large-scale services, such as Microsoft Azure, Amazon Web Services, and VMware products, have so many components that they split into different modules focused on specific areas.

The modules available on a system can be discovered using the `Get-Module` command.

The Get-Module command

`Get-Module` is used to find the modules either in the current PowerShell session or available on the current system.

PowerShell itself comes with several built-in modules, including `PowerShellGet`, `ThreadJob`, `PSReadLine`, and the commands in the `Microsoft.PowerShell.*` modules.

The Windows platform, especially the most recent versions, comes with a wide variety of modules to manage components of the operating system. These, as well as any other available modules, can be viewed using the `Get-Module -ListAvailable` command.

By default, `Get-Module` returns information about each module that has been imported (either automatically or by using `Import-Module`). For example, if the command is run from PowerShell 7, it shows that the `PSReadLine` module has been loaded:

```
PS C:\> Get-Module

ModuleType Version    PreRelease Name
```

```
---------- -------          ---------- ----
Script     2.3.6                       PSReadLine
```

The `ListAvailable` parameter shows the list of modules that are available on the system instead of just those that have been imported:

```
Get-Module -ListAvailable
```

Modules are discovered using the paths in the `PSModulePath` environment variable, which contains a delimited list of paths for PowerShell to search.

`Get-Module` will show all instances of a module regardless of the path and version when using the All parameter:

```
Get-Module <ModuleName> -All -ListAvailable
```

Modules that are available on a system can be imported either by running `Import-Module` or by running a command from the module.

The Import-Module command

PowerShell 3 and later attempts to automatically load modules if a command from that module is used and the module is under one of the paths in the `$env:PSModulePath` environment variable. Explicit use of the `Import-Module` command is less important than it was before Windows PowerShell 3.

For example, if PowerShell is started and the `CimCmdlets` module is not imported, running the `Get-CimInstance` command will cause the module to be automatically imported. This is shown in the following example:

```
PS> Get-Module CimCmdlets
PS> Get-CimInstance Win32_OperatingSystem | Out-Null
PS> Get-Module CimCmdlets

ModuleType Version    PreRelease Name
---------- -------    ---------- ----
Binary     7.0.0.0               CimCmdlets
```

The autoloader may be disabled using the `$PSModuleAutoLoadingPreference` variable as shown here:

```
$PSModuleAutoLoadingPreference = 'None'
```

Modules can be explicitly imported in PowerShell using the `Import-Module` command. Modules may be imported using a name or with a full path, as shown in the following example:

```
Import-Module -Name ThreadJob
Import-Module -Name $PSHome\Modules\ThreadJob\ThreadJob.psd1
```

Importing a module using a path is only required if the module is not in a discoverable path.

Once a module has been imported, the commands within the module may be listed using `Get-Command` as follows:

```
Get-Command -Module ThreadJob
```

Note

Modules, Get-Command, and auto-loading

As the commands exported by a module are only identified by PowerShell importing the module, the previous command will also trigger an automatic import.

If the module autoloading is disabled, the command above will not list any commands (and will not write any errors).

Modules installed in Windows PowerShell 5 and later are placed in a folder named after the module version, for example, `Modules\ModuleName\1.0.0\<ModuleContent>`. This allows multiple versions of the same module to coexist, as shown in the following example:

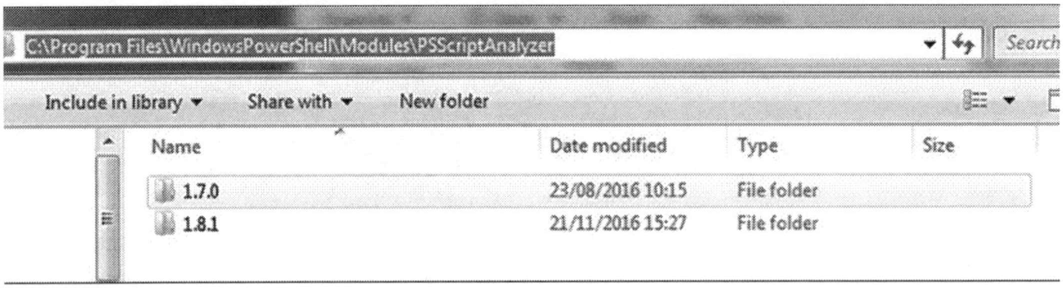

Figure 2.1: Side-by-side versioning

Version 1.8.1 of `PSScriptAnalyzer` will be imported by default, as it is the highest version number. It is possible to import a specific version of a module using the `MinimumVersion` and `MaximumVersion` parameters:

```
Import-Module PSScriptAnalyzer -MaximumVersion 1.7.0
```

Modules that have been imported can be removed from a PowerShell session using the `Remove-Module` command.

The Remove-Module command

The `Remove-Module` command removes a previously imported module from the current session.

For binary modules or manifest modules that incorporate a **Dynamic Link Library (DLL)**, commands are removed from PowerShell but DLLs are not unloaded. DLL files used in a PowerShell session cannot be unloaded without restarting the PowerShell process.

`Remove-Module` does not remove or delete the files that make up a module from a computer.

Each of the preceding commands, by default, interacts with modules saved in the `PSModulePath` environment variable.

PSModulePath in PowerShell

`PSModulePath` is a delimited list of paths that can be used to store modules. Modules can import modules in these paths by name, and they will be automatically loaded when a command from the module is used.

PowerShell 7 and Windows PowerShell have different module paths. Abstracting the specific paths, PowerShell 7 can be expected to include:

- The current user's `Documents\PowerShell\Modules` folder: User-specific modules.
- `Program Files\PowerShell\Modules`: Computer-specific modules.
- `Program Files\PowerShell\7\Modules`: Modules installed with PowerShell 7.
- `Windows\System32\WindowsPowerShell\v1.0\Modules`: Modules installed with the operating system.

Windows PowerShell has a slightly different set of paths:

- The current user's `Documents\WindowsPowerShell\Modules`
- `Program Files\WindowsPowerShell\Modules`
- `Windows\System32\WindowsPowerShell\v1.0\Modules`

PowerShell allows the value of `$env:PSModulePath` to be set using user- and machine-scoped environment variables. By default, the machine-scoped variable should include the following paths, which are used by Windows PowerShell and by PowerShell 7 for compatibility:

```
C:\Program Files\WindowsPowerShell\Modules
C:\Windows\System32\WindowsPowerShell\v1.0\Modules
```

If environment variables do not exist, PowerShell 7 uses the default values:

```
PS> $env:PSModulePath -split [System.IO.Path]::PathSeparator
C:\Users\whoami\Documents\PowerShell\Modules
C:\Program Files\PowerShell\Modules
C:\program files\powershell\7\Modules
C:\WINDOWS\system32\WindowsPowerShell\v1.0\Modules
```

The default values in the preceding list are included regardless of the value of the environment variable.

When using module paths, it is important to note that PowerShell does not search all paths for the latest version of a module.

When loading a module, PowerShell searches the list of paths in the order they appear in the `PSModulePath` environment variable. If a module is listed in more than one path, the most recent version from the first discovered path is used.

For example, if the current user path contains a module with version 1.0.0, and the Program Files path contains the same module but with version 2.0.0, PowerShell will prefer to load version 1.0.0 because the current user path is searched first. The `Version` or `MinimumVersion` parameter must be used with `Import-Module` if a specific version of a module is required.

If both Windows PowerShell and PowerShell 7 are in use in an environment, care must be taken when updating the `PSModulePath` environment variable. The behavior described previously differs from Windows PowerShell. In Windows PowerShell:

- If the user environment variable is set, it completely replaces the user value, which defaults to `C:\Users\whoami\Documents\WindowsPowerShell\Modules`.
- If the machine environment variable is set, it replaces the system32 path: `C:\windows\system32\windowspowershell\v1.0\Modules`.
- In all cases, the `C:\Program Files\WindowsPowerShell\Modules` path remains.

The `C:\windows\system32\windowspowershell\v1.0\Modules` path should be included in the machine environment variable to allow PowerShell 7 to load modules, either directly or using a Windows PowerShell compatibility session.

The value of `$env:PSModulePath` may be safely modified within all PowerShell versions and all platforms, for example, by using a profile script. Changes made to `$env:PSModulePath` are scoped to the process and only affect the current PowerShell session and any child processes; the changes do not persist.

As modules are stored in specific places on the file system, it can be said that most modules consist only of files.

Module content

A module is typically made up of several files stored in a directory. For instance, a module might include:

- A manifest, a `.psd1` file, which defines metadata like version, author, and so on.
- A root module, as either a `.psm1` file or `.dll` file. Most often named after the module directory.
- A set of `.xml` files used to hold help content, formatting data, and so on.
- Any other supporting files required by the module.

In many cases, this means that modules are self-contained and can be copied from one location to another, or from one computer to another, without needing an explicit installation step. This self-contained feature is the basis for the `Save-PSResource` command introduced later in this chapter.

Several modules are not self-contained and require content beyond the module directories.

The modules preinstalled by Microsoft as part of the operating system, such as `NetAdapter`, `SmbShare`, `Storage`, and so on, are not portable. They depend on **WMI (Windows Management Instrumentation)** classes installed into the operating system.

Similarly, modules installed as Windows features or components, such as the `ActiveDirectory` module, are also not portable.

PowerShell 7 can use modules intended for Windows PowerShell either directly or by using a Windows PowerShell compatibility session.

Using Windows PowerShell modules in PowerShell 7

Many modules available to Windows PowerShell are compatible with PowerShell 7 without requiring any changes.

If a module is not compatible with the Core edition (PowerShell 6 and higher), PowerShell 7 will automatically attempt to load the module in a Windows compatibility session. The compatibility session allows PowerShell 7 to communicate with Windows PowerShell somewhat transparently.

The `ConfigDefender` module does not support PowerShell 7; it does not state that it supports the Core edition of PowerShell, as shown by `Get-Module`:

```
PS> Get-Module ConfigDefender -ListAvailable -SkipEditionCheck

    Directory: C:\Windows\System32\WindowsPowerShell\v1.0\Modules

ModuleType Version    PreRelease Name                PSEdition
---------- -------    ---------- ----                ---------
Manifest   1.0                   ConfigDefender      Desk
```

In Windows 11 and PowerShell 7.5, if a command from the module is used, PowerShell automatically creates a compatibility session and makes commands accessible. PowerShell 7 will show a different version of the module as a result:

```
PS> Get-MpPreference | Out-Null
PS> Get-Module ConfigDefender

ModuleType Version    PreRelease Name
---------- -------    ---------- ----
Script     1.0                   ConfigDefender
```

In Windows 10 and PowerShell 7.5, the module will not automatically load. The module can be explicitly loaded into the compatibility session:

```
PS> Import-Module ConfigDefender -UseWindowsPowerShell
PS> Get-Module ConfigDefender

ModuleType Version    PreRelease Name
---------- -------    ---------- ----
Script     1.0                   ConfigDefender
```

The compatibility session can be seen using the `Get-PSSession` command after the module has been imported:

```
Get-PSSession -Name WinPSCompatSession
```

In some cases, a module has simply not been tested and marked as compatible with PowerShell 7 by the module author. A module can be explicitly loaded in PowerShell 7 regardless of the stated compatible editions:

```
Import-Module ConfigDefender -SkipEditionCheck
```

Modules may fail when they import; for example, the RemoteDesktop module will raise a few errors, including one about a missing referenced assembly shown in part below:

```
PS> Import-Module RemoteDesktop -SkipEditionCheck
Add-Type: (35,16): error CS0012: The type 'Enum' is defined in an assembly that is
not referenced. You must add a reference to
assembly 'mscorlib, Version=4.0.0.0, Culture=neutral,
PublicKeyToken=b77a5c561934e089'.
```

Even if a module successfully imports without explicitly stating support, ensure thorough testing of any intended process.

When a module is automatically imported because a command from the module is used, PowerShell does not indicate that the module has been loaded using a compatibility session.

When `Import-Module` is explicitly used, a warning is displayed:

```
PS> Import-Module Appx
WARNING: Module Appx is loaded in Windows PowerShell using WinPSCompatSession
remoting session; please note that all input and output of commands from this
module will be deserialized objects. If you want to load this module into
PowerShell please use 'Import-Module -SkipEditionCheck' syntax.
```

The impact of this warning depends on how the module has been written to work in PowerShell. There is a significant risk that the module functionality will be impaired.

Microsoft maintains a list of modules (written by Microsoft) and their compatibility state:

`https://learn.microsoft.com/en-us/powershell/windows/module-compatibility`.

The effect of an impaired command can be demonstrated by using `Get-WmiObject`. `Get-WmiObject` is not available in PowerShell 7 and cannot be directly used; PowerShell will automatically load the command using the compatibility session. The following command will therefore be executed successfully:

```
Get-WmiObject Win32_Process -Filter "ProcessID=$PID"
```

If the `Get-WmiObject` command is run in Windows PowerShell, it will have several methods available. One of these methods is `GetRelated`, which is typically used as follows when used in Windows PowerShell:

```
$process = Get-WmiObject Win32_Process -Filter "ProcessID=$PID"
$process.GetRelated('Win32_Session')
```

Because PowerShell 7 has a copy of the properties only, the method does not exist, and an error will be displayed. The functionality of the command is impaired because it has been used via the compatibility session.

```
PS> $process = Get-WmiObject Win32_Process -Filter "ProcessID=$PID"
PS> $process.GetRelated('Win32_Session')
InvalidOperation: Method invocation failed because
[Deserialized.System.Management.ManagementObject#root\cimv2\Win32_Process] does
not contain a method named 'GetRelated'.
```

In Windows PowerShell, the command above would successfully return the session associated with the process.

The compatibility feature is incredibly useful but does not replace native compatibility with modern versions of PowerShell.

PowerShell on the Windows platform has a wide variety of modules available, or available through installable applications and features to interact with other systems. New modules can also be installed from resources such as the PowerShell Gallery.

Finding and installing modules

PowerShell includes a module named `PowerShellGet`, which can be used to register repositories and search for and install modules.

By default, `PowerShellGet` searches the PowerShell Gallery.

What is the PowerShell Gallery?

The PowerShell Gallery is a Microsoft-run repository and distribution platform for PowerShell scripts and modules written by Microsoft or other users.

The PowerShell Gallery has parallels in other scripting languages, as shown in the following examples:

- Perl has cpan.org
- Python has PyPI
- Ruby has RubyGems

The PowerShell Gallery may be searched using `https://www.powershellgallery.com` as shown in the following screenshot:

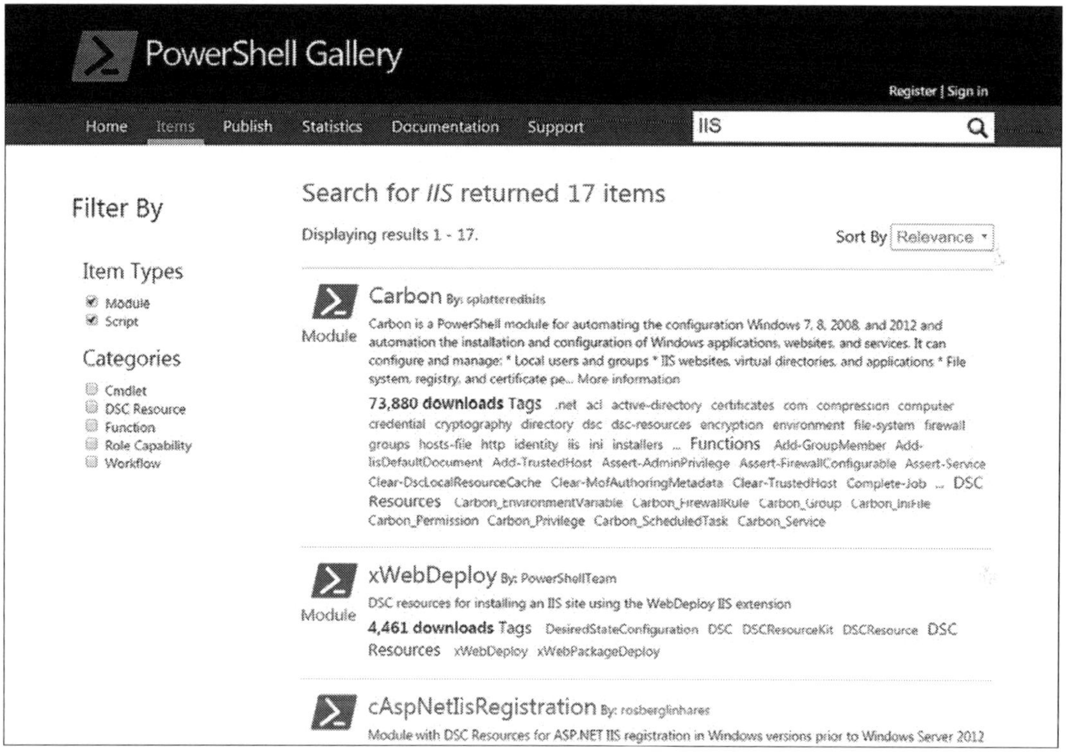

Figure 2.2: Searching the PowerShell Gallery

Support for the gallery is included by default in PowerShell 5 using the `PowerShellGet` module. For Windows PowerShell 3 and 4, `PowerShellGet` must be installed as described in Microsoft Learn: `https://learn.microsoft.com/en-us/powershell/gallery/powershellget/install-on-older-systems`.

The `PowerShellGet` module has since been superseded by the `Microsoft.PowerShell.PSResourceGet` module, which is preinstalled in PowerShell 7.

In the sections that follow, `Microsoft.PowerShell.PSResourceGet` is referred to as `PSResourceGet`.

Getting PSResourceGet

As noted above, PowerShell 7 comes with the `PSResourceGet` module. No further action is required. This section is intended to help bootstrap `PSResourceGet` in Windows PowerShell.

Windows PowerShell does not come with the `PSResourceGet` module; it must be copied or installed. There are several ways to approach this, and this section walks through some of the options available.

If the `PowerShellGet` module is installed, `PowerShellGet` can be used to install the newer module:

```
Install-Module Microsoft.PowerShell.PSResourceGet
```

The module content can be manually downloaded using the **Manual Download** option in the PowerShell gallery and unzipped: `https://www.powershellgallery.com/packages/Microsoft.PowerShell.PSResourceGet/`.

If PowerShell 7 is installed on the system, Windows PowerShell can use the version of the module by importing with a path:

```
Import-Module 'C:\Program
Files\PowerShell\7\Modules\Microsoft.PowerShell.PSResourceGet'
```

The module folder can be copied from the PowerShell 7 location (or any other file system location where it is available, including another computer) to a Windows PowerShell native location. Doing so will require a shell running as administrator. For example, it can be copied to the equivalent module path for Windows PowerShell:

```
$params = @{
     Path        = 'C:\Program
Files\PowerShell\7\Modules\Microsoft.PowerShell.PSResourceGet'
    Destination = 'C:\Program Files\WindowsPowerShell\Modules'
    Recurse     = $true
}
Copy-Item @params
```

Administrative rights are not required if copying to the module path for the current user.

The final option is a lot more advanced and intended as a bootstrapping script where neither `PowerShellGet` nor an existing `Microsoft.PowerShell.PSResourceGet` installation is available. It is possible to directly download the module content from the PowerShell Gallery without using `PowerShellGet`.

```
$module = 'Microsoft.PowerShell.PSResourceGet'
# Find the module in the gallery
$params = @{
    Uri = 'https://www.powershellgallery.com/api/v2/FindPackagesById()'
    Body = @{
        '$filter' = 'IsLatestVersion eq true'
        id  = "'$module'" # Extra quotes are required.
    }
}
$searchResult = Invoke-RestMethod @params
# Download the module archive
Invoke-RestMethod $searchResult.content.src -OutFile module.zip
# Expand the archive to a versioned folder.
$params = @{
    Path        = 'module.zip'
    Destination = 'C:\Program Files\WindowsPowerShell\Modules' |
        Join-Path -ChildPath $module |
        Join-Path -ChildPath $searchResult.properties.version
}
Expand-Archive @params
# Clean up redundant package files.
Get-ChildItem $params.Destination |
    Where-Object Name -in @(
        '_rels'
        'package'
        '[Content_Types].xml'
        "$module.nuspec"
    ) |
    Remove-Item -Recurse
# Remove downloaded archive
Remove-Item module.zip
```

Once PSResourceGet is installed, the PowerShell Gallery or another repository can be registered using the Register-PSResourceRepository command:

```
Register-PSResourceRepository -PSGallery
```

The Find-PSResource command can be used to search the PowerShell Gallery, or any registered repository, instead of using the web page.

The Find-PSResource command

Find-PSResource is used to search registered PowerShell repositories. Modules are identified by name, as shown in the following example:

```
Find-PSResource Carbon
Find-PSResource -Name Carbon
Find-PSResource -Name Az.*
```

The Tag parameter may be used to search for a specific system or service:

```
Find-PSResource -Tag IIS
```

Tags may also be combined to search for a module with a more specific focus:

```
Find-PSResource -Tag excel, import, export
```

The first result is the popular and comprehensive ImportExcel module. However, ordering is coincidental; it being first is not reflective of popularity or publication date. If the import and export tags were omitted, the module would appear in the middle of a block of others. Research outside of the PowerShell console is required when assessing if a module is suitable.

The Find-PSResource command cannot filter by PowerShell edition, and the result of the search does not state which version the module might work with.

Once found, a module can be installed using the Install-PSResource command.

Version ranges

Find-PSResource allows wildcards to be used for the Version parameter; using * will return all available versions except pre-release. The Prerelease parameter may be added to include those:

```
Find-PSResource -Name PowerShellGet -Version *
```

A range of versions may be defined using the range syntax used by NuGet, which is described in the following document: `https://learn.microsoft.com/nuget/concepts/package-versioning#version-ranges-and-wildcards`.

For example, the highest version of PowerShellGet available between 1.0 (inclusive) and 2.0 (exclusive) may be found using this:

```
Find-PSResource -Name PowerShellGet -Version '[1.0,2.0)'
```

The search can be changed to be inclusive by changing the closing `)` to `]`. For example, the following command will find version 2.0.0 of `PowerShellGet`:

```
Find-PSResource -Name PowerShellGet -Version '[1.0,2.0]'
```

The same syntax will be available when declaring dependencies between modules.

The Install-PSResource command

The `Install-PSResource` command installs modules from the PowerShell Gallery or any other configured repository. By default, `Install-PSResource` installs modules to the path for `CurrentUser`, at `C:\Users\user\Documents\Modules` on Windows and at `/home/.local/share/powershell/Modules` on Ubuntu.

Modules may also be installed in `AllUsers` scope if a module is to be shared by all users on a system. Installing in `AllUsers` scope requires administrative access.

```
Install-PSResource carbon -Scope AllUsers
```

For example, the `posh-git` module may be installed using either of the following two commands:

```
Find-PSResource -Name posh-git | Install-PSResource
Install-PSResource posh-git
```

If the most recent version of a module is already installed, the command ends without providing feedback. If a newer version is available, it will be automatically installed alongside the original.

The `Reinstall` parameter may be used to reinstall a module:

```
Install-PSResource posh-git -Reinstall
```

The `Install-PSResource` command does not provide an option to install modules under the `$PSHOME` directory. The `$PSHOME` directory is reserved for modules that are shipped with the PowerShell installer, or for Windows PowerShell, those that are shipped with the Windows operating system.

The Update-PSResource command

Use the `Update-PSResource` command to update any module installed using the `Install-PSResource` command.

In both Windows PowerShell and PowerShell 7, `Update-PSResource` attempts to update the specified module to the latest or specified version.

The Save-PSResource command

The `Save-PSResource` command downloads the module from the PowerShell Gallery (or any other registered repository) to a path without installing it.

Installation often only means downloading content to a specific location (one of the paths in `$env:PSModulePath`); there is rarely a traditional installation step as would be seen by installing an application such as Microsoft Office. The `Save-PSResource` command is therefore almost no different from `Install-PSResource`; the key difference is that a target path is required when saving module content.

The following example command downloads the `Carbon` module into a "Modules" directory in the root of the `C:` drive:

```
Save-PSResource -Name Carbon -Path C:\Modules
```

`Save-PSResource` will download the module and overwrite any previously saved version in the specified path. The command ignores other downloaded versions of the module.

The Uninstall-PSResource command

The `Uninstall-PSResource` command can be used to remove a previously installed module from disk. By default, the command searches CurrentUser scope for a module; the Scope parameter must be used if a module was installed in `AllUsers` scope.

```
Uninstall-PSResource carbon -Scope AllUsers
```

The uninstall command checks to see if another module is dependent before removal.

Ultimately any module, except pre-installed modules, can be deleted by removing the module folder from disk.

The PowerShell Gallery is a Microsoft-provided repository; other repositories can be created.

PowerShell repositories

Each of the examples from the previous section uses the PowerShell Gallery as a source for installing modules. This is an important resource, but in a business setting, it may be desirable to reduce the dependency on the PowerShell Gallery. Instead, an internal repository that holds curated or internally developed content may be implemented to share content.

Creating an SMB repository

An SMB file share is a simple way to share PowerShell content. A file share may be registered as a repository as follows:

```
$params = @{
    Name    = 'Internal'
    Uri     = '\\server\share\directory'
    Trusted = $true
}
Register-PSResourceRepository @params
```

Existing modules can be published to the repository using the `Publish-PSResource` command. For example, if the module Pester 5.7.1 is installed, it may be published to the newly created internal repository:

```
$module = Get-Module Pester -List | Where-Object Version -eq 5.7.1
Publish-PSResource -Path $module.ModuleBase -Repository Internal
```

Published modules must have a module manifest (for example, `Pester.psd1`) including ModuleVersion, GUID, Author, and Description. Existing modules installed from the gallery will already have these fields.

`Where-Object` is required if more than one version of the module (in this case Pester) exists on the system publishing the module. Once published, a `nupkg` file will appear in the file share. The Pester module is now available for installation by anyone else with the repository registered.

Users installing content from an SMB share must be authenticated and must have at least read access to the share. Guest access may be granted to avoid the authentication requirement.

NuGet repositories

NuGet is a package manager for .NET. PowerShellGet can use a NuGet repository as a source for PowerShell modules. The PowerShell Gallery is a NuGet repository.

NuGet offers greater flexibility when dealing with authentication or package life cycles when compared with SMB shares.

At the simple end, the `Chocolatey.Server` package available from chocolatey.org may be used to configure an **Internet Information Services** (**IIS**) website to act as a NuGet repository: `https://chocolatey.org/packages/chocolatey.server`

> Note
>
> **About Chocolatey**
>
> Chocolatey is a package manager for Windows. See `https://chocolatey.org` for further information.

More advanced servers include Sonatype Nexus and ProGet. Both offer free-to-use servers which may be locally deployed. These services must be configured, and once configured, packages will typically be published by using an API key to authenticate.

About snap-ins

Snap-ins and the commands for interacting with snap-ins are only available in Windows PowerShell; they are not present in PowerShell 7 and the commands used below will not work.

A snap-in is the predecessor to a module. It was the mechanism available to extend the set of commands in PowerShell 1 and was deprecated with the release of PowerShell 2. Unfortunately, a small number of organizations persist in offering PowerShell commands via a snap-in.

The list of installed snap-ins may be viewed using the following command:

```
Get-PSSnapIn -Registered
```

If the `Registered` parameter is excluded, `Get-PSSnapIn` will show the snap-ins that have been imported into the current PowerShell session.

PowerShell does not automatically load commands from a snap-in. All snap-ins must be explicitly imported using the `Add-PSSnapIn` command:

```
Add-PSSnapIn WDeploySnapin3.0
```

Once a snap-in has been installed (registered) and added, `Get-Command` can be used to list the commands as if the snap-in were a module:

```
Get-Command -Module WDeploySnapin3.0
```

The snap-in shown will only be visible if the Web Deployment Toolkit 3.0 is installed.

Summary

Modules are a vital part of PowerShell. Modules allow users to extend the commands available within PowerShell, allowing PowerShell to work with many different systems from many different vendors.

The commands explored in this chapter have demonstrated how to discover and use locally available modules along with the commands each module contains. The PowerShell Gallery has been introduced as a public repository of modules, extending PowerShell further still.

`PowerShellGet` has been a feature of PowerShell since PowerShell 3 but has now been replaced by `Microsoft.PowerShell.PSResourceGet`, which is faster, simpler to set up, and offers more advanced filtering capabilities.

SMB and NuGet-based repositories were briefly introduced for those looking to establish private repositories for use within an organization. This allows administrators to create private repositories with curated content, reducing exposure to unknown modules.

Snap-ins, an artifact of PowerShell 1 that is limited to Windows PowerShell, were very briefly demonstrated for the products where snap-ins remain important.

3

Variables, Arrays, and Hashtables

A variable in a programming language is used to give a name to a piece of information or data. A variable can be used and reused in the console, script, or function, or any other piece of code.

A variable may be of any .NET type or object instance. It may contain a string such as `"Hello World"`, an integer such as `42`, a decimal such as `3.141`, an array, a hashtable, a ScriptBlock, and so on. Everything a variable might refer to is an object when used in PowerShell.

This chapter covers the following topics:

- Naming and creating variables
- Variables in strings
- Variable types
- Variable commands
- Variable providers
- Variable scope
- About arrays
- About hashtables
- About Ordered

A variable must be given a name when it is created.

Note

Download the PDF version of this book

Your purchase includes a DRM-free PDF copy of this book, the code bundle, and a range of exclusive benefits. To unlock everything, follow the *Free benefits with your book* section in the *Preface*.

Naming and creating variables

Variables in PowerShell are preceded by the dollar symbol ($), for example:

```
$MyVariable
```

Values are assigned to variables using the assignment operator, =:

```
$MyVariable = 'Hello World'
```

It is possible to assign the same value to several variables in one statement. For example, this creates two variables, first and second, both with a value of 0:

```
$first = $second = 0
```

The name of a variable may contain numbers, letters, underscores, and question marks. For example, each of the following is a valid name:

- `$123`
- `$x`
- `$my_variable`
- `$variable`
- `$varIABle`
- `$Path_To_File`

The following are invalid names, each includes a character outside of the set above:

- `$a-b`
- `$variable!`
- `$a{b}c`

Variables are frequently written in either camel case or Pascal case. For example:

- `$myVariable` is camel case.
- `$MyVariable` is Pascal case.

PowerShell does not enforce a naming convention, nor does it consistently use a convention in the automatic variables.

One of the most common practices is that variables used as parameters must use Pascal case. Variables used only within a script or a function must use camel case.

All variables should ideally have a descriptive name. In general, PowerShell is a verbose descriptive language.

It is possible to use more complex variable names, such as one containing normally forbidden characters, by surrounding the variable name in curly braces.

For example, the variables below include characters that would not normally be permitted, such as space and hyphen:

```
${My Variable}
${My-Variable}
```

In general, variables should not include special characters.

The only special character that cannot be used between curly braces, as shown in the example above, is a colon (`:`). When a colon is used, the variable becomes a reference to a provider path.

Provider variables

When a colon is included in a variable, the value, or values, on the left of the colon are read as provider names.

For example, an environment variable is accessed using the env: drive:

```
${env:ProgramFiles(x86)}
```

The braces around the name are necessary here because of the (x86) part of the name.

This type of notation is often seen with environment variables and quite often used to access function definitions. The example below shows the code for the built-in `mkdir` function in Windows:

```
${function:mkdir}
```

It can also be used to change something. In the example below, a function is created:

```
${function:Write-HelloWorld} = { Write-Host 'Hello world' }
```

This is not a great way to create a function, but it will work.

One far less common use of this approach is to change content on the filesystem. The example below will create a new file in `C:\Windows\Temp`. Any path can be used:

```
${C:\Windows\Temp\variable.txt} = "New value"
```

While it is relatively common to see this notation for the env and function providers, it is rare to find this used to manage file content.

Curly braces can be used when expanding variables inside double-quoted strings.

Variables in strings

In PowerShell, variables can be included within any double-quoted string. The value of that variable will expand when the string is created.

For example:

```
$count = 5
$string = "There are $count items"
```

Variables will not expand inside single-quoted or literal strings.

Provider-specific values will also expand inside a double-quoted string:

```
"Computer Name: $env:COMPUTERNAME"
```

The example above uses a colon to split the provider name, env, from the variable name, `COMPUTERNAME`. If a colon is present after a variable name, PowerShell will always interpret it as a provider name.

In the following example, the first variable in the string ends with a colon, which causes a parser error:

```
PS> $computerName = $env:COMPUTERNAME
PS> "$ComputerName: Running PS $PSEdition"
ParserError:
Line |
```

```
1 |  "$ComputerName: Running PS $PSEdition"
  |   ~~~~~~~~~~~~~~
  | Variable reference is not valid. ':' was not followed by
  | a valid variable name character. Consider using ${} to
  | delimit the name.
```

In both PowerShell 7 and Windows PowerShell, the error message includes the solution to the problem. Surrounding the variable name with curly braces will correctly define the extent of the name:

```
$computerName = $env:COMPUTERNAME
"${ComputerName}: Running PS $PSEdition"
```

A sub-expression would also have been effective in this case:

```
$computerName = $env:COMPUTERNAME
"$($ComputerName): Running PS $PSEdition"
```

The sub-expression is not required in this case, a sub-expression would be required if a more complex expression were included in the string. In the example below, the length of the computer name string is used in a sub-expression:

```
"${ComputerName}: $($ComputerName.Length) characters long"
```

Sub-expressions may contain any arbitrary code, including their own quoted values (further escaping is not required).

Variable types

Values in PowerShell all have a .NET type. A .NET type describes what a value is. This affects what can be done with or to the value.

In the example below, the .NET type will be string, the .NET type `System.String`:

```
$variable = "Hello world"
```

This may be seen using the `Get-Member` command:

```
PS> $variable | Get-Member | Select-Object -First 1

   TypeName: System.String
```

```
Name  MemberType Definition
----  ---------- ----------
Clone Method     System.Object Clone(), System.Object ICloneab...
```

The `Clone` method shown in the example above can be ignored at this point.

One method that is useful at this point is the `GetType` method. This reveals the .NET type of a value. The method is available on any value that is not null and is used as shown below:

```
PS> $variable.GetType()

IsPublic IsSerial Name       BaseType
-------- -------- ----       --------
True     True     String     System.Object
```

In the output from the example above, the value of Name is the most important. This shows that the value type is string, or the .NET type `System.String`. The `FullName` property of the type will show this value:

```
PS> $variable.GetType().FullName
System.String
```

Assigning a numerical value instead will change the value type that is held in the variable:

```
$variable = 1
```

Using `Get-Member` or the `GetType` method will show that the value is now `System.Int32`.

PowerShell is not a statically typed language. When a language is statically typed, the type of a variable cannot be changed as a program or script runs. PowerShell allows the value type assigned to a variable to be changed at any point.

It is sometimes necessary to ensure a variable is of a specific type. This is most often done for parameters of functions or scripts.

A type can be given to a value of a variable on either the left- or right-hand side of the assignment.

Assignment with types on the right

When a type is used on the right-hand side of an assignment, the type affects the current value only.

In the example below, an integer value on the right-hand side of an assignment operation is coerced to a string:

```
$variable = [string]1
```

The `[string]` part of this expression is a type accelerator for `System.String`.

The type used in this assignment affects the value on the right-hand side for the current assignment. It does not prevent different value types from being assigned.

If a script later makes the following assignment, the value type will once again be `System.Int32`:

```
PS> $variable = 1
PS> $variable.GetType()

IsPublic IsSerial Name      BaseType
-------- -------- ----      --------
True     True     Int32     System.ValueType
```

The type may also be placed on the left of an assignment.

Assignment with types on the left

When a type is used on the left-hand side of an assignment, the type affects the current value and all subsequent assigned values.

For example, the following statement assigns the value `1` to a variable called `typedVariable`:

```
[string]$typedVariable = 1
```

The integer value will immediately be converted to `System.String`.

Any other value assigned to the same variable later will also be converted to a string:

```
PS> $typedVariable = 1
PS> $typedVariable.GetType()

IsPublic IsSerial Name      BaseType
-------- -------- ----      --------
True     True     String    System.Object
```

The type assigned persists for the lifetime of a variable, or until a new type is assigned on the left of an assignment. In the following example, the `string` type is replaced with an `int` type by the second assignment:

```
[string]$typedVariable = 1
[int]$typedVariable = 1
```

To avoid confusion, if a variable is given a type, it should not be reused to hold values of another type.

As mentioned at the start of this section, the type of a value affects what can be done with the value. This introduces the concept of value types and reference types.

Value and reference types

In .NET languages, a variable may be assigned a value type or a reference type. This is a concept that applies to many different languages and might be considered to describe how the computer holds a value in memory.

It is easiest to explain the difference between the two by looking at reference types first.

A hashtable, which is explored later in this chapter, is a good example of a reference type. When a hashtable is assigned to a variable, the variable maintains a reference to the location in memory of the hashtable:

```
$first = @{ Key = 'value' }
```

If a second variable is created and assigned the value of first, PowerShell will have two variables referencing the same hashtable, the same location in memory:

```
$second = $first
```

The same applies if two variables are created with the same value in a single statement:

```
$first = $second = @{ Key = 'value' }
```

If the second variable is used to make a change to the hashtable, the change will be reflected in the first variable:

```
PS> $second.Key = 'newValue'
PS> $first.Key
newValue
```

The variable holds a reference to the value. Assigning to a new variable does not implicitly create a copy of the value.

Conversely, a variable holding a value type will have an independent copy of the value.

An integer is an example of a value type. Even if two variables are created from the same value, each variable has a distinct instance of that value:

```
$first = $second = 2
```

Strings are not value types but behave in the same way as the value type in practice:

```
$first = $second = 'value'
```

Strings are immutable; a string cannot be changed without creating a new string.

Changing the value of either variable will result in the creation of a new string. The other variable will maintain the current value:

```
PS> $second = 'newValue'
PS> $first
value
```

When a value assigned to a variable must be converted to a different type, PowerShell will attempt several different operations.

Type conversion

PowerShell has an extensive set of operations, which are performed when a value is converted from one type to another.

Type conversion in PowerShell is exceptionally powerful. A great deal of work is hidden behind a simple use of a type against a value. The PowerShell team wrote a short blog post listing the steps taken when PowerShell attempts to cast or coerce a value: `https://devblogs.microsoft.com/powershell/understanding-powershells-type-conversion-magic/`

While old, this article is still relevant except for "Static Create Conversion", which is no longer in use.

`Trace-Command` can be used to attempt to see how PowerShell is converting a value from one type to another.

For example, converting the string "1/1/1970" to a DateTime type implicitly calls the `Parse` method of `DateTime`. `Trace-Command` will show a message stating that the conversion is a Parse result:

```
PS> Trace-Command -Expression { [DateTime]'1/1/1970' } -Name TypeConversion -
PSHost
DEBUG: 2024-02-11 13:16:43.5705 TypeConversion Information: 0 : Parse result:
01/01/1970 00:00:00

01 January 1970 00:00:00
```

This, in turn, means it was the result of calling the static parse method with the value. This is equivalent to the expression below:

```
[DateTime]::Parse('1/1/1970')
```

Ultimately, this means that PowerShell will try a lot harder to convert from one type to another than a more strongly typed language.

When a variable has been assigned a type on the left, PowerShell will step through the same process of attempting to convert the variable value:

```
[DateTime]$dateTime = Get-Date
Trace-Command -Expression { $dateTime = '1/1/1970' } -Name TypeConversion -PSHost
```

The command above will show the debug output shown below:

```
DEBUG: 2024-03-24 12:27:29.2837 TypeConversion Information: 0 : Converting
"1/1/1970" to "System.DateTime".
DEBUG: 2024-03-24 12:27:29.2884 TypeConversion Information: 0 :     Parse result:
01/01/1970 00:00:00
```

The presence of the type converter on a variable can be seen by making use of `Get-Variable`.

Variable commands

The variable commands may be used to explore and interact with variables defined in PowerShell. However, these commands are rarely used to declare variables when writing scripts or functions. They may be useful to explore, or as a reference, if the commands are present in other code.

PowerShell optimizes code when it can, specifically in this section around the use of local variables. Using the `*-Variable` commands in a script block disables optimization, which will have an impact on the performance of a script.

The following commands are used to work with variables:

- `Get-Variable`
- `New-Variable`
- `Set-Variable`
- `Remove-Variable`
- `Clear-Variable`

When using the variable commands, the `$` preceding the variable name is not considered part of the name; `$` tells PowerShell what follows is a variable name.

Get-Variable

The `Get-Variable` command provides access to any variable that has been created in the current session as well as the default (automatic) variables created by PowerShell. For further information on automatic variables, refer to `Get-Help about_Automatic_Variables`.

Default or automatic variables often have descriptions; these may be seen by using the `Get-Variable` command and selecting the description:

```
Get-Variable | Select-Object Name, Description
```

The following example shows the first few variables with descriptions:

```
PS> Get-Variable | Select-Object Name, Description

Name                     Description
----                     -----------
?                        Status of last command
^
$
args
ConfirmPreference        Dictates when confirmation should...
DebugPreference          Dictates the action taken when a ...
```

Metadata, such as a variable description, can only be set when creating a variable using the `New-Variable` command.

New-Variable

The `New-Variable` command can be used to create a variable:

```
New-Variable -Name today -Value (Get-Date)
```

The preceding command is the equivalent of using the following simpler assignment:

```
$today = Get-Date
```

In both cases, the outcome is the creation of a variable holding the current date. The format of the date may vary depending on the date time format settings of the operating system:

```
PS> $today
24 March 2024 12:37:46
```

`Get-Variable` may also be used to review the created variable:

```
PS> Get-Variable today

Name                           Value
----                           -----
today                          24/03/2024 12:37:46
```

`New-Variable` gives more control over the created variable, including adding metadata such as descriptions. For example, it may be used to create a constant, a variable that cannot be changed after creation:

```
New-Variable -Name startTime -Value (Get-Date) -Option Constant
```

The default output for `Get-Variable` will not show that the variable above is a constant, the Options for the variable may be shown using `Select-Object *` or, as used in the example below, `Format-List`:

```
PS> Get-Variable startTime | Format-List

Name        : startTime
Description :
Value       : 24/03/2024 12:41:08
Visibility  : Public
```

```
Module      :
ModuleName  :
Options     : Constant
Attributes  : {}
```

Any attempt to modify the variable after creation results in an error message. This includes changing the variable value or its properties and attempting to remove the variable, as shown here:

```
PS> New-Variable -Name var -Value 1 -Option Constant
PS> $var = 2
WriteError: Cannot overwrite variable var because it is read-only or constant.
```

A variable cannot be changed into a constant after creation. `Set-Variable` may be used to change other variable metadata.

Set-Variable

The `Set-Variable` command allows certain properties of an existing variable to be changed. For example, the following sets the description of an existing variable:

```
$objectCount = 42
Set-Variable objectCount -Description 'The number of objects in the queue'
```

`Set-Variable` can be used to change a variable's scope to private:

```
Set-Variable objectCount -Option Private
```

None of the commands above has output, the result of this sequence of changes may be reviewed using `Get-Variable`. `Format-List` is used to see the properties that are not automatically displayed:

```
PS> Get-Variable objectCount | Format-List

Name        : objectCount
Description : The number of objects in the queue
Value       : 42
Visibility  : Public
Module      :
ModuleName  :
```

```
Options     : Private
Attributes  : {}
```

Private scope is accessible using `$private:objectCount`. Use of the `Set-Variable` command is not required.

Remove-Variable

As the name suggests, the `Remove-Variable` command removes a variable. If this is the only variable referring to an object, the object will be removed from memory shortly afterward.

The `Remove-Variable` command is used as follows:

```
$psProcesses = Get-Process pwsh
Remove-Variable psProcesses
```

If more than one variable refers to an object, the object will not be removed, removal only occurs when all references to the object are removed. For example, the following command shows the name of the first process running (conhost.exe, in this case):

```
PS> $object1 = $object2 = Get-Process | Select-Object -First 1
PS> Remove-Variable object1
PS> Write-Host $object2.Name
conhost
```

It is rarely necessary to explicitly remove a variable in a script or function. Variables defined in a block of code fall out of scope at the end of the block in most cases.

Clear-Variable

The `Clear-Variable` command removes the value from any existing variable. `Clear-Variable` does not remove the variable itself. For example, the following example calls `Write-Host` to show the value of the variable:

```
PS> $temporaryValue = "Some-Value"
PS> Write-Host $temporaryValue -ForegroundColor Green
Some-Value
```

As with the other variable commands, it is better to assign null if there is a specific need to empty a variable:

```
$temporaryValue = $null
```

`Clear-Variable` removes the value of the variable. The command below will display a blank line as the output:

```
Clear-Variable temporaryValue
Write-Host $temporaryValue -ForegroundColor Green
```

`Get-Variable` can be used to show that the variable exists:

```
PS> Get-Variable temporaryValue

Name                           Value
----                           -----
temporaryValue
```

The variable commands are one way of interacting with existing variables; the PowerShell provider for variables is another.

Variable provider

PowerShell includes a provider and a drive, which allows variables to be listed, created, and changed using `Get-ChildItem`, `Test-Path`, and so on.

`Get-ChildItem` may be used to list all the variables in the current scope by running the command shown as follows:

```
Get-ChildItem variable:
```

The first few variables returned by the command above are shown below. This is the same output as would be seen with `Get-Variable`:

```
Name                           Value
----                           -----
?                              True
^                              if
$                              }
args                           {}
ConfirmPreference              High
DebugPreference                SilentlyContinue
```

The output shown includes the built-in variables, user-created variables, and any added modules that might have been imported.

As the provider behaves much like a filesystem, `Test-Path` may be used to determine whether a variable exists. `Get-Variable` may be used instead, but `Get-Variable` will throw an error if the variable does not exist:

```
Test-Path variable:\VerbosePreference
```

`Set-Item` may be used to change the value of a variable or create a new variable:

```
Set-Item variable:\new -Value variable
```

`Get-Content` can also be used to retrieve the content of any existing variable.

```
PS> Get-Content variable:\PSHome
C:\Program Files\PowerShell\7
```

The backslash character used in the preceding examples is optional. The following command has the same output:

```
PS> Get-Content variable:PSHome
C:\Program Files\PowerShell\7
```

Additional scope modifiers can be included in the variable path. `PSHome` is globally scoped, and the global scope modifier can be added to the command:

```
PS> Get-Content variable:global:PSHome
C:\Program Files\PowerShell\7
```

Variables are created in local scope by default.

Variable scope

PowerShell uses scopes to limit access to variables (and other items, such as functions). Scopes are layered one on top of another; child scopes inherit from parent scopes. Parent scopes cannot access variables created in child scopes.

Scopes are also used by PowerShell when optimizing blocks. Locally scoped variables can be optimized for performance, but variables from parent scopes cannot be.

There are three named scopes:

- Global
- Script
- Local

`Global` is the topmost scope; it is the scope the prompt in the console uses and is available to all child scopes.

The `Script` scope, as the name suggests, is specific to a single script. Script scoped items are available to all child scopes (such as functions) within that script. The Script scope is also available in modules, making it an ideal place to store variables that should be shared within a module.

`Local` is the current scope and is therefore relative. In the console, the `Local` scope is also the `Global` scope. In a script, the `Local` scope is the `Script` scope. Functions and script blocks also have a `Local` scope of their own.

The sections that follow demonstrate how scopes affect variable lookups. More examples are available in the `about_Scopes` help document.

By default, variables are created in the current scope, the Local scope. However, variables can be accessed from the Local scope or any parent scope.

Accessing variables

When PowerShell retrieves the value for a variable, it starts by looking for the variable in the Local scope. If the variable does not exist in the Local scope, it looks through parent scopes until it either finds the variable or runs out of scopes to search.

The following script uses two variables. The variable `$local` exists inside the `Write-VariableValue` function only. The variable `$parent` exists outside, in the parent scope, but can be used inside the function:

```
function Write-VariableValue {
    $local = 'value from inside the function'
    Write-Host "Local: $local"
    Write-Host "Parent: $parent"
}
$parent = 'value from parent scope'
```

Running the function will show both values:

```
PS> Write-VariableValue
Local: value from inside the function
Parent: value from parent scope
```

If the preceding content is run in the console, the parent scope is the `Global` scope. If the function and the call to the function are inside a script, the parent scope is the Script scope.

If the parent variable were explicitly added to the `Write-VariableValue` function, the locally scoped value would be used instead. For example:

```
function Write-VariableValue {
    $local = 'value from inside the function'
    $parent = 'a new value for parent'
    Write-Host "Local: $local"
    Write-Host "Parent: $parent"
}
$parent = 'value from parent scope'
```

The variable `$parent` inside the function is locally scoped. Assigning a value inside the function has no effect on the value of the variable outside the function. A new variable is created when a value is assigned to a variable for the first time in that scope.

Scope modifiers can be used to explicitly define the scope of a variable.

Scope modifiers

A scope modifier is placed before the variable name and is followed by a colon. For example, the following variable will always be created in the `Global` scope:

```
$Global:variableName = 123
```

Scope modifiers are available for the scopes defined above, `Global`, `Local`, and `Script`. Scope modifiers may also be used for the private variable option and provider namespaces such as `alias`, `env`, `function`, and `variable`. The private option is explored later in this topic.

Any child scope accessing the variable may repeat the same scope modifier both to make it clear where the variable is from and to avoid using a variable of the same name in the Local (or another parent) scope.

> **Note**
>
> **Non-local scoped variables in scripts and functions**
>
> Using user-defined (not automatic) variables from other scopes in scripts and functions can make code very difficult to follow and test.
>
> Adding a scope modifier improves the situation as it clearly shows the origin. However, it is still better to avoid out-of-scope variables where possible.

The creation of a child scope is dependent on where the function or script is called, not where it is written.

Numeric scopes

The `Get-Variable` command allows a numeric value to be used for the `Scope` parameter. The numeric value describes how far away from the current scope the variable is. `Get-Variable` may be used when accessing variables in parent scopes, even when a variable of the same name exists in the `Local` scope.

In the example below, each function defines one unique variable name and reuses a variable name:

```
function first {
    $first = $name = 'first'
    Write-Host "first: Name: $name; First: $first"
    second
}
function second {
    $second = $name = 'second'
    Write-Host "second: Name: $name; Second: $second"
    third
}
function third {
    $third = $name = 'third'
    Write-Host "third: Name: $name; Third: $third"
}
```

When the function `first` is called, `first` will call `second`, and `second` will call `third`. The output from running `first` is shown below:

```
PS> first
first: Name: first; First: first
second: Name: second; Second: second
third: Name: third; Third: third
```

This shows that the value of the variable `$name` changes in each case. The `$name` variable is in `Local` scope in each case.

The scopes for these functions are stacked one on top of the other in the order shown in the following list:

- Global or script
- Local scope for first
- Local scope for second
- Local scope for third

Each function can access variables defined in the parent scope. That is, the function `third` can access variables defined in the function `second`, variables defined in the function `first`, as well as any variables in the `Global` or `Script` scope.

The variables `$first`, `$second`, and `$third` are unique in the script and are therefore accessible in any child scope. The function third can access the value of `$first` with no special effort as shown here:

```
function first {
    $first = $name = 'first'
    second
}
function second {
    $second = $name = 'second'
    third
}
function third {
    "The value of first is $first"
}
first
```

Accessing the value of the $name variable from a specific parent scope requires the Get-Variable command. As described previously, the Scope parameter accepts a numeric value, defined by the number of scopes the given variable is away from the current scope.

In the function third, the value of the variable $name in second is 1 scope away; the value of the variable $name in first is two scopes away. The changes to the function third below show how Get-Variable can be used to access those variables:

```
function first {
    $first = $name = 'first'
    second
}
function second {
    $second = $name = 'second'
    third
}
function third {
    "The value of name in first is {0}" -f @(
        Get-Variable -Name name -Scope 2 -ValueOnly
    )
    "The value of name in second is {0}" -f @(
        Get-Variable -Name name -Scope 1 -ValueOnly
    )
}
first
```

In the preceding example, if the function second or third is run directly, an error will be displayed. For example, running third directly will show the following errors:

```
PS> third
Get-Variable:
Line |
   3 |          Get-Variable -Name name -Scope 2 -ValueOnly
     |          ~~~~~~~~~~~~~~~~~~~~~~~~~~~~~~~~~~~~~~~~~~~
     | The scope number '2' exceeds the number of active scopes. (Parameter
'Scope')
Actual value was 2.
Get-Variable:
Line |
   6 |          Get-Variable -Name name -Scope 1 -ValueOnly
```

```
     |              ~~~~~~~~~~~~~~~~~~~~~~~~~~~~~~~~~~~~~~~~~~~~~~~~~~~~~~
     | Cannot find a variable with the name 'name'.
```

The technique used in the preceding example is instructive but is rarely found in production code.

The ability to access variables from parent scopes is affected by the private option, which may be used when creating a variable.

Private variables

A private variable is hidden from child scopes. A private variable may either be created using `New-Variable` or by using the private scope modifier, as shown in the following examples:

```
New-Variable -Name thisValue -Option Private
$private:thisValue = "Some value"
```

In the following example, a `$name` variable is set in the first two functions. The variable is private in the function second.

```
function first {
    $name = 'first'
    second
}
function second {
    $private:name = 'second'
    third
}
function third {
    "In the function third the value of name is $name"
}
```

When the function `third` uses the `$name` variable, PowerShell searches through parent scopes since the variable does not exist in the local scope. As the `$name` variable is private in the function `second`, that variable value is ignored. PowerShell retrieves the value of the `$name` variable from the scope for the function `first`.

The output from calling `first` is shown below:

```
PS> first
In the function third the value of name is first
```

It is still possible to get the value of the private variable using a numeric scope with the `Get-Variable` command as demonstrated in the previous section.

Scopes are an important part of PowerShell and are used by more than variables. Certain settings, such as strict mode, are scoped, as are preference variables and functions.

About arrays

An array contains a collection of objects. Each entry in the array is called an element, and each element has an index (position). Indexing in an array starts from 0.

Arrays are an important part of PowerShell. When the return from a command is assigned to a variable, an array will be the result if the command returns more than one object. For example, the following command will yield an array of objects:

```
$processes = Get-Process
```

Arrays created in PowerShell use a non-specific type.

Array type

In PowerShell, arrays are, by default, given the `System.Object[]` type. This is an array of the `System.Object` type, where `[]` is used to signify that it is an array.

> Note
>
> **Why System.Object?**
>
> All object instances are derived from a .NET type or class, and, in .NET, every object instance is derived from `System.Object` (including strings and integers). Therefore, a `System.Object` array in PowerShell can hold just about anything.

Arrays in PowerShell (and .NET) have a fixed size. The size is declared on creation and cannot be changed. A new array must be created if an element is to be added or removed.

The array operations described next are considered less efficient for large arrays because of the recreation overhead involved in changing the array size.

The following sections explore creating arrays, assigning a type to the array, and selecting elements, as well as adding and removing elements.

When the result of a command is assigned to a variable, and the command returned more than one item, an array is created. For example:

```
$processes = Get-Process
```

This can be seen using the `GetType` method on the variable:

```
PS> $processes.GetType()

IsPublic IsSerial Name       BaseType
-------- -------- ----       --------
True     True     Object[]   System.Array
```

If the command emitted a single value only, the result would be a scalar, a single item of whatever type the command returns:

```
PS> $processes = Get-Process -Id $PID
PS> $processes.GetType()

IsPublic IsSerial Name       BaseType
-------- -------- ----       --------
True     False    Process    System.ComponentModel.Component
```

Enclosing the command in the array sub-expression operator would ensure the value was an array regardless of how many values the command returns (zero, one, or many):

```
$processes = @(Get-Process -Id $PID)
```

Before considering how to explicitly create an array, it is worth considering if it is necessary at all.

Creation by assignment

In PowerShell, all statements can be assigned. It is common to find arrays created and filled as shown below:

```
$array = @()
foreach ($value in 1..5) {
    $array += [PSCustomObject]@{
        Value = $value
```

```
    }
}
```

A simpler and more efficient way to write the same statement is shown here:

```
$array = foreach ($value in 1..5) {
    [PSCustomObject]@{
        Value = $value
    }
}
```

Assigning the loop (in this case) immediately avoids the problem of deciding what kind of array to create and how to fill it. The PowerShell engine takes care of that, and the result is assigned when the loop completes.

If necessary, it is also possible to create and slowly fill an array.

Creating an array

There are several ways to create arrays. An empty array (containing no elements) can be created by using the array sub-expression operator:

```
$myArray = @()
```

An empty array of a specific size may be created using the `new` method. Using `[]` after the name of the type denotes that it is an array, and the number following sets the array size:

```
$myArray = [object[]]::new(10)          # 10 objects
$byteArray = [byte[]]::new(100)         # 100 bytes
$ipAddresses = [IPAddress[]]::new(5)    # 5 IP addresses
```

It is typically not necessary to create an array in advance like this.

An array with a few strings in it can be created by assigning values directly to a variable:

```
$myGreetings = "Hello world", "Hello sun", "Hello moon"
```

Alternatively, the array sub-expression operator can be used:

```
$myGreetings = @("Hello world", "Hello sun", "Hello moon")
```

An array may be spread over multiple lines in either the console or a script, which may make it easier to read in a script:

```
$myGreetings = @(
    "Hello world"
    "Hello sun"
    "Hello moon"
)
```

Elements with different types can be mixed in a single array:

```
$myThings = "Hello world", 2, 34.23, (Get-Date)
```

When splitting over lines inside the array sub-expression operator, the parentheses around the `Get-Date` command are not required:

```
$myThings = @(
    "Hello world"
    2
    34.23
    Get-Date
)
```

If the content of the variable is displayed, it will show that each expression has been executed. Each item in the array is displayed on a new line:

```
PS> $myThings
Hello world
2
34.23

24 March 2024 13:17:34
```

Arrays may be cast to a specific type by including the array type on the left or right of an assignment.

Arrays with a type

An array may be given a type in a similar manner to a variable holding a single value. The difference is that the type name is followed by [ ], as was the case when creating an empty array of a specific size. For example, each of these is an array type that may appear before a variable name:

```
[string[]]      # An array of strings
[ulong[]]       # An array of unsigned 64-bit integers
[xml[]]         # An array of XML documents
```

If a type is set for the array, more care must be taken as regards assigning values. If a type is declared, PowerShell attempts to convert any value assigned to an array element into that type.

In this example, `$null` will become `0` and `3.45` (a double) will become `3`. PowerShell uses banker's rounding (round-half-to-even) when converting to integers:

```
[int[]]$myNumbers = 1, 2, $null, 3.45
```

The following example shows an error being thrown, as a string cannot be converted into an integer:

```
PS> [int[]]$myNumbers = 1, 2, $null, "A string"
MetadataError: Cannot convert value "A string" to type "System.Int32". Error:
"Input string was not in a correct format."
```

Elements may be added to an array using the addition operator.

Adding elements to an array

A single item, or another array, can be added to the end of an array using the assignment by addition operator:

```
$myArray = @()
$myArray += 'New value'
```

The preceding command is equivalent to the following:

```
$myArray = $myArray + 'New value'
```

The addition operator can be used to join one array to another, as shown below:

```
$firstArray = 1, 2, 3
$secondArray = 4, 5, 6
$mergedArray = $firstArray + $secondArray
```

Looking at the content of `$mergedArray` will show it contains all the values from `$firstArray` and `$secondArray`:

```
PS> $mergedArray
1
2
3
4
5
6
```

Using the array sub-expression, `@()` around a set of elements or expressions is often the cleanest way to merge values into a single array:

```
$firstArray = 1, 2, 3
$mergedArray = @(
    Get-Date
    'someString'
    $firstArray
)
```

Each of the statements in the array sub-expression will be evaluated. The content of the `$mergedArray` variable can be shown:

```
PS> $mergedArray

24 March 2024 13:22:24
someString
1
2
3
```

For arrays of a few elements, the cost to add elements like this is trivial and can be ignored. Arrays scaling up to hundreds or thousands of elements may need a different approach.

List and ArrayList

If an array must be created, and it cannot be created by assigning a statement (such as a loop), it is frequently better to make use of a resizable collection. For example, a script might want to separate values into two separate arrays inside a loop.

A `List` can be created which holds objects; this is more modern than the `ArrayList` used later in this section:

```
$list = [System.Collections.Generic.List[object]]::new()
```

Then, elements may be added to this collection using the `Add` or `AddRange` methods:

```
$list.Add('New value')
```

This avoids the recreation penalty associated with adding to a fixed-size array.

When using `AddRange` with a List, the array type being added must be of the same type as the list.

For example, if a list of strings is created, any array being added must be of the same type:

```
$stringList = [System.Collections.Generic.List[string]]::new()
$array = 'one', 'two'
$stringList.AddRange([string[]]$array)
```

If the cast to a string array is omitted from the example above, an error will be raised:

```
PS> $stringList.AddRange($array)
MethodException: Cannot convert argument "collection", with value:
"System.Object[]", for "AddRange" to type
"System.Collections.Generic.IEnumerable`1[System.String]": "Cannot convert the
"System.Object[]" value of type "System.Object[]" to type
"System.Collections.Generic.IEnumerable`1[System.String]"."
```

A popular, but older, alternative to the generic list is an `ArrayList`:

```
$arrayList = [System.Collections.ArrayList]::new()
```

Elements can be added to the list using the `Add` or `AddRange` methods:

```
$arrayList.Add('New value')
```

With the `ArrayList`, adding an element returns the index of the added element. Therefore, it is often necessary to suppress output. The example below makes use of `Out-Null` for this, which is a good option in PowerShell 7:

```
$arrayList.Add('New value') | Out-Null
```

Assigning to null or casting to void is another solution, and a fast approach for Windows PowerShell:

```
$null = $arrayList.Add('New value')
[void]$arrayList.Add('New value')
```

Unassigned output from methods like this will otherwise become output from the function or script.

Lists like these do not need to be explicitly created and filled; they can be created when assigning a value. For example, when assigning output from a command:

```
[System.Collections.Generic.List[object]]$processes = Get-Process
```

The same applies when assigning the output from a loop:

```
[System.Collections.Generic.List[object]]$list =
    foreach ($value in 1..5) {
        [PSCustomObject]@{
            Value = $value
        }
    }
```

This allows immediate use of the advanced features of these collections.

`Get-Member` may be used to view the methods available on either collection type. Note that the example below explicitly uses the `InputObject` parameter. This avoids getting the members of the elements in the collection.

```
Get-Member -InputObject $list
Get-Member -InputObject $arrayList
```

Elements in an array have an index, a zero-based position.

Selecting elements from an array

Individual elements from an array may be selected by index. The first and second elements are available using index `0` and `1`:

```
PS> $myArray = 1, 2, 3, 4, 5, 6, 7, 8, 9, 10
PS> $myArray[0]
1
PS> $myArray[1]
2
```

In a similar manner, array elements can be accessed counting backward from the end. The last element is available using `-1` as the index, and the penultimate element using `-2` as the index. For example:

```
PS> $myArray[-1]
10
PS> $myArray[-2]
9
```

Ranges of elements may be selected either going forward (starting from `0`) or going backward (starting with `-1`):

```
PS> $myArray[2..4]
3
4
5
PS> $myArray[-1..-5]
10
9
8
7
6
```

More than one range can be selected in a single statement:

```
PS> $myArray[0..2 + 6..8 + -1]
1
2
3
7
```

```
8
9
10
```

This requires some care. The first part of the index set must be an array for the addition operation to succeed; an array cannot be added to an integer. The expression in square brackets is evaluated first and converted into a single array (of indexes) before any elements are selected from the array:

```
PS> $myArray[0 + 6..8 + -1]
InvalidOperation: Method invocation failed because [System.Object[]] does not
contain a method named 'op_Addition'.
```

The same error would be shown when running the expression within square brackets alone:

```
0..2 + 6..8 + -1
```

The following modified command shows three different ways to achieve the intended result:

```
$myArray[@(0) + 6..8 + -1]
$myArray[0..0 + 6..8 + -1]
$myArray[@(0; 6..8; -1)]
```

Each of the examples above will show the output below:

```
1
7
8
9
10
```

As well as selecting elements by index, elements may be selected by value in several different ways.

The `IndexOf` method may be used to find the position of a value within the array, then the value may be accessed:

```
PS> $index = $myArray.IndexOf(5)
PS> $index
4
```

```
PS> $myArray[$index]
5
```

If the value of `$index` is -1, the value does not exist within the array. For example:

```
PS> $myArray.IndexOf(11)
-1
```

Comparison operators may be used to select elements from the array. For example, using the `-gt` operator:

```
PS> $myArray -gt 5
6
7
8
9
10
```

Alternatively, the `-lt` operator can be used:

```
PS> $myArray -lt 3
1
2
```

Comparisons can be chained together to build more complex expressions, provided each part of the expression continues to return an array:

```
PS> $myArray -gt 3 -lt 7
4
5
6
```

For more complex filtering expressions, `Where-Object` may be used:

```
PS> $myArray | Where-Object { $_ -lt 3 -or $_ -gt 7 }
1
2
8
9
10
```

The `Where` method may also be used to filter the array, this example has the same output as the `Where-Object` version:

```
$myArray.Where{ $_ -lt 3 -or $_ -gt 7 }
```

The `Where` method is faster than `Where-Object` but will raise an error if the variable is not an array.

Changing element values in an array

Elements within an array may be changed by assigning a new value to a specific index, for example:

```
$myArray = 1, 2, 9, 4, 5
$myArray[2] = 3
```

Elements in an array may be changed within a loop. The following example sets all elements in the array to 9:

```
$myArray = 1, 2, 3, 4, 5
for ($i = 0; $i -lt $myArray.Count; $i++) {
    $myArray[$i] = 9
}
```

Removing elements from a fixed-size array requires recreation of the array.

Removing elements

Elements cannot be removed from a fixed-size array except by recreating the array. This is an extension of selecting elements from an array.

Elements can be removed from `List` and `ArrayList` collections by making use of the different `Remove` methods.

For example, with a list of strings, the `Remove` method can remove by value:

```
$list = [System.Collections.Generic.List[string]]@('a', 'b', 'c')
$list.Remove('a')
```

Alternatively, the `RemoveAt` method can remove a value at a specific index:

```
$list.RemoveAt(0)
```

After these two operations, the list will only contain the value c.

For fixed-size arrays, it is possible to remove elements by filtering (see *Selecting elements from an array*), or by omitting specific indexes in a copy.

Removing elements by index

Removing elements based on an index requires the creation of a new array and the omission of the value in the element in that index. In each of the following cases, an array with 100 elements will be used as an example; the element at index 49 (with a value of 50) will be removed:

```
$oldArray = 1..100
```

The following example uses indexes to access and add everything we want to keep:

```
$newArray = $oldArray[0..48] + $oldArray[50..99]
```

Another approach uses the .NET `Array.Copy` static method.

The example below uses the `Copy` method to fill a new array with part of the original:

```
$newArray = [Object[]]::new($oldArray.Count - 1)
# Before the index
[Array]::Copy(
    $oldArray,     # Source
    $newArray,     # Destination
    49             # Number of elements to copy
)
# After the index
[Array]::Copy(
    $oldArray,     # Source
    50,            # Copy from index of Source
    $newArray,     # Destination
    49,            # Copy to index of Destination
    50             # Number of elements to copy
)
```

This operation is relatively complex, and it may be better to consider using a resizable collection instead.

Arrays and collections can be used to set the value of multiple variables.

Filling variables from arrays

It is possible to create two (or more) variables by assigning an array to a comma-separated list (an array) of variables:

```
$i, $j = 1, 2
```

Looking at the value of each variable will show it has a value assigned from the array on the right. For example, the value of the variable `$i`:

```
PS> $i
1
```

Assigning variables from an array can be useful when splitting a string, the `-split` operator is explored in more detail in *Chapter 5, Operators*:

```
$firstName, $lastName = -split "First Last"
$firstName, $lastName = "First Last".Split()
```

If the array is longer than the number of variables, all remaining elements are assigned to the last variable. For example, the variable $k will contain 3, 4, and 5, as can be seen as follows:

```
PS> $i, $j, $k = 1, 2, 3, 4, 5
PS> $k
3
4
5
```

If there are too few elements, the remaining variables will not be assigned a value. In this example, $k will be null:

```
$i, $j, $k = 1, 2
```

If it is desirable to discard part of a split operation, one or more of the variables on the left can be `$null`:

```
$firstName, $null, $lastName = -split "First A. Last"
```

First and Last can be shown to have values:

```
PS> [PSCustomObject]@{ First = $firstName; Last = $lastName }

First Last
----- ----
First Last
```

The value A. in this example will be assigned to null and therefore discarded.

It is possible to create multi-dimensional arrays in PowerShell.

Multi-dimensional and jagged arrays

Given that an array contains objects, an array can therefore also contain other arrays.

For example, an array that contains other arrays (a multi-dimensional array) might be created as follows:

```
$arrayOfArrays = @(
    @(1, 2, 3),
    @(4, 5, 6),
    @(7, 8, 9)
)
```

Be careful to ensure that the comma following each of the nested arrays (except the last) is in place. If that comma is missing, the entire structure will be flattened, merging the three inner arrays.

Elements in the preceding array are accessed by indexing into each array in turn (starting with the outermost). The element with the value 2 is accessible using the following notation:

```
PS> $arrayOfArrays[0][1]
2
```

This states that we wish to retrieve the first element (which is an array) and the second element of that array.

The element with the value 6 is accessible using the following:

```
PS> $arrayOfArrays[1][2]
6
```

If the array were created without the extra commas the second element would not exist and there would be no output from the example below:

```
$arrayOfArrays = @(
    @(1, 2, 3)
    @(4, 5, 6)
    @(7, 8, 9)
)
$arrayOfArrays[0][1]  # No output
```

A jagged array is a specific type of multi-dimensional array. An example of a jagged array is as follows:

```
$arrayOfArrays = @(
    @(1,  2),
    @(4,  5,  6,  7,  8,  9),
    @(10, 11, 12)
)
```

As in the first example, it is an array containing arrays. Instead of containing inner arrays, which all share the same size (dimension), the inner arrays have no consistent size (hence, they are jagged).

In this example, the element with the value 9 is accessed as follows:

```
PS> $arrayOfArrays[1][5]
9
```

Multi-dimensional arrays are rarely used in PowerShell. PowerShell tends to flatten arrays, which can make working with complex array structures difficult.

About hashtables

A hashtable is an associative array or an indexed array. Values in the hashtable are added with a unique key. Each key has a value associated with it; this is also known as a key-value pair. Keys cannot be duplicated within the hashtable.

A hashtable is one of several collections broadly known as dictionaries. In each case, the dictionary uses a key to identify a value in the collection.

Hashtables, and dictionaries in general, are incredibly widely used in PowerShell.

For example, *Chapter 1, Introduction to PowerShell* made use of hashtables when exploring splatting.

They can be used as arguments for parameters by commands such as `Select-Object`, `Sort-Object`, `Group-Object`, `Format-List`, and `Format-Table`. They are also used by many others to accept generic sets of arguments.

Hashtables are used repeatedly throughout this book.

An empty hashtable can be created, or a set of initial values can be set.

Creating a hashtable

An empty Hashtable is created in much the same way as an empty array. The at symbol followed by curly braces is used to denote that this is a hashtable:

```
$hashtable = @{}
```

Alternatively, a hashtable may be created with specific keys and values:

```
$hashtable = @{ Key1 = "Value1"; Key2 = "Value2" }
```

Elements in a Hashtable may be spread across multiple lines to make it easier to read:

```
$hashtable = @{
    Key1 = 'Value1'
    Key2 = 'Value2'
}
```

In both cases, the hashtable will display as having names (keys) and values:

```
PS> $hashtable

Name                           Value
----                           -----
Key1                           Value1
Key2                           Value2
```

Unlike fixed-size arrays, hashtables may have keys and values added or removed without penalty.

Adding, changing, and removing keys

The most common way of adding an element to a hashtable is to assign a value to a key. This can make use of the index operator:

```
PS> $hashtable = @{}
PS> $hashtable['Key1'] = 'Value1'
PS> $hashtable

Name                           Value
----                           -----
Key1                           Value1
```

Or a key can be created using the property dereference operator, a dot:

```
$hashtable = @{}
$hashtable.Key1 = "Value1"
```

In either case, if the key exists in the hashtable, the value will be overwritten.

Alternatively, the `Add` method may be used:

```
PS> $hashtable = @{}
PS> $hashtable.Add("Key1", "Value1")
PS> $hashtable

Name                           Value
----                           -----
Key1                           Value1
```

If the key already exists, using `Add` generates an error (as shown here):

```
PS> $hashtable = @{ Existing = "Value0" }
PS> $hashtable.Add("Existing", "Value1")
MethodInvocationException: Exception calling "Add" with "2" argument(s): "Item has
already been added. Key in dictionary: 'Existing'  Key being added: 'Existing'"
```

The `Contains` or `ContainsKey` methods can be combined with any of the approaches above to control when a value is added, changed, or read:

```
$hashtable = @{
    Key1 = 'Value1'
    Key2 = 'Value2'
}
if (-not $hashtable.Contains('Key3')) {
    $hashtable.Key3 = 'Value3'
}
```

`ContainsKey` is used in the same way, but while `Contains` is implemented by a hashtable, `ContainsKey` is implemented by all dictionary types:

```
if (-not $hashtable.ContainsKey('Key3')) {
    $hashtable.Key3 = 'Value3'
}
```

Keys can be removed from the hashtable using the `Remove` method:

```
$hashtable.Remove('Key3')
```

Hashtables can be used in PowerShell as an incredibly powerful filtering technique.

Using a hashtable to filter

The lookup of a key in a hashtable is extremely fast; this makes it an exceptional choice for filtering or finding the intersection of two collections of values.

This snippet below creates two relatively large arrays where a subset of values overlap:

```
$left = 1..10000 | ForEach-Object {
    [PSCustomObject]@{ UserID  = "User$_" }
}
$right = 6400..20000 | ForEach-Object {
    [PSCustomObject]@{ UserID = "User$_" }
}
```

The arrays used here are deliberately large, and the point they overlap is arbitrary.

The goal in this example is to find the overlap between left and right. This is an inner join.

One simple, but slow, approach is to use `Where-Object` and the `In` parameter:

```
$left | Where-Object UserID -in $right.UserID
```

A rough approximation of the time required can be found using Measure-Object. The actual time will depend on the hardware PowerShell has access to:

```
Measure-Command { $left | Where-Object UserID -in $right.UserID }
```

This approach will work, but it is slow. It will easily take several seconds to complete.

Each incoming element from left must be compared against all values from right, until it finds the first match. For User10000, it must search through and reject 99,999 other elements before it finds a match.

More broadly, the operation must loop through the content of `$right` 10,000 times, once for each value in `$left`.

This operation can be made significantly faster by making use of a hashtable. First, a lookup hashtable is created from `$right`:

```
$rightLookup = @{}
$right | ForEach-Object {
    $rightLookup[$_.UserID] = $_
}
```

Then the lookup hashtable is used to test for the value:

```
$left | Where-Object { $rightLookup.Contains($_.UserID) }
```

This has the same result as the version making use of `In`, but the operation executes in a fraction of the time. The time required should be measurable in a relatively small number of milliseconds.

The speed of this operation is somewhat affected by the loop style. In this case, `Where-Object` is used to iterate over each element in the array. A keyword loop such as foreach would be faster still. Loops are explored in *Chapter 6, Conditional Statements and Loops*.

So far, this approach has been used to find the intersection of two sets. It can be extended to join data together. For example, if `$left` and `$right` hold a few unique properties:

```
$left = 1..10000 | ForEach-Object {
    [PSCustomObject]@{
        UserID  = "User$_"
        Country = "UK"
    }
}
$right = 6400..20000 | ForEach-Object {
    [PSCustomObject]@{
        UserID = "User$_"
        City   = "Manchester"
    }
}
```

Assuming the `Country` and `City` values are different for each user, the related values from each set are required to join the sets together.

The example below extends on filtering the set, to adding a `City` value to each user from `$left`. The matched values are returned as output:

```
$rightLookup = @{}
$right | ForEach-Object {
    $rightLookup[$_.UserID] = $_
}
$left |
    Where-Object { $rightLookup.Contains($_.UserID) } |
    ForEach-Object {
        $_.City = $rightLookup[$_.UserID].City
        $_
    }
```

This allows the two sets to be joined very efficiently.

It is often necessary to enumerate the values within a hashtable.

Enumerating a hashtable

The content of a hashtable can be enumerated in several different ways. The most common way is to make use of the `GetEnumerator` method, which turns the keys and values into an array:

```
$hashtable = @{
    Key1 = 'Value1'
    Key2 = 'Value2'
}
```

Using the method on the hashtable above will result in an array of names and values:

```
PS> $hashtable.GetEnumerator()

Name                           Value
----                           -----
Key2                           Value2
Key1                           Value1
```

The `Name` property may also be referred to as `Key`. `Name` is an alias for the `Key` property.

It is also possible to access the `Keys` and `Values` properties of the hashtable to get keys only or values only respectively:

```
PS> $hashtable.Keys
Key2
Key1
```

The `Values` property returns values only; the key holding the value is not accessible when using this property:

```
PS> $hashtable.Values
Value2
Value1
```

When using these properties, it is possible to bump into a problem if one of the keys in the hashtable is named `Keys`, or one of the keys is named `Values`.

For example, consider the following hashtable:

```
$user = @{
    UserID = 'User1'
    Keys     = 'Office', 'Workshop'
}
```

If the Keys property is accessed, PowerShell hides it behind the key in the hashtable itself:

```
PS> $user.Keys
Office
Workshop
```

To work around this problem, the hidden get_Keys method can be used instead:

```
PS> $user.get_Keys()
Keys
UserID
```

At this point, it should be noted that the order of keys in a hashtable is not guaranteed. They appear in hash order, which is not very predictable and should not be depended upon.

If the order of a hashtable is important, then an OrderedDictionary should be used.

About Ordered

OrderedDictionary is made available in PowerShell by using the [Ordered] keyword. This was introduced along with PSCustomObject in PowerShell 3.

An OrderedDictionary preserves the order in which keys were added. For example:

```
$ordered = [Ordered]@{
    One   = 1
    Two   = 2
    Three = 3
}
```

Viewing the value of $ordered will show the keys appear in the same order they were entered:

```
PS> $ordered

Name                           Value
```

```
----                           -----
One                            1
Two                            2
Three                          3
```

Conversely, a hashtable may show the keys in a different order:

```
PS> @{ One = 1; Two = 2; Three = 3 }

Name                           Value
----                           -----
Two                            2
Three                          3
One                            1
```

In PowerShell 7, a type accelerator exists for `[Ordered]`, which makes the derivation of the type fairly easy to understand.

In Windows PowerShell, the following code will succeed:

```
[Ordered]@{ One = 1 }
```

But attempting to directly access `[Ordered]` as a type will fail:

```
PS> [Ordered]
Unable to find type [Ordered].
At line:1 char:1
+ [Ordered]
+ ~~~~~~~~~
    + CategoryInfo          : InvalidOperation: (Ordered:TypeName) [],
RuntimeException
    + FullyQualifiedErrorId : TypeNotFound
```

`Ordered` is a parser instruction. It can order values only because it sends the parser down a very specific branch of code which creates keys in the order entered. The error above is a symptom of the partial implementation in Windows PowerShell and can be ignored.

Note that the `PSCustomObject` type accelerator is also a parser instruction and uses much the same code to preserve order.

Beyond the parser specialization, `OrderedDictionary` may be used in the same way as hashtable. It is a great way to build up custom objects when the list of properties is not known in advance.

This small example shows that new properties can be added in the order they are listed in the array. The actual values are based on the PowerShell executable path:

```
$properties = @(
    'FullName'
    'Length'
)

$item = Get-Item (Get-Process -Id $PID).Path

$customObject = [Ordered]@{}
$properties | ForEach-Object {
    $customObject.$_ = $item.$_
}
[PSCustomObject]$customObject
```

Ordered is used widely in PowerShell to dynamically build objects where the properties might not be known in advance.

Summary

In this chapter, we explored the creation of and interaction with variables in PowerShell, a fundamental part of any scripting language.

Variables can be used in strings to create dynamic content in code. The use of provider-specific variables in strings was explored.

Variable commands can be used to interact with variables beyond changing the value, such as setting a description, making a variable in a specific scope, or exploring the facets of a variable.

Variable scope was explored, and scope modifiers were introduced, which can affect the scope in which a variable is set.

Arrays and more advanced collections were introduced as a means of storing large sets of data. The idea of assigning statements instead of explicitly building arrays was introduced as the simplest and most performance-friendly approach.

Finally, hashtables and ordered dictionaries were explored. Hashtables are very widely used in PowerShell for multiple purposes and can be used as indexed lookups to build fast comparisons.

The next chapter explores working with objects in PowerShell.

4

Working with Objects in PowerShell

Everything in PowerShell revolves around working with objects. An object is a representation of a thing, and realistically that can be anything. However, at this stage it is better to stick with things PowerShell already does.

The `Get-Process` command in PowerShell returns objects that represent running processes in the operating system. The processes are broadly described by the `Process` Type.

Type is a term .NET uses to describe the abstract representation of a thing. It is abstract because it does not represent any single process (in this case), but how a process should look to the programming language (like PowerShell).

A single specific process is represented by an instance of the `Type`.

At this point, it can be said that running `Get-Process` returns instances of the `Process` Type. Each `Process` instance is therefore a single object.

Instances of a `Type`, like the Process object, have what are known as `Members`. There are different types of `Members`, two of which are called `Properties` and `Methods` (in PowerShell). These are the only two `Member` types explored in this chapter.

An object is a representation of a thing, for example, this book might be represented as an object in PowerShell.

A book is an object that can have properties that describe its physical characteristics, such as the number of pages, the weight, or physical size. It has metadata (information about data) properties that describe the author, the publisher, the table of contents, and so on.

The book might also have methods. A method might affect the state of an object. For example, there might be methods to open or close the book or methods to jump to different chapters. A method might also convert an object into a different format. For example, there might be a method to copy a page, or even destructive methods such as one to split or dispose of the book.

Properties are therefore used to describe information about a thing. For example, the `Process` object includes `Properties` that hold the process name, the amount of memory the process is using, and so on.

Methods are used to act, to change something about the object, or to make something new. The `Process` object includes methods that can be used to `Close` or `Kill` the process. It also includes a `ToString` method to convert the (representation of the) `Process` object into a string.

PowerShell has a variety of commands to work with objects, either for the purpose of discovery such as `Get-Member`, or to select, filter, format, and so on. These commands are typically used in a pipeline.

This chapter covers the following topics:

- Pipelines
- Members
- Enumerating and filtering
- Selecting and sorting
- Grouping and measuring
- Comparing
- Importing, exporting, and converting
- Formatting

The commands in this chapter are generally activity focused. The table below summarizes usage when commands are used in a pipeline:

Goal	Command
Explore shape and structure	`Get-Member`
Loop over items	`ForEach-Object`
Filter	`Where-Object`
Add or remove properties or limit number of items	`Select-Object`

Goal	Command
Sort based on one or more properties	`Sort-Object`
Group based on one or more properties	`Group-Object`
Measure the size of items	`Measure-Object`
Compare sets of objects	`Compare-Object`
Export data	`Export-Csv` and `ConvertTo-Csv`
Import data	`Import-Csv` and `ConvertFrom-Csv`
Format for console display	`Format-Table` and `Format List`

Table 4.1: Commands and their usage

Pipelines in PowerShell allow output from one command to be passed to another.

Pipelines

The pipeline is one of the most prominent features of PowerShell. The pipeline is used to send output from one command to another command as input.

There are different kinds of output in PowerShell. Each of these different types of output is sent to a different stream, allowing each to be read separately. In PowerShell, the streams are Success, Error, Warning, Verbose, Debug, Information, and Progress.

Most of the output from a command is sent to what is known as the `Success` stream, synonymous with `stdout` (standard output).

Success stream

When assigning the output of a command to a variable, the assigned value is taken from the success stream of a command. For example, the following command assigns the data from the standard output to a variable:

```
$computerSystem = Get-CimInstance -ClassName Win32_ComputerSystem
```

Other streams such as Verbose will not be assigned to the variable.

Other streams

In PowerShell, each of the streams has a command associated with it and most have a stream number:

Stream	Command	Stream number
Success	Write-Output	1
Error	Write-Error	2
Warning	Write-Warning	3
Verbose	Write-Verbose	4
Debug	Write-Debug	5
Information	Write-Information	6
Progress	Write-Progress	None

Table 4.2: Streams and their associated commands

In PowerShell 5 and later, the `Write-Host` command is a wrapper for `Write-Information`. It sends output to the information stream.

Prior to Windows PowerShell 5, `Write-Host` did not have a dedicated stream; the output could only be captured via a transcript, that is, by using the `Start-Transcript` command to log console output to a file.

For example, if the Verbose switch is added to the preceding command, more information is shown. This extra information is not held in the variable; it is sent to a different stream:

```
PS> $computerSystem = Get-CimInstance Win32_ComputerSystem -Verbose
VERBOSE: Perform operation 'Enumerate CimInstances' with following parameters,
''namespaceName' = root\cimv2,'className' = Win32_ComputerSystem'.
VERBOSE: Operation 'Enumerate CimInstances' complete.
```

The content of the variable can be reviewed afterward, showing it does not contain the verbose message.

```
PS> $computerSystem
```

```
Name  PrimaryOwnerName  Domain     TotalPhysicalMemory  Model
----  ----------------  ------     -------------------  -----
NAME  Username          WORKGROUP  17076875264          Model
```

PowerShell is not limited to sending strings between commands in a pipeline.

The Object pipeline

Languages such as Batch scripting (on Windows) or tools on Linux and Unix often use a pipeline to pass text between commands. When the output (stdout) from one command is piped to another, it is up to the next command in the pipeline to figure out what the text from the input pipeline means.

PowerShell, on the other hand, sends objects from one command to another when using the pipeline via the success stream.

The pipe (|) symbol is used to send the standard output between commands.

In the following example, the output of `Get-Process` is sent to the `Where-Object` command, which applies a filter. The filter used in the example below returns only processes that are using more than 50 MB of memory according to the `WorkingSet64` property:

```
Get-Process | Where-Object WorkingSet64 -gt 50MB
```

Any number of commands can be added to the pipeline, each command filtering, selecting, sorting, or changing the output from the command before it.

As pipelines can be long, it can be useful to add a line break between commands.

```
Get-Process |
    Where-Object WorkingSet64 -gt 50MB |
    Select-Object -Property Name, ID
```

Or, in PowerShell 7, the pipe may be placed at the start of the following line within a script or script block. To demonstrate in the console, hold *Shift* and press *Return* at the end of each line; the prompt will change to >> for each subsequent line:

```
Get-Process
    | Where-Object WorkingSet64 -gt 50MB
    | Select-Object Name, ID
```

When the pipe is placed at the end of a line, the command can be pasted or typed in the console as-is. When using a pipe at the beginning of a new line, Shift + Return must be used in the console to add the new line without ending the code block.

No special action is required in a script or function to use the pipe at the beginning of the line.

Two generalized rules can be applied to any pipeline created in PowerShell:

- Filter as far left in a pipeline as possible.
- Format as far right in a pipeline as possible.

If the first command in a pipeline can filter, then filtering should be done there if possible. Otherwise, a command like `Where-Object`, explored in more detail later in this chapter, might be added as the second command in a pipeline.

In the example above, the `WorkingSet64` name is a `Property`, one of the members of the object returned by the `Get-Process` command.

Members

Members, as described at the beginning of this chapter, are used to interact with an object.

Members of objects in PowerShell have several possible origins:

- Members are defined by a .NET Type.
- Members can be added by PowerShell (essentially by the PowerShell Team).
- Members can be added by a user or developer in PowerShell.

The `Get-Member` command is one of the most important discovery tools available in PowerShell.

The Get-Member command

The `Get-Member` command can be used to view the different members of an object. For example, it can be used to list the members of a `Process` object returned by `Get-Process`. The automatic variable `$PID` holds the process ID of the current PowerShell process:

```
PS> Get-Process -Id $PID | Get-Member

    TypeName: System.Diagnostics.Process

Name                 MemberType     Definition
----                 ----------     ----------
Handles              AliasProperty  Handles = Handlecount
Name                 AliasProperty  Name = ProcessName
```

```
NPM                    AliasProperty  NPM = NonpagedSystemMemorySize64
PM                     AliasProperty  PM = PagedMemorySize64
SI                     AliasProperty  SI = SessionId
```

In this case, the first few members are `AliasProperty`. This is an example of a member that has been added by the command developer.

`Get-Member` offers filters using its parameters (`MemberType`, `Static`, and `View`). For example, to view the properties of the PowerShell process object, the following can be used:

```
Get-Process -Id $PID | Get-Member -MemberType Property
```

The first few lines of output are shown below again. This time, each of the members is a `Property`:

```
   TypeName: System.Diagnostics.Process

Name                   MemberType Definition
----                   ---------- ----------
BasePriority           Property   int BasePriority {get;}
Container              Property   System.ComponentModel.IContai...
EnableRaisingEvents    Property   bool EnableRaisingEvents {get...
ExitCode               Property   int ExitCode {get;}
ExitTime               Property   datetime ExitTime {get;}
```

Wildcards can be used with the `MemberType` parameter. Using `*Property*` would have included the original `AliasProperty` members in the result.

The `View` parameter is set to `All` by default. It has three additional values:

- **Base**: This shows properties that are derived from a .NET object, omitting members defined by PowerShell (such as the Alias Property members).
- **Adapted**: This shows members handled by the **Adapted Type System (ATS)** in PowerShell, which is often the same as the Base properties.
- **Extended**: This shows members added by the **Extended Type System (ETS)** in PowerShell. AliasProperty members will, for example, show here.

Note

ATS and ETS

ATS and ETS make it easy to work with object frameworks other than .NET in PowerShell, for example, objects returned by ADSI, COM, WMI, or XML. Each of these frameworks is discussed later in this book.

Microsoft published an article on ATS and ETS in 2011 that is still relevant today: `https://learn.microsoft.com/en-us/archive/blogs/besidethepoint/psobject-and-the-adapted-and-extended-type-systems-ats-and-ets`

All objects in PowerShell implement several properties provided by the type systems above, which are typically not visible. These include `PSBase`, `PSObject`, and `PSTypeNames`. These properties may be displayed by adding the `Force` parameter to `Get-Member`, which causes the command to display all hidden members:

```
Get-Process -Id $PID | Get-Member PS* -Force
```

These hidden properties are used in more than one chapter in this book as objects are used in increasingly complex ways.

Properties of objects can be directly accessed using a dot or period.

Accessing object properties

The properties of an object in PowerShell may be accessed by writing the property name after a period. For example, the `Name` property of the current PowerShell process may be accessed by using the following code:

```
$process = Get-Process -Id $PID
$process.Name
```

PowerShell also allows us to access these properties by enclosing a command in parentheses:

```
(Get-Process -Id $PID).Name
```

The properties of an object are objects themselves. For example, the `StartTime` property of a process is a `DateTime` object. `Get-Member` can be used to show information about the property:

```
PS> Get-Process -Id $PID | Get-Member -Name StartTime

   TypeName: System.Diagnostics.Process

Name      MemberType Definition
----      ---------- ----------
StartTime Property   datetime StartTime {get;}
```

The `DateTime` object in turn has properties and methods. `Get-Member` can be used again:

```
(Get-Process -Id $PID).StartTime | Get-Member -MemberType Property
```

One of the properties shown is `DayOfWeek`. The value of `DayOfWeek` may be accessed using the following example:

```
$process = Get-Process -Id $PID
$process.StartTime.DayOfWeek
```

The variable assignment step may be skipped if parentheses are used:

```
(Get-Process -Id $PID).StartTime.DayOfWeek
```

The examples above will show the day on which the current PowerShell process started. As this content was written on a Sunday, they show that value:

```
Sunday
```

The ability to assign a property or assign a new value to a property is governed by the accessor for a property.

Access modifiers

An accessor for a property has two possible values: `Get`, indicating that the property can be read; and `Set`, indicating that the property can be written to (changed).

Depending on the type of object, properties may be read-only or read/write. These may be identified using `Get-Member` and by inspecting the accessor.

In the following example, the value in curly braces at the end of each line is the accessor:

```
PS> $File = New-Item NewFile.txt
PS> $File | Get-Member -MemberType Property

   TypeName: System.IO.FileInfo

Name              MemberType    Definition
----              ----------    ----------
Attributes        Property      System.IO.FileAttributes Attributes {get;set;}
CreationTime      Property      datetime CreationTime {get;set;}
CreationTimeUtc   Property      datetime CreationTimeUtc {get;set;}
Directory         Property      System.IO.DirectoryInfo Directory {get;}
DirectoryName     Property      string DirectoryName {get;}
Exists            Property      bool Exists {get;}
```

When the accessor is `{get;}`, the property value is read-only; attempting to change the value results in an error:

```
PS> $File = New-Item NewFile.txt -Force
PS> $File.Name = 'NewName'
InvalidOperation: 'Name' is a ReadOnly property.
```

When the modifier is `{get;set;}`, the property value may be read and changed. In the preceding example, `CreationTime` has the `set` accessor. The value can be changed; in this case, it may be set to any date after January 1, 1601:

```
$File = New-Item NewFile.txt -Force
$File.CreationTime = Get-Date -Day 1 -Month 2 -Year 1692
```

The result of the preceding command can be seen by reviewing the properties for the file in PowerShell:

```
Get-Item NewFile.txt | Select-Object -ExpandProperty CreationTime
```

This command will show the date that was assigned above:

```
01 February 1692 09:14:27
```

The value displayed will change depending on the date and time formatting configuration of the operating system.

Alternatively, **File Explorer** can be used to view the properties of a file, as shown in *Figure 4.1*:

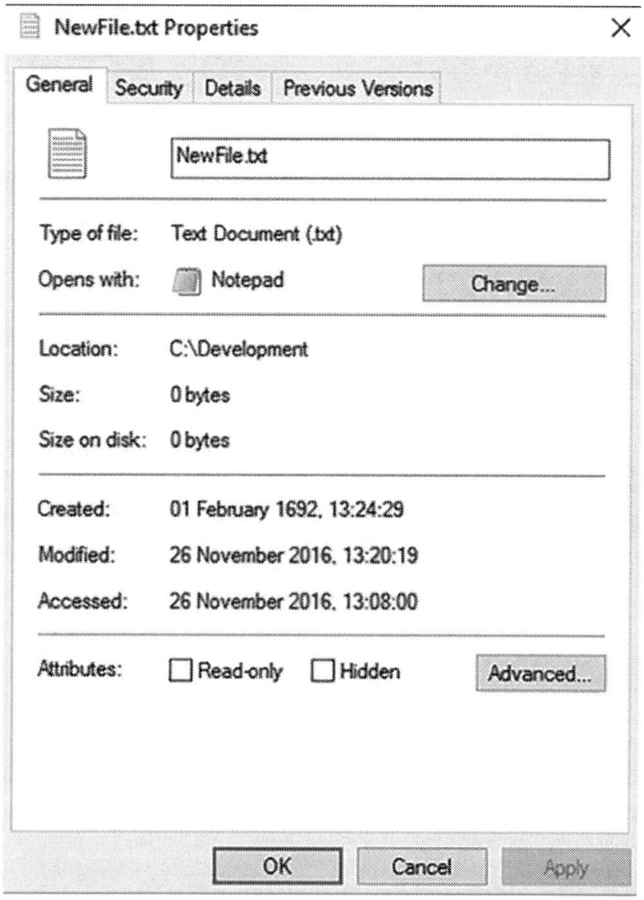

Figure 4.1: Changing the created date

In the preceding example, the change made to `CreationTime` is passed from the object representing the file to the file itself. The object used here, based on the .NET `System.IO.FileInfo` class, is written in such a way that it supports the change. A property may indicate that it can be changed (by supporting the set access modifier in `Get-Member`) and still not pass the change back to whatever the object represents.

Using methods

Methods perform an action, such as creating something new or effecting a change in state.

Methods are called using the following notation in PowerShell:

```
<Object>.Method()
```

The methods available on an object are specific to that object type. For example, a string has several methods that can be used to create a new string based on the current string.

The methods available for a `String` can be seen using the `Get-Member` command:

```
'any string' | Get-Member -MemberType Method
```

For example, a method can be used to convert an uppercase or mixed-case string to a lowercase string. This causes the creation of a new string:

```
'CaT'.ToLower()
```

Methods often accept arguments. For example, the `Replace` method on a string can be given arguments to describe an old value to find, and a new value to insert:

```
'My pet is a cat'.Replace('cat', 'dog')
```

This results in the following string:

```
My pet is a dog
```

The result of this operation can be considered somewhat like using the `-replace` operator. The most notable difference with this simple replacement is that the `Replace` method is case-sensitive and the `-replace` operator is not:

```
'My pet is a cat' -replace 'cat', 'dog'
```

There are more differences between the two approaches and the `-replace` operator is discussed in more detail in *Chapter 5, Operators*.

Methods often allow more than one set of arguments. When a method is called without parentheses, PowerShell will show the overload definitions. Overloading a method is a .NET concept; it comes into play when two or more methods share the same name but have different arguments and implementations.

The example below shows the possible arguments for the `Substring` method:

```
PS> 'thisString'.Substring

OverloadDefinitions
-------------------
string Substring(int startIndex)
string Substring(int startIndex, int length)
```

It is possible to use `Substring` to get characters from a starting point to the end:

```
'My cat'.Substring(3)
```

This returns the word "cat", starting from the fourth character of the string.

Or `Substring` can be used with both `startIndex` and `length`, where indexing starts at 0:

```
'My cat is gray'.Substring(3, 3)
```

This also returns the word "cat", but this time by finding the fourth character and getting the following 3 characters.

One very common use of methods in PowerShell comes when working with dates. The `Get-Date` command can be used to get a date. If no parameters are used, it gets the current date and time:

```
$date = Get-Date
```

The `DateTime` object returned by this command has properties and methods that can be used to change the value. As with the string examples above, the `Get-Member` command may be used to show the available properties. In this example, it just shows the Date property:

```
PS> Get-Date | Get-Member -Name Date -MemberType Property

   TypeName: System.DateTime

Name MemberType Definition
---- ---------- ----------
Date Property   datetime Date {get;}
```

The Date property can be used to go to the start of the day:

```
$date = Get-Date
$date.Date
```

DateTime also includes methods that can be used to move backward or forward in time:

```
PS> $date | Get-Member -Name Add* -MemberType Method

   TypeName: System.DateTime

Name            MemberType Definition
----            ---------- ----------
Add             Method     datetime Add(timespan value)
AddDays         Method     datetime AddDays(double value)
AddHours        Method     datetime AddHours(double value)
AddMicroseconds Method     datetime AddMicroseconds(double value)
AddMilliseconds Method     datetime AddMilliseconds(double value)
AddMinutes      Method     datetime AddMinutes(double value)
AddMonths       Method     datetime AddMonths(int months)
AddSeconds      Method     datetime AddSeconds(double value)
AddTicks        Method     datetime AddTicks(long value)
AddYears        Method     datetime AddYears(int value)
```

These methods accept positive numerical values to go forward in time and negative numeric values to go backward:

```
$date.Date.AddDays(1)
$date.Date.AddDays(-1)
```

The output from Get-Member above shows both the value type returned by the method and the permissible types for the arguments.

Return types and argument types

The output from Get-Member also shows the type of object returned by the method:

```
PS> Get-Date | Get-Member -Name AddDays -MemberType Method

   TypeName: System.DateTime

Name            MemberType Definition
```

```
----              ---------- ----------
AddDays           Method     datetime AddDays(double value)
```

The same information is visible by using AddDays on a DateTime object without using parentheses and arguments:

```
PS> (Get-Date).AddDays

OverloadDefinitions
-------------------
datetime AddDays(double value)
```

In the definitions above:

- `datetime` is the type of the value that the method returns.
- `AddDays` is the name of the method.
- `double` (`System.Double`) is the type name of the argument. Double allows values with a decimal point such as 1.5, 9.8, and so on. Whole numbers may be used as well; for example, 1.0 or 1.

The return value, `datetime`, in this case means that it is possible to use more than one method (or property) in a single statement. Each method used returns a new `DateTime` instance.

For example, the command below finds the start date (the `Date` property), then goes back one second (using `AddSeconds` with a negative value), then forward one and a half days:

```
$date = Get-Date
$date.Date.AddSeconds(-1).AddDays(1.5)
```

The result will be `11:59:59` tomorrow.

Objects in PowerShell may be created or changed either directly or within a pipeline.

Creating and modifying objects

This section focuses on creating custom objects and includes an exploration of approaches used in the past that still find their way into modern code. `New-Object` and `Add-Member` are briefly introduced in relation to custom object creation.

A custom object is one where the properties shown are defined by the author of a piece of code (a script, a function, or just something in the console). Custom objects are frequently used to create output from commands, for instance to generate a report.

The `[PSCustomObject]` type accelerator is frequently used to create a custom object.

Using PSCustomObject

PowerShell 3 introduced the ability to create a custom object using the `[PSCustomObject]` type in front of a hashtable (`@{}`). Hashtables were introduced in *Chapter 3, Variables, Arrays, and Hashtables*. A hashtable contains key and value pairs. For example, the command below creates a custom object with a single property, `Email`:

```
[PSCustomObject]@{
    Email = 'name@domain.com'
}
```

The resulting object can be used with any of the commands in this chapter.

> Note
>
> **PSCustomObject is parser magic**
>
> The `[PSCustomObject]` statement, and the `[Ordered]` statement used later in this section, are instructions to the parser.
>
> PowerShell does include a type accelerator for `PSCustomObject` which resolves to `System.Management.Automation.PSObject` shown when running:
>
> ```
> [PSCustomObject].FullName
> ```
>
> However, the statement below will create a custom object from a hashtable:
>
> ```
> [PSCustomObject]@{ Name = 'Value' }
> ```
>
> Using the apparent full name will not change the hashtable into a custom object at all:
>
> ```
> [System.Management.Automation.PSObject]@{
>     Name = 'Value'
> }
> ```

Any number of properties can be defined within the hashtable, a second property is shown below:

```
[PSCustomObject]@{
    Username = 'username'
    Email    = 'name@domain.com'
}
```

Properties are displayed in the same order they are typed. The output from the statement is shown below:

```
Username Email
-------- -----
username name@domain.com
```

In the preceding example, all properties are expected to be known in advance. Properties can be set (or changed) after the object has been created:

```
$customObject = [PSCustomObject]@{
    Username = 'username'
    Email    = ''
}
$customObject.Email = 'name@domain.com'
```

Properties can be filled based on conditions or other decisions made by the script.

If the properties that should be added cannot be known in advance, an `OrderedDictionary` can be created first. Conditional statements can be used to test if a property should be added; then, once the object is complete, it can be converted into a `PSCustomObject`:

```
$customObject = [Ordered]@{
    Username = 'username'
}
if ($email) {
    $customObject.Email = $email
}
$customObject = [PSCustomObject]$customObject
```

Custom objects can also be created using the `New-Object` command.

The New-Object command

The `New-Object` command in PowerShell can be used to create instances of .NET objects and COM objects.

Custom object creation using `New-Object` was added in PowerShell 2 and effectively deprecated by the introduction of `[PSCustomObject]` and `[Ordered]` in PowerShell 3.

Custom objects can be created with `New-Object`, as shown below:

```
New-Object -TypeName PSObject -Property @{
    Username = 'username'
    Email    = 'name@domain.com'
}
```

A limitation of this approach is that the order in which properties have been written may not be reflected in the resulting object. The example below shows the possible output from the command:

```
Email           Username
-----           --------
name@domain.com username
```

In PowerShell 3 and above it is possible to add the `[Ordered]` type to the hashtable to maintain order. However, if PowerShell 3 or above is available, `[PSCustomObject]` should be used instead.

Another common approach is to create an empty object then add properties (members) to the object afterward using the `Add-Member` command.

The Add-Member command

`Add-Member` allows new members (including `Properties` and `Methods`) to be added to existing objects.

`Add-Member` can be useful if the object type must be preserved. `Select-Object` can often be used to achieve a similar outcome, but it changes the object type when doing so; `Select-Object` is explored later in this chapter.

`Add-Member` can be used to add arbitrary properties to an existing object. The example below takes the output of `Get-ChildItem`, then adds a property called `ComputerName` to each item:

```
$dir = Get-ChildItem
$dir | Add-Member -NotePropertyName ComputerName -NotePropertyValue
$env:COMPUTERNAME
```

The new property can be seen using `Get-Member` based on the example above:

```
PS> $dir | Get-Member ComputerName

   TypeName: System.IO.DirectoryInfo

Name         MemberType   Definition
----         ----------   ----------
ComputerName NoteProperty string ComputerName=PSTEST

   TypeName: System.IO.FileInfo

Name         MemberType   Definition
----         ----------   ----------
ComputerName NoteProperty string ComputerName=PSTEST
```

Because the `Get-ChildItem` command, in this case, finds both files and directories, two entries are seen in the output from `Get-Member`.

Add-Member and custom objects

The `Add-Member` command was popularized as part of a way of creating custom objects when it was released with PowerShell 2. In some cases, it was used to overcome the ordering problem when using `New-Object`.

Using the custom object example above, `Add-Member` might be used as follows:

```
$customObject = New-Object Object
$customObject | Add-Member -Name Username -Value 'username' -MemberType
NoteProperty
$customObject | Add-Member -Name Email -Value 'name@domain.com' -MemberType
NoteProperty
$customObject
```

Alternatively, the NotePropertyName and NotePropertyValue parameters might be used:

```
$customObject = New-Object Object
$customObject | Add-Member -NotePropertyName Username -NotePropertyValue
'username'
$customObject | Add-Member -NotePropertyName Email -NotePropertyValue
'name@domain.com'
$customObject
```

This series of commands results in an object with the requested properties:

```
Username Email
-------- -----
username name@domain.com
```

Add-Member also has a PassThru parameter, which allows the statements above to be used in a pipeline:

```
New-Object Object |
    Add-Member -NotePropertyName Username -NotePropertyValue 'username' -PassThru
|
    Add-Member -NotePropertyName Email -NotePropertyValue 'name@domain.com' -
PassThru
```

The named parameters can be replaced with positional parameters to reduce the length of the statements above:

```
New-Object Object |
    Add-Member Username 'username' -PassThru |
    Add-Member Email 'name@domain.com' -PassThru
```

As with the previous series of commands, this creates an object with each property:

```
Username Email
-------- -----
username name@domain.com
```

As with the New-Object style of creating a custom object, the approach should be replaced with [PSCustomObject] as it is simpler and faster.

`Add-Member` has uses beyond custom objects. It can add arbitrary members to an existing object, which is useful if the object type must be preserved.

As well as being used to present information to an end user, the properties and methods of an object are used when enumerating and filtering collections of objects.

Enumerating and filtering

Enumerating, or listing, the objects in a collection in PowerShell does not need a specialized command. For example, if the results of `Get-PSDrive` were assigned to a variable, enumerating the content of the variable is as simple as writing the variable name and pressing Return, allowing the values to be viewed:

```
PS> $drives = Get-PSDrive
PS> $drives

Name     Used (GB)     Free (GB)     Provider       Root
----     ---------     ---------     --------       ----
Alias                                Alias
C           319.37        611.60     FileSystem     C:\
Cert                                 Certificate    \
Env                                  Environment
...
```

`ForEach-Object` may be used to work on an existing collection of objects or used to work on the output from another command in a pipeline.

`Where-Object` may be used to filter an existing collection or objects, or it may be used to filter the output from another command in a pipeline.

The ForEach-Object command

`ForEach-Object` is used to work on each object in an input pipeline. For example, the following command works on each of the results from `Get-Process` in turn by running the specified script block (enclosed in `{ }`):

```
Get-Process | ForEach-Object {
    Write-Host $_.Name -ForegroundColor Green
}
```

The `ForEach-Object` command is often interchangeable with the foreach keyword. The `foreach` keyword is explored in *Chapter 6, Conditional Statements and Loops.*

It is mentioned here because `foreach` is also an alias for the `ForEach-Object command, which can be confusing.`

Use of the alias is shown below:

```
Get-Process | foreach {
    Write-Host $_.Name -ForegroundColor Green
}
```

The example above is still using the `ForEach-Object` command. The alias is used because "foreach" is used in a context where it can only be a command (on the right of a pipe).

A foreach loop equivalent of the command above is written as follows; it does not accept pipeline input:

```
foreach ($value in Get-Process) {
    Write-Host $value.Name -ForegroundColor Green
}
```

The script block used above, an arbitrary block of code, is used as an argument for the `Process` parameter. The preceding command may explicitly include the `Process` parameter name shown here:

```
Get-Process | ForEach-Object -Process {
    Write-Host $_.Name -ForegroundColor Green
}
```

The script block executes once for each object in the input pipeline, that is, once for each object returned by `Get-Process`. The special `$_` variable is used to access the current object.

The `$PSItem` variable may be used in place of `$_` if desired. There is no difference between the two variable names. `$_` is the more commonly used name.

The `Process` parameter is accompanied by the `Begin` and `End` parameters. `Begin` and `End` are used to run script blocks before the first value is sent to the `Process` script block, and after the last value has been received.

Begin and End parameters

If `ForEach-Object` is given a single script block as an argument, it is passed to the `Process` parameter. The `Process` script block runs once for each object in the input pipeline.

`ForEach-Object` also supports `Begin` and `End` parameters. `Begin` runs once before the first value in the pipeline is passed. `End` runs once after the last value has been received from the input pipeline.

The behavior of these parameters is shown in the following example:

```
1..5 | ForEach-Object -Begin {
    Write-Host "Starting the pipeline. Creating value."
    $value = 0
} -Process {
    Write-Host "Adding $_ to value."
    $value += $_
} -End {
    Write-Host "Finished the pipeline. Displaying value."
    $value
}
```

The command above will generate the following output:

```
Starting the pipeline. Creating value.
Adding 1 to value.
Adding 2 to value.
Adding 3 to value.
Adding 4 to value.
Adding 5 to value.
Finished the pipeline. Displaying value.
15
```

The trailing `15` is the value of the variable `$value` from the `End` block.

The parameters above match the names of named blocks used by other commands acting in a pipeline.

Note

Positional parameters

The `ForEach-Object` command is written to allow all parameters to be passed based on position. The first positional parameter is `Process`. However, `ForEach-Object` will switch parameters around based on the number of arguments:

```
1 | ForEach-Object { "Process: $_" }
```

> If more than one script block is passed, the first position is passed to the `Begin` parameter:
>
> ```
> 1 | ForEach-Object { "Begin" } { "Process: $_" }
> ```
>
> If a third script block is added, it will be passed to the `End` parameter:
>
> ```
> 1 | ForEach-Object {
>     "Begin"
> } {
>     "Process: $_"
> } {
>     "End"
> }
> ```

The `parallel` parameter was added to `ForEach-Object` in PowerShell 7 as a convenient way of running operations in parallel.

The Parallel parameter

In PowerShell 7, `ForEach-Object` gains a `Parallel` parameter. This, as the name suggests, can be used to run process blocks in parallel rather than one after another.

By default, `ForEach-Object` runs 5 instances of the process block at a time; this is controlled by the `ThrottleLimit` parameter. The limit may be increased (or decreased) depending on where the bottleneck is with a given process.

Running a simple `ForEach-Object command` with a `Start-Sleep` statement shows how the output is grouped together as each set of jobs completes:

```
1..10 | ForEach-Object -Parallel {
    Start-Sleep -Seconds 2
    $_
}
```

When using `ForEach-Object` without the `Parallel` parameter, variables created before the command are accessible without any special consideration:

```
$string = 'Hello world'
1 | ForEach-Object {
    # The string variable can be used as normal
```

```
    $string
}
```

When using Parallel, each parallel script block runs in a separate thread. Variables created outside the `ForEach-Object` command must be accessed by prefixing the variable name with the `$using` scope modifier, as shown here:

```
$string = 'Hello world'
1 | ForEach-Object -Parallel {
    # The $string variable is only accessible if using is used.
    $using:string
}
```

For the most part, the `$using` scope modifier is one-way. That is, values may be read from the scope, but new values cannot be set. For example, the following attempt to write a value to `$using:newString` will fail:

```
1 | ForEach-Object -Parallel {
    $using:newString = $_
}
```

This example causes the following error:

```
ParserError:
Line |
   2 |         $using:newString = $_
     |         ~~~~~~~~~~~~~~~~
     | The assignment expression is not valid. The input to an
     | assignment operator must be an object that is able to
     | accept assignments, such as a variable or a property.
```

Advanced array types and hashtables can be changed; however, parentheses are required around the variable name, or the value must be assigned to another variable first. For example:

```
$values = @{}
1..5 | ForEach-Object -Parallel {
    ($using:values).Add($_, $_)
}
$values
```

While it is possible to access the hashtable like this, a hashtable is not built to be changed from multiple threads (it is not thread-safe).

Output from a parallel `ForEach-Object` should ideally be sent to the output pipeline. For example:

```
$output = 1..5 | ForEach-Object -Parallel { $_ }
```

`ForEach-Object` is most often used to add complexity when processing the output from another command, or when working on a collection. `ForEach-Object` may also be used to read a single property or execute a method of every object in a collection.

The MemberName parameter

`ForEach-Object` may also be used to get a single property or execute a single method on each of the objects. For example, `ForEach-Object` may be used to return only the Path property when using `Get-Process`:

```
Get-Process | ForEach-Object -MemberName Path
```

Or `ForEach-Object` may be used to run the `ToString` method on a set of dates:

```
@(
    Get-Date '01/01/2019'
    Get-Date '01/01/2020'
) | ForEach-Object ToString('yyyyMMdd')
```

This will result in strings based on each date:

```
20190101
20200101
```

`ForEach-Object` is frequently used alongside `Where-Object`.

The Where-Object command

Filtering the output from commands may be performed using `Where-Object`. For example, processes might be filtered for those started after 9 am today. If there are no processes matching the filter, then the statement will not return anything:

```
Get-Process | Where-Object StartTime -gt (Get-Date 9:00:00)
```

The syntax shown in help for `Where-Object` does not quite match the syntax used here. The help text is as follows:

```
Where-Object [-Property] <String> [[-Value] <Object>] -GT ...
```

In the preceding example, we see the following:

- `StartTime` is the argument for the `Property` parameter (first argument by position).
- The comparison is greater than, as signified by the `gt` switch parameter.
- The date (using the `Get-Date` command) is the argument for the `Value` parameter (second argument by position).

Based on the points above, the example might be written as follows:

```
Get-Process |
    Where-Object -Property StartTime -Value (Get-Date 9:00:00) -GT
```

However, it is arguably easier to read "StartTime is greater than <some date>", so most examples tend to follow that pattern.

`Where-Object` also accepts filters using the `FilterScript` parameter. `FilterScript` is often used to describe more complex filters and filters where more than one term is used:

```
Get-Service | Where-Object {
     $_.StartType -eq 'Manual' -and
     $_.Status -eq 'Running'
}
```

In this example, a list of services satisfying the filter will be shown. The services listed will depend on those available on the computer running the command. The output will be like this partial example:

```
Status   Name               DisplayName
------   ----               -----------
Running  Appinfo            Application Information
Running  AppXSvc            AppX Deployment Service (AppXSVC)
Running  BluetoothUserServ… Bluetooth User Support Service_535639
Running  BTAGService        Bluetooth Audio Gateway Service
```

When a filter like this is used, the conditions are evaluated in the order they are written. This can be used to avoid conditions that may otherwise cause errors.

In the following example, `Test-Path` is used before `Get-Item`, which is used to test the last time a file was written on a remote computer (via the administrative share):

```
$date = (Get-Date).AddDays(-90)
'Computer1', 'Computer2' | Where-Object {
    (Test-Path "\\$_\c$\temp\file.txt") -and
    (Get-Item "\\$_\c$\temp\file.txt").LastWriteTime -lt $date
}
```

If `Test-Path` is removed, the snippet will throw an error if either the computer or the file does not exist.

Selecting and sorting

`Select-Object` acts on an input pipeline, either an existing collection of objects, or the output from another command. `Select-Object` can be used to select a subset of properties, to change properties, or to add new properties. `Select-Object` also allows a user to limit the number of objects returned.

`Sort-Object` can be used to perform both simple and complex sorting based on an input pipeline.

Using `Select-Object` is a key part of working with PowerShell; output can be customized to suit circumstances in several ways.

The Select-Object command

`Select-Object` is an extremely versatile command as shown by each of the following short examples, which demonstrate some of the simpler uses of the command.

`Select-Object` can be used to explore what is available on an object by using a wildcard for the `Property` parameter:

```
Get-Process -Id $PID | Select-Object *
```

This can be a handy way of viewing all available properties and sometimes a useful alternative to `Get-Member`.

`Select-Object` may be used to limit the properties returned by a command by name:

```
Get-Process | Select-Object -Property Name, Id
```

In this case, output will be formatted as shown below, although the process names and IDs will differ:

```
Name                              Id
----                              --
Aac3572DramHal_x86              9904
Aac3572MbHal_x86               11868
AacKingstonDramHal_x64          5144
AacKingstonDramHal_x86         11724
AcPowerNotification            11752
```

`Select-Object` can limit the properties returned from a command using wildcards:

```
Get-Process | Select-Object -Property Name, *Memory*
```

As more than one property is matched by the `Memory` wildcard, and there are more than 4 selected properties, the output from the command above will be displayed as a list instead of a table.

The first result is shown below. The result will depend on locally executing processes:

```
Name                          : Aac3572DramHal_x86
NonpagedSystemMemorySize64 : 10728
NonpagedSystemMemorySize   : 10728
PagedMemorySize64          : 1572864
PagedMemorySize            : 1572864
PagedSystemMemorySize64    : 103744
PagedSystemMemorySize      : 103744
PeakPagedMemorySize64      : 2154496
PeakPagedMemorySize        : 2154496
PeakVirtualMemorySize64    : 77770752
PeakVirtualMemorySize      : 77770752
PrivateMemorySize64        : 1572864
PrivateMemorySize          : 1572864
VirtualMemorySize64        : 51818496
VirtualMemorySize          : 51818496
```

`Select-Object` can list everything but a few properties:

```
Get-Process | Select-Object -Property * -ExcludeProperty *Memory*
```

The first few properties of the output from the command above are shown below:

```
Name                 : Aac3572DramHal_x86
Id                   : 9904
PriorityClass        :
FileVersion          :
HandleCount          : 195
WorkingSet           : 10051584
TotalProcessorTime   :
```

`Select-Object` can get the first few objects in a pipeline:

```
Get-ChildItem C:\ -Recurse | Select-Object -First 2
```

Or `Select-Object` can select the last few objects in a pipeline:

```
Get-ChildItem C:\ | Select-Object -Last 3
```

`Select-Object` can skip items at the beginning; in this example, it returns the fifth item:

```
Get-ChildItem C:\ | Select-Object -Skip 4 -First 1
```

Or it can Skip items at the end. This example returns the third from the end:

```
Get-ChildItem C:\ | Select-Object -SkipLast 2 -Last 1
```

`Select-Object` can get an object from a pipeline by index:

```
Get-ChildItem C:\ | Select-Object -Index 3, 4, 5
```

In PowerShell 7 and above, `Select-Object` can omit certain indexes:

```
Get-ChildItem C:\ | Select-Object -SkipIndex 3, 4, 5
```

`Select-Object` also offers several more advanced uses. The following sections describe calculated properties, the `ExpandProperty` parameter, the `Unique` parameter, and property sets.

Calculated properties are perhaps one of the most used features of `Select-Object`.

Calculated properties

`Select-Object` can be used to add new properties to or rename existing properties on objects in an input pipeline.

Calculated properties are described using a hashtable with specific key names. The format is described in the help for `Select-Object`. In addition to names, the following hashtable formats are acceptable for the `Property` parameter:

```
@{ Name = 'PropertyName'; Expression = { 'PropertyValue' } }
@{ Label = 'PropertyName'; Expression = { 'PropertyValue' } }
@{ n = 'PropertyName'; e = { 'PropertyValue' } }
@{ l = 'PropertyName'; e = { 'PropertyValue' } }
```

The expression is most often a script block; this allows other commands to be executed, mathematical operations to be performed, substitutions to be made, and so on.

If a property is being renamed, a quoted string can be used instead of the script block. The following two examples have the same result:

```
Get-Process | Select-Object @{ Name = 'ProcessID'; Expression = 'ID' }
Get-Process | Select-Object @{ Name = 'ProcessID'; Expression = { $_.ID } }
```

If the list of properties is long, it can be better to enclose the list in `@()`, the array sub-expression operator, allowing the properties to be spread across different lines:

```
Get-Process | Select-Object -Property @(
    'Name'
    @{Name = 'ProcessId'; Expression = 'ID' }
    @{Name = 'FileOwner'; Expression = {
        (Get-Acl $_.Path).Owner
    }}
)
```

Any number of properties might be added in this manner. The preceding example includes the output from `Get-Acl`. If more than one property were required, `ForEach-Object` might be added to the command:

```
Get-Process | Where-Object Path | ForEach-Object {
    $acl = Get-Acl $_.Path
    Select-Object -InputObject $_ -Property @(
```

```
        'Name'
        @{Name = 'ProcessId'; Expression = 'ID' }
        @{Name = 'FileOwner'; Expression = { $acl.Owner }}
        @{Name = 'Access';    Expression = { $acl.AccessToString }}
    )
}
```

When `Select-Object` is used with the `Property` parameter, a new custom object is always created. If the existing object type must be preserved, `Add-Member` should be used instead. For example, if the object includes methods that must be accessible later in a script, the `Property` parameter of `Select-Object` should not be used.

The following example shows that the object type is preserved if the `Property` parameter is not used. The following command shows that the type is `Process`, which allows any of the methods, such as `WaitForExit`, to be used later in a script:

```
(Get-Process | Select-Object -First 1).GetType()
```

If the `Property` parameter is used, the output is the `PSCustomObject` type. The resulting object will not have any of the methods specific to the Process type:

```
(Get-Process | Select-Object -Property Path, Company -First 1).GetType()
```

Calculated properties are extremely flexible, allowing an object to be modified, or a more complex object to be created with a relatively small amount of code.

The ExpandProperty parameter

The `ExpandProperty` parameter of Select-Object may be used to expand one property of an object. This might be used to expand a property containing a string, leaving the output as an array of strings:

```
Get-Process | Select-Object -First 5 -ExpandProperty Name
```

If `ExpandProperty` is omitted, the returned object will be a `PSCustomObject` with a `Name` property rather than the simpler array of strings.

Expanding a single property containing a string, or a numeric value, or an array of either, is the most common use of the `ExpandProperty` parameter.

Occasionally, it may be desirable or necessary to expand a property containing a more complex object. The members of the expanded property are added to the custom object:

```
Get-ChildItem $env:SYSTEMROOT\*.dll |
    Select-Object FullName, Length -ExpandProperty VersionInfo |
    Format-List *
```

Conflicting property names will cause an error to be raised; an existing property is not replaced.

It is possible, if unusual, to use this technique to build up a single custom object based on the output from multiple commands:

```
$computerInfo = Get-CimInstance Win32_ComputerSystem |
    Select-Object -Property @(
        @{n='ComputerName';e={ $_.Name }}
        'DnsHostName'
        @{n='OSInfo';e={ Get-CimInstance Win32_OperatingSystem }}
    ) |
    Select-Object * -ExpandProperty OSInfo |
    Select-Object -Property @(
        'ComputerName'
        'DnsHostName'
        @{n='OperatingSystem';e='Caption'}
        'SystemDirectory'
    )
```

The resulting object will contain two properties from `Win32_ComputerSystem` and two properties from `Win32_OperatingSystem`. This is shown in list format below:

```
PS> $computerInfo | Format-List

ComputerName    : NAME
DnsHostName     : Name.domain.com
OperatingSystem : Microsoft Windows 11 Pro
SystemDirectory : C:\WINDOWS\system32
```

A common requirement is to make a list of objects unique; `Select-Object` has a parameter to help with this.

The Unique parameter

`Select-Object` returns unique values from arrays of simple values with the Unique parameter:

```
1, 1, 1, 3, 5, 2, 2, 4 | Select-Object -Unique
```

> Note
>
> **About Get-Unique**
>
> `Get-Unique` may also be used to create a list of unique elements. When using `Get-Unique`, a list must be sorted first, for example:
>
> ```
> 1, 1, 1, 3, 5, 2, 2, 4 | Sort-Object | Get-Unique
> ```

In the following example, an object is created with one property called `Number`. The value for the property is 1, 2, or 3. The result is two objects with a value of 1, two with a value of 2, and so on:

```
1, 2, 3, 1, 2, 3 | ForEach-Object {
    [PSCustomObject]@{
        Number = $_
    }
}
```

This statement creates an array of custom objects as shown below:

```
Number
------
     1
     2
     3
     1
     2
     3
```

`Select-Object` can remove the duplicates from the set in this example using the `Unique` parameter if a list of properties (or a wildcard for the properties) is set:

```
1, 2, 3, 1, 2, 3 | ForEach-Object {
    [PSCustomObject]@{
```

```
        Number = $_
    }
} | Select-Object -Property * -Unique
```

This causes the removal of any instance where all properties match:

```
Number
------
     1
     2
     3
```

`Select-Object` builds up a collection of unique objects by comparing each property of each object to every unique object that came before it in a pipeline. This allows `Select-Object` to work without relying on an ordered collection (as `Get-Unique` requires).

When working with strings, the comparison used by `Select-Object` is case-sensitive. In the statement below, the two occurrences of `Mouse` will be retained.

```
'dog', 'dog', 'cat', 'cat', 'mouse', 'Mouse' |
    Select-Object -Unique
```

`Select-Object` may be used to select property sets, although this is rarely used in practice.

Property sets

A property set is a pre-defined list of properties that might be used when exploring an object. The property set is stored with the object itself. `Select-Object` can be used to select the properties within a specified property set.

In the following example, `Get-Member` is used to view the property sets available on the objects returned by `Get-Process`:

```
PS> Get-Process -Id $PID | Get-Member -MemberType PropertySet

    TypeName: System.Diagnostics.Process

Name               MemberType     Definition
----               ----------     ----------
PSConfiguration    PropertySet    PSConfiguration {Name, Id, ...
PSResources        PropertySet    PSResources {Name, Id, Hand...
```

`Select-Object` may then be used to display one of the property sets, `PSConfiguration`:

```
PS> Get-Process -Id $PID | Select-Object -Property PSConfiguration

Name   Id PriorityClass FileVersion
----   -- ------------- -----------
pwsh 2220        Normal 7.4.1.500
```

Objects, including selected objects, may be sorted using the `Sort-Object` command.

The Sort-Object command

The `Sort-Object` command allows objects to be sorted. By default, `Sort-Object` will sort objects in ascending order:

```
PS> 5, 4, 3, 2, 1 | Sort-Object
1
2
3
4
5
```

Strings are sorted in ascending order, irrespective of uppercase or lowercase:

```
PS> 'ccc', 'BBB', 'aaa' | Sort-Object
aaa
BBB
ccc
```

When dealing with more complex objects, `Sort-Object` may be used to sort based on a named property. For example, processes may be sorted based on the `Id` property:

```
Get-Process | Sort-Object -Property Id
```

Objects may be sorted using more than one property; for example, a list of files may be sorted on `LastWriteTime` and then on `Name`:

```
Get-ChildItem C:\Windows\System32 |
    Sort-Object LastWriteTime, Name
```

In the preceding example, items are first sorted on `LastWriteTime`. Items that have the same value for `LastWriteTime` are then sorted based on `Name`.

`Sort-Object` is not limited to sorting on existing properties. A script block (a fragment of script, enclosed in curly braces) can be used to create a calculated value for sorting. For example, it is possible to order items based on a word, as shown in this example:

```
$examResults = @(
    [PSCustomObject]@{ Exam = 'Music';   Result = 'N/A';  Mark = 0 }
    [PSCustomObject]@{ Exam = 'History'; Result = 'Fail'; Mark = 23 }
    [PSCustomObject]@{ Exam = 'Biology'; Result = 'Pass'; Mark = 78 }
    [PSCustomObject]@{ Exam = 'Physics'; Result = 'Pass'; Mark = 86 }
    [PSCustomObject]@{ Exam = 'Maths';   Result = 'Pass'; Mark = 92 }
)
$examResults | Sort-Object {
    switch ($_.Result) {
        'Pass' { 1 }
        'Fail' { 2 }
        'N/A'  { 3 }
    }
}
```

The result of sorting the objects is shown here:

```
Exam       Result   Mark
----       ------   ----
Maths      Pass       92
Physics    Pass       86
Biology    Pass       78
History    Fail       23
Music       N/A        0
```

In the preceding example, when `Sort-Object` encounters a `Pass` result it is given the lowest numerical value (`1`) to sort on. As `Sort-Object` defaults to ascending order, this means exams with a result of `Pass` appear first in the list. This process is repeated to give a numeric value to each of the other possible results.

Sorting within each Result set varies depending on the version of PowerShell. Windows PowerShell changes the order of the elements within each set, listing Maths, Physics, then Biology. PowerShell 6 and above, on the other hand, maintains the original order, listing Biology, then Physics, then Maths within the pass set.

As Sort-Object is capable of sorting on more than one property, the preceding example can be taken further to sort on mark next. This makes the output order entirely predictable, regardless of the version of PowerShell:

```
$examResults | Sort-Object {
    switch ($_.Result) {
        'Pass' { 1 }
        'Fail' { 2 }
        'N/A'  { 3 }
    }
}, Mark
```

The result is a table sorted by Result, then by Mark:

```
Exam     Result  Mark
----     ------  ----
Biology    Pass    78
Physics    Pass    86
Maths      Pass    92
History    Fail    23
Music       N/A     0
```

Adding the Descending parameter to Sort-Object will reverse the order of both fields:

```
$examResults | Sort-Object {
    switch ($_.Result) {
         'Pass' { 1 }
         'Fail' { 2 }
         'N/A'  { 3 }
    }
}, Mark -Descending
```

The output from the command is sorted again, this time in descending order for both Result and Mark:

```
Exam     Result  Mark
----     ------  ----
Music       N/A     0
History    Fail    23
Maths      Pass    92
```

```
Physics    Pass     86
Biology    Pass     78
```

The ordering behavior can be made property-specific using the notation that is shown in the following example. `@()` is used to try and make the property list easier to read:

```
$examResults | Sort-Object @(
    {
        switch ($_.Result) {
            'Pass' { 1 }
            'Fail' { 2 }
            'N/A'  { 3 }
        }
    }
    @{ Expression = { $_.Mark }; Descending = $true }
)
```

This example shows different sorting for the two properties:

```
Exam      Result   Mark
----      ------   ----
Maths       Pass     92
Physics     Pass     86
Biology     Pass     78
History     Fail     23
Music        N/A      0
```

The hashtable, `@{}`, is used to describe an expression (a calculated property; in this case, the value for Mark) and the sorting order, which is either ascending or descending.

In the preceding example, the first sorting property, based on the `Result` property, is sorted in ascending order as this is the default. The second property, Mark, is sorted in descending order.

Like `Select-Object`, `Sort-Object` can be used to find unique values.

The Unique parameter

`Sort-Object` can be used to make a set of values unique, but unlike `Select-Object`, comparisons between objects are not case-sensitive:

```
'dog', 'dog', 'cat', 'cat', 'mouse', 'Mouse' |
    Sort-Object -Unique
```

Of course, unlike `Select-Object`, the resulting collection will be sorted as shown below:

```
cat
dog
mouse
```

Once a set of data has been prepared by selecting and sorting, grouping and measuring can be used to work on the collection.

Grouping and measuring

`Group-Object` is a powerful command that allows objects to be grouped together under a single property name or an expression.

`Measure-Object` supports several simple mathematical operations, such as counting the number of objects, calculating an average, calculating a sum, and so on. `Measure-Object` also allows characters, words, or lines to be counted in text fields.

The Group-Object command

The `Group-Object` command shows a `Group` and `Count` for each occurrence of a value in a collection of objects.

Given the sequence of numbers shown, Group-Object creates a Name that holds the value it is grouping, a Count as the number of occurrences of that value, and a Group property as the set of similar values:

```
PS> 6, 7, 7, 8, 8, 8 | Group-Object

Count   Name                Group
-----   ----                -----
    1   6                   {6}
    2   7                   {7, 7}
    3   8                   {8, 8, 8}
```

The `Group` property may be removed using the `NoElement` parameter, which simplifies the output of the command:

```
PS> 6, 7, 7, 8, 8, 8 | Group-Object -NoElement

Count   Name
-----   ----
```

```
    1   6
    2   7
    3   8
```

`Group-Object` can group based on a specific property. For example, it might be desirable to list the number of occurrences of a file in an extensive folder structure. In the following example, the `C:\Windows\Assembly` folder contains different versions of DLLs for different versions of packages, including the .NET Framework:

```
Get-ChildItem C:\Windows\Assembly -Filter *.dll -Recurse |
    Group-Object Name
```

Combining `Group-Object` with commands such as `Where-Object` and `Sort-Object` allows reports about the content of a dataset to be generated extremely quickly; for example, a report on the names of the top five files that appear more than once in a file tree:

```
Get-ChildItem C:\Windows\Assembly -Filter *.dll -File -Recurse |
    Group-Object Name -NoElement |
    Where-Object Count -gt 1 |
    Sort-Object Count, Name -Descending |
    Select-Object Name, Count -First 5
```

The output from the preceding command will vary from one computer to another; it depends on the installed software, development kits, .NET Framework version, and so on. The output from the preceding command might be like the following example:

```
Name                                              Count
----                                              -----
Microsoft.Web.Diagnostics.resources.dll           14
Microsoft.Web.Deployment.resources.dll            14
Microsoft.Web.Deployment.PowerShell.resources.dll 14
Microsoft.Web.Delegation.resources.dll            14
Microsoft.Web.PlatformInstaller.resources.dll     13
```

As was seen with `Sort-Object`, `Group-Object` can group on more than one property. For example, we might group on both a filename and the size of a file (the `Length` property of a file):

```
Get-ChildItem C:\Windows\Assembly -Filter *.dll -Recurse |
    Group-Object Name, Length -NoElement |
```

```
    Where-Object Count -gt 1 |
    Sort-Object Name -Descending |
    Select-Object Name, Count -First 5
```

As with the previous example, the output from the command will vary from one computer to another:

```
Name                                                Count
----                                                -----
WindowsFormsIntegration.Package.ni.dll, 100352          2
Templates.Editorconfig.Wizard.resources.ni.dll, 9216   13
Templates.Editorconfig.Wizard.resources.ni.dll, 8192   13
System.Web.ni.dll, 16939008                             2
System.Web.ni.dll, 14463488                             2
```

In the preceding example, `System.Web.ni.dll` is listed twice (with a count of two in each case). Each pair of files has the same file size.

Like `Sort-Object`, `Group-Object` is not limited to properties that already exist. Calculated properties can be used to create a new value to group on. For example, grouping on an email domain in a list of email addresses might be useful. The domain is obtained by splitting on the @ character:

```
'one@one.example', 'two@one.example', 'three@two.example' |
    Group-Object { ($_ -split '@')[1] }
```

The created groups are shown below:

```
Count  Name                 Group
-----  ----                 -----
    2  one.example          {one@one.example, two@one.example}
    1  two.example          {three@two.example}
```

In this example, the split operator is used to split on the @ character; everything to the left is stored in index `0`, while everything to the right is stored in index `1`.

By default, `Group-Object` returns the collection of objects shown in each of the preceding examples. `Group-Object` can also return a hashtable using the `AsHashtable` parameter.

When using the `AsHashTable` parameter, the `AsString` parameter can be added, which ensures that keys in the resulting hashtable are always strings. This parameter ensures that a group can be accessed after the grouping operation is complete. For example:

```
$hashtable = @(
    [IPAddress]'10.0.0.1'
    [IPAddress]'10.0.0.2'
    [IPAddress]'10.0.0.1'
) | Group-Object -AsHashtable -AsString
```

`AsString` allows the use of a string instead of an `IPAddress` instance to access values:

```
PS> $hashtable['10.0.0.1']

AddressFamily       : InterNetwork
ScopeId             :
IsIPv6Multicast     : False
IsIPv6LinkLocal     : False
IsIPv6SiteLocal     : False
IsIPv6Teredo        : False
IsIPv6UniqueLocal   : False
IsIPv4MappedToIPv6  : False
Address             : 16777226
IPAddressToString   : 10.0.0.1

AddressFamily       : InterNetwork
ScopeId             :
IsIPv6Multicast     : False
IsIPv6LinkLocal     : False
IsIPv6SiteLocal     : False
IsIPv6Teredo        : False
IsIPv6UniqueLocal   : False
IsIPv4MappedToIPv6  : False
Address             : 16777226
IPAddressToString   : 10.0.0.1
```

If the AsString parameter was excluded from the preceding example, the value used to access the key would have to be an IPAddress type. For example:

```
$hashtable = @(
    [IPAddress]'10.0.0.1'
    [IPAddress]'10.0.0.2'
    [IPAddress]'10.0.0.1'
) | Group-Object -AsHashtable
```

Then the key used to access the value must also match the type:

```
$hashtable[[IPAddress]'10.0.0.1']
```

In the preceding example, attempting to access the key without the [IPAddress] type will fail; no value will be returned, and no error will be shown.

By default, Group-Object is not case sensitive. The strings one, ONE, and One are all considered equal when grouping. The CaseSensitive parameter forces Group-Object to differentiate between items where cases differ:

```
PS> 'one', 'ONE', 'One' | Group-Object -CaseSensitive

Count Name                      Group
----- ----                      -----
    1 one                       {one}
    1 ONE                       {ONE}
    1 One                       {One}
```

Group-Object can be used to count occurrences of a value within a collection of objects. Measure-Object is useful when it is necessary to analyze the values, such as when determining the average of a specific property.

The Measure-Object command

When used without any parameters, Measure-Object returns a value for Count, which is the number of items passed in using the pipeline, for example:

```
PS> 1, 5, 9, 79 | Measure-Object

Count    : 4
Average  :
```

```
Sum       :
Maximum   :
Minimum   :
Property  :
```

Each of the remaining properties is empty, unless requested using their respective parameters. For example, `Sum` may be requested:

```
PS> 1, 5, 9, 79 | Measure-Object -Sum
Count      : 4
Average    :
Sum        : 94
Maximum    :
Minimum    :
Property   :
```

Adding the remaining parameters adds values to the rest of the fields (except `Property`):

```
PS> 1, 5, 9, 79 | Measure-Object -Average -Maximum -Minimum -Sum

Count       : 4
Average     : 23.5
Sum         : 94
Maximum     : 79
Minimum     : 1
Property    :
```

The value for `Property` is added when Measure-Object is asked to work against a particular property (instead of a set of numbers). For example:

```
PS> Get-Process | Measure-Object WorkingSet -Average

Count       : 135
Average     : 39449395.2
Sum         :
Maximum     :
Minimum     :
Property    : WorkingSet
```

When working with text, `Measure-Object` can count characters, words, or lines. For example, it can be used to count the number of lines, words, and characters in a text file:

```
Get-Content C:\Windows\WindowsUpdate.log |
    Measure-Object -Line -Word -Character
```

This time, an object is shown that describes the content of the text file.

```
Lines  Words  Characters  Property
-----  -----  ----------  --------
    3     32         268
```

`Group-Object` and `Measure-Object` are essential parts of a PowerShell toolkit. They can significantly simplify analyzing collections of data for repetition or performing simple mathematical operations. Each of these commands is used against a single collection of objects; when working with more than one collection of objects, it may be necessary to compare.

Comparing

The `Compare-Object` command can be used to compare two collections of objects with one another.

`Compare-Object` must be supplied with values for the `ReferenceObject` and `DifferenceObject` parameters, which are normally collections or arrays of objects. If either value is null, then an error will be displayed. If both values are equal, `Compare-Object` does not return anything by default. For example, the reference and difference objects in the following example are identical:

```
Compare-Object -ReferenceObject 1, 2 -DifferenceObject 1, 2
```

If there are differences, `Compare-Object` displays the results, as shown here:

```
PS> Compare-Object -ReferenceObject 1, 2, 3, 4 -DifferenceObject 1, 2

InputObject SideIndicator
----------- -------------
          3 <=
          4 <=
```

This shows that `ReferenceObject` (the collection on the left, denoted by the direction of the `<=` arrow) has the values, but `DifferenceObject` (the collection on the right) does not.

`Compare-Object` has several other parameters that may be used to change the output. The `IncludeEqual` parameter adds values that are present in both collections to the output:

```
$params = @{
    ReferenceObject  = 1, 2, 3, 4
    DifferenceObject = 1, 2
    IncludeEqual     = $true
}
Compare-Object @params
```

The result from this command will show the values that are equal as requested:

```
InputObject SideIndicator
----------- -------------
          1 ==
          2 ==
          3 <=
          4 <=
```

`ExcludeDifferent` will omit the results that differ. This parameter makes sense if `IncludeEqual` is also set; without this, the command will always return nothing.

The `PassThru` parameter is used to return the original object instead of the representation showing the differences. In the following example, it is used to select values that are common to both the reference and difference objects:

```
$params = @{
    ReferenceObject  = 1, 2, 3, 4
    DifferenceObject = 1, 2
    ExcludeDifferent = $true
    IncludeEqual     = $true
    PassThru         = $true
}
Compare-Object @params
```

This example shows the values only:

```
1
2
```

`Compare-Object` can compare based on properties of objects, as well as the simpler values in the preceding examples. This can be a single property or a list of properties. For example, the following command compares the contents of `C:\Windows\System32` with `C:\Windows\SysWOW64`, returning files that have the same name and are the same size in both:

```
$params = @{
    ReferenceObject  = Get-ChildItem C:\Windows\System32 -File
    DifferenceObject = Get-ChildItem C:\Windows\SysWOW64 -File
    Property         = 'Name', 'Length'
    IncludeEqual     = $true
    ExcludeDifferent = $true
}
Compare-Object @params
```

By default, `Compare-Object` writes an error if either the reference or difference objects are null. If `Compare-Object` is used when there is a chance of either being empty, the following technique can be used to avoid an error being generated, provided neither contains an explicit null value:

```
$reference = Get-ChildItem C:\Windows\System32\tcpmon*.ini
$difference = Get-ChildItem C:\Windows\SysWOW64\tcpmon*.ini
Compare-Object @($reference) @($difference) -Property Name
```

The array operator (`@()`) around each parameter value will be discarded by PowerShell. If `$difference` is empty, it will be treated as an empty array instead of it being a null value.

Collections of objects generated by any of the preceding commands might be exported to move data outside of PowerShell. The result of any of these operations might be exported to a file for another user, system, or program to use.

Importing, exporting, and converting

Getting data in and out of PowerShell is a critical part of using the language. There are several commands dedicated to this task, including:

- `Export-Csv`

- `ConvertTo-Csv`
- `Import-Csv`
- `ConvertFrom-Csv`
- `Export-CliXml`
- `ConvertTo-CliXml`
- `Import-CliXml`
- `ConvertFrom-CliXml`
- `Tee-Object`

Other PowerShell modules, such as the `ImportExcel` module, available in the PowerShell Gallery, can be used to extend the output formats available.

The Export-Csv and ConvertTo-Csv commands

The `Export-Csv` command writes data from objects to a text file, for example:

```
Get-Process | Export-Csv processes.csv
```

By default, `Export-Csv` writes a comma-delimited file using UTF8NoBOM encoding in PowerShell 6 and later, or ASCII encoding in Windows PowerShell, and completely overwrites any file using the same name.

`Export-Csv` may be used to add lines to an existing file using the `Append` parameter. When the `Append` parameter is used, the input object must have each of the fields listed in the CSV header or an error will be thrown, unless the `Force` parameter is used.

For example, if a CSV file is created with `Name` and `Id` headers, as shown below:

```
Get-Process -ID $PID |
    Select-Object Name, Id |
    Export-Csv .\Processes.csv
```

Then a second command with a different set of properties is run to add to the CSV:

```
Get-Process explorer |
    Select-Object Name |
    Export-Csv .\Processes.csv -Append
```

Then the following error will be shown:

```
Export-Csv: Cannot append CSV content to the following file: .\Processes.csv. The
appended object does not have a property that corresponds to the following column:
Id. To continue with mismatched properties, add the -Force parameter, and then
retry the command.
```

If the `Append` parameter is used and the input object has more fields than the CSV, the extra fields are silently dropped when writing the CSV file, resulting in data loss. For example, the value held in `Id` is ignored when writing the results to the existing CSV file:

```
Get-Process pwsh |
    Select-Object Name | Export-Csv .\Processes.csv
Get-Process explorer |
    Select-Object Name, Id |
    Export-Csv .\Processes.csv -Append
```

`Export-Csv` in Windows PowerShell writes a header line to each file, which details the .NET type it has just exported. If the preceding example was used in Windows PowerShell, the header line would be as follows:

```
#TYPE Selected.System.Diagnostics.Process
```

In PowerShell 6 and later, this header is included only when explicitly using the `IncludeTypeInformation` parameter.

`Export-Csv` in Windows PowerShell can be instructed to exclude this header using the `NoTypeInformation` parameter:

```
Get-Process | Export-Csv processes.csv -NoTypeInformation
```

`ConvertTo-Csv` in Windows PowerShell is like `Export-Csv`, except that instead of writing content to a file, content is written as command output:

```
PS> Get-Process powershell | Select-Object Name, Id | ConvertTo-Csv
#TYPE Selected.System.Diagnostics.Process
"Name","Id"
"pwsh","404"
```

Both Export-Csv and ConvertTo-Csv are limited in what they can do with arrays of objects in properties. For example, ConvertTo-Csv is unable to display the values that are in an array:

```
[PSCustomObject]@{
    Name = "Numbers"
    Value = 1, 2, 3, 4, 5
} | ConvertTo-Csv -NoTypeInformation
```

PowerShell will write Numbers as System.Object[] as shown below:

```
"Name","Value"
"Numbers","System.Object[]"
```

The value of the Value property in the CSV content is taken from the ToString method, which is called on the property named Value; for example:

```
$object = [PSCustomObject]@{
    Name = "Numbers"
    Value = 1, 2, 3, 4, 5
}
$object.Value.ToString()
```

This will display the System.Object[] text.

If a CSV file is expected to hold the content of an array, code must be written to convert it into a suitable format. For example, the content of the array can be written after converting it to a string:

```
[PSCustomObject]@{
    Name  = "Numbers"
    Value = 1, 2, 3, 4, 5
} | ForEach-Object {
    $_.Value = $_.Value -join ', '
    $_
} | ConvertTo-Csv -NoTypeInformation
```

Creating the joined string allows the value to be represented in the CSV content:

```
"Name","Value"
"Numbers","1, 2, 3, 4, 5"
```

In the preceding example, the value of the property is joined using a comma followed by a space. The modified object (held in `$_`) is passed on to the `ConvertTo-Csv` command.

The Import-Csv and ConvertFrom-Csv commands

Comma-Separated Value (CSV) files are structured text. Applications such as Microsoft Excel can work with CSV files without changing the file format, although Excel's advanced features cannot be saved to a CSV file.

By default, Import-Csv expects the input to have a header row and be comma-delimited. In PowerShell 6 and later, the default encoding is UTF8NoBOM; Windows PowerShell uses the active system code page. If any of these items are different, the command parameters may be used. For example, a tab may be set as the delimiter:

```
Import-Csv TabDelimitedFile.tsv -Delimiter `t
```

A tick (grave accent) followed by t (` t) is used to represent the tab character in PowerShell.

Data imported using `Import-Csv` will always be formatted as a string. If `Import-Csv` is used to read a file containing the following text, each of the numbers will be treated as a string:

```
Name,Position
Jim,35
Matt,3
Dave,5
```

Attempting to use `Sort-Object` on the imported CSV file results in values being sorted as if they were strings, not numbers:

```
PS> Import-Csv .\positions.csv | Sort-Object Position

Name   Position
----   --------
Matt   3
Jim    35
Dave   5
```

`Sort-Object` can use an expression in a script block to coerce the value of the `Position` property to an integer:

```
PS> Import-Csv .\positions.csv | Sort-Object { [Int]$_.Position }
```

```
Name Position
---- --------
Matt  3
Dave  5
Jim   35
```

This conversion problem exists regardless of whether the data in a CSV file is numerical, a date, or any type other than a string.

The `ConvertFrom-Csv` command is like `Import-Csv` in that it reads CSV content and creates custom objects from that content. The difference is that `ConvertFrom-Csv` reads strings from standard input instead of a file. In the following example, a string is converted into a custom object using the `ConvertFrom-Csv` command with the Header parameter:

```
PS> "powershell,404" | ConvertFrom-Csv -Header Name, Id

Name          Id
----          --
powershell    404
```

`ConvertFrom-Csv` expects either an array of strings or a single string with line-breaks. The following example includes a header in the string:

```
"Name,Id
Powershell,404" | ConvertFrom-Csv
```

CSV is a simple and accessible format. However, CSV is a pure-text format; it cannot express different value types (such as numbers and dates) – all data is a string. The `CliXml` format is at the other end of the spectrum: it can be used to store complex data types.

The Clixml commands

The **CLI** acronym stands for **Common Language Infrastructure**, a technical standard developed by Microsoft. `Export-Clixml` is extremely useful where type information about each property must be preserved.

`Export-Clixml` creates representations of objects in XML files. For example, the following object may be exported using `Export-Clixml`:

```
[PSCustomObject]@{
    Integer = 1
    Decimal = 2.3
```

```
    String  = 'Hello world'
} | Export-Clixml .\object.xml
```

The resulting XML file shows the type for each of the properties it has just exported:

```
PS> Get-Content object.xml
<Objs Version="1.1.0.1" xmlns="http://schemas.microsoft.com/powershell/2004/04">
  <Obj RefId="0">
    <TN RefId="0">
      <T>System.Management.Automation.PSCustomObject</T>
      <T>System.Object</T>
    </TN>
    <MS>
      <I32 N="Integer">1</I32>
      <Db N="Decimal">2.3</Db>
      <S N="String">Hello world</S>
    </MS>
  </Obj>
</Objs>
```

`ConvertTo-Clixml`, added in PowerShell 7.5, may be used if the file is not required:

```
[PSCustomObject]@{
    Integer = 1
    Decimal = 2.3
    String  = 'Hello world'
} | ConvertTo-Clixml
```

`ConvertTo-Clixml` will write the same XML content shown in the file to the success stream.

In the preceding example, `I32` is a 32-bit integer (`Int32`). `Db` is a double-precision floating-point number (double). `S` is a string.

With this extra information in the file, PowerShell can rebuild the object, including the different types, using `Import-Clixml`, as follows:

```
$object = Import-Clixml .\object.xml
```

If the serialized content were in a string instead, `ConvertFrom-Clixml` may be used. `ConvertFrom-Clixml` was added in PowerShell 7.5.

```
$string = [PSCustomObject]@{
    Integer = 1
    Decimal = 2.3
    String  = 'Hello world'
} | ConvertTo-Clixml
$object = $string | ConvertFrom-Clixml
```

Once imported, the value types can be inspected using the `GetType` method:

```
PS> $object.Decimal.GetType()

IsPublic  IsSerial  Name          BaseType
--------  --------  ----          --------
   True      True   Double        System.ValueType
```

The ability to rebuild the original object allows `Export-CliXml` to convert credential objects to text. When it does so, password values are encrypted using **Data Protection API (DPAPI)** on Windows. For example, providing a username and password when prompted will create an XML file holding the encrypted password:

```
Get-Credential | Export-CliXml -Path secret.xml
```

The file can be opened in a text editor to view the encrypted password. The credential can be imported again using `Import-CliXml`:

```
$credential = Import-CliXml -Path secret.xml
```

And from there, the password may be viewed by making use of the `GetNetworkCredential` method:

```
$credential.GetNetworkCredential().Password
```

The password for the credential is encrypted using the current user account (protected by the login password). The key used is held in the user profile; the resulting file can only be decrypted on the computer it was created on (without a roaming profile).

Note that while the command above can be used on Linux and macOS, the password value in the XML file will be in plain text.

The Tee-Object command

The `Tee-Object` command is used to send output to two places at the same time. `Tee-Object` is used to write output to a console and a file or variable.

For example, the following command both displays the output of `Get-Process` on the screen and writes the content to a `$processes` variable:

```
Get-Process | Tee-Object -Variable processes
```

The first few values from the `$processes` variable are shown below:

```
PS> $processes

NPM(K)  PM(M)    WS(M)   CPU(s)      Id  SI ProcessName
------  -----    -----   ------      --  -- -----------
    10   1.50     9.59     0.00    9904   0 Aac3572DramHal_x86
    13   2.38    10.60     0.00   11868   0 Aac3572MbHal_x86
    10   1.70     8.63     0.00    5144   0 AacKingstonDramHal_x64
    11   1.64     9.63     0.00   11724   0 AacKingstonDramHal_x86
    32  33.48    10.23     0.06   11752   1 AcPowerNotification
```

`Tee-Object` writes file output as the console sees it (table or list) rather than writing in CSV or another format:

```
Get-Process | Tee-Object -FilePath .\processes.txt
```

The first few lines of the file are shown in *Figure 4.2*:

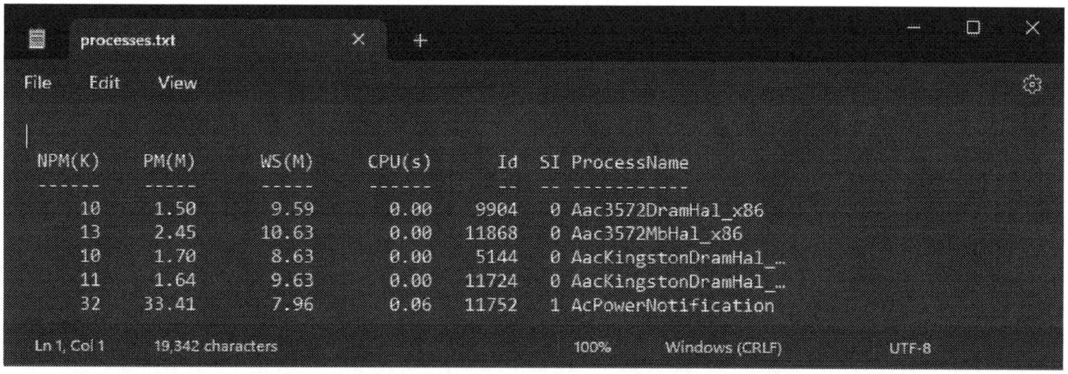

Figure 4.2: Tee-Object file formatting

It is important to note here that some of the lines end with ellipses ("..."). The output format `Tee-Object` generates is governed by the width of the console. This can be good for debugging or even logging, but it is not a good thing if something else is supposed to act on this file output.

The output shown above is part of the larger topic on formatting in PowerShell.

Formatting

Formatting in PowerShell encompasses the use of the `Format-` and `Out-` commands from the built-in `Microsoft.PowerShell.Utility` module.

PowerShell includes a complex formatting system that allows command authors to dictate the default appearance of objects in the console. Objects shown in the console almost always have more properties available than are displayed by default.

Formatting and exporting

It is important to note that format commands shown in this section should not be used alongside commands like `Export-Csv`. Formatting commands completely change the objects they receive into a set of formatting instructions.

This can be seen by combining `Format-Table` and `ConvertTo-Csv` in the example pipeline below:

```
Get-Process |
    Select-Object Name, ID, WorkingSet -First 2 |
    Format-Table |
    ConvertTo-Csv
```

This example will generate output like that shown below:

```
"ClassId2e4f51ef21dd47e99d3c952918aff9cd","pageHeaderEntry","pageFooterEntry","aut
osizeInfo","shapeInfo","groupingEntry"
"033ecb2bc07a4d43b5ef94ed5a35d280",,,,"Microsoft.PowerShell.Commands.Internal.Form
at.TableHeaderInfo",
"9e210fe47d09416682b841769c78b8a3",,,,,
"27c87ef9bbda4f709f6b4002fa4af63c",,,,,
"27c87ef9bbda4f709f6b4002fa4af63c",,,,,
"4ec4f0187cb04f4cb6973460dfe252df",,,,,
"cf522b78d86c486691226b40aa69e95c",,,,,
```

The output from the format commands can be used alongside commands such as `Out-String` and `Out-File`, but not with `Add-Content`, `Set-Content`, and `Out-GridView` (which can be used to display a user interface).

As shown above, `Format-Table` can be used to create tabular formats.

The Format-Table command

`Format-Table` can be used in a pipeline to request the table format of an object. As this is the default for `Get-Process` it has no significant effect on the output below:

```
PS> Get-Process -Id $PID | Format-Table

 NPM(K)    PM(M)      WS(M)     CPU(s)      Id  SI ProcessName
 ------    -----      -----     ------      --  -- -----------
    107   120.85     201.59       2.30    5512   1 pwsh
```

`Format-Table`, much like `Select-Object`, can request specific properties to display:

```
PS> Get-Process -Id $PID | Format-Table ProcessName, Path

ProcessName Path
----------- ----
pwsh        C:\Program Files\PowerShell\7\pwsh.exe
```

Wildcards may be used for the property name. If a wildcard is used and table format is requested, PowerShell will fit as many properties in the table as it is able to fit in the console:

```
Get-Process | Format-Table *
```

`Format-Table` allows custom properties to be defined in much the same way as `Select-Object`:

```
Get-Process | Format-Table -Property @(
    'Name'
    @{ Name = 'Started'; Expression = { $_.StartTime } }
)
```

However, as `Format-Table` is writing something to display, it includes several additional keys that may be defined in the custom property.

For example, the `Width` option can be added:

```
Get-Process | Format-Table -Property @(
    @{ Expression = 'Name'; Width = 30 }
    @{ Name = 'Started'; Expression = 'StartTime' }
)
```

It is also possible to dictate a format for fields using the `FormatString` key, which applies a specific format to a value:

```
Get-Process | Format-Table -Property @(
    @{ Expression = 'Name'; Width = 30 }
    @{ Expression = 'StartTime'; FormatString = '{0:HH:mm}' }
)
```

The format string used above is a composite format, commonly used with the `-f` operator. Composite formatting and the `-f` operator are explored in *Chapter 5, Operators*

Additional parameters, such as `AutoSize` and `Wrap`, may be used to further affect the format.

`Format-List` can be used to generate a vertical view instead of a horizontal tabular view.

The Format-List command

The `Get-Process` command includes both table (the default) and list views. If run in a pipeline with no arguments, `Format-List` requests that any list format that may exist is applied:

```
PS> Get-Process -Id $PID | Format-List

Id      : 5512
Handles : 1062
```

```
CPU     : 9.859375
SI      : 1
Name    : pwsh
```

Because list formats do not have a width constraint, using a wildcard for the property can be used to display all properties of an object:

```
Get-Process -Id $PID | Format-List *
```

Like both `Select-Object` and `Format-Table`, custom properties may be created using a hashtable. As `Format-List` is generating a vertical view it does not support defining a `Width`.

`FormatString` is supported by `Format-List` in the same way as `Format-Table`:

```
Get-Process | Format-List -Property @(
    'Name'
    @{ Expression = 'StartTime'; FormatString = '{0:HH:mm}' }
)
```

Formatted output, often created using `Select-Object`, is frequently mixed with informational output in interactive scripts; scripts that prompt for user input or write informational messages for the user to read.

Select-Object, Write-Host, and inline output

Because PowerShell wants to make informed decisions about how to display something, a 300 ms (millisecond) delay is implemented before something is displayed in the console.

If the example below is run in the console, the output will not be displayed in the order the commands imply:

```
& {
    $counter = @{ index = 0 }

    Write-Host 'Item picker'
    Write-Host '==========='
    $process = Get-Process | Select-Object -First 3
    $process | Select-Object -Property @(
        @{ Name = 'Option'; Expression = { ($counter.index++) }}
        'ProcessName'
        'ID'
        'StartTime'
```

```
    )
    [int]$picked = Read-Host 'Please select an item'

    Write-Host 'Thank you, you picked:'
    $process[$picked - 1]
}
```

Instead of showing the process list before the prompt to pick an item, the prompt is shown first, and the result of the `Select-Object` command is shown at the end:

```
Item picker
===========


Please select an item: 1
Thank you, you picked:
Option ProcessName    Id StartTime
------ -----------    -- ---------
     1 powershell   5768 01/05/2023 11:17:38
     2 pwsh         5512 01/05/2023 09:31:20
     3 pwsh        12384 01/05/2023 11:02:04
       powershell   5768 01/05/2023 11:17:38
```

There are several ways to prevent this problem.

`Out-Host` might be added to the `Select-Object` pipeline to immediately display values in the console rather than allowing PowerShell to delay this:

```
& {
    $counter = @{ index = 0 }

    Write-Host 'Item picker'
    Write-Host '==========='
    $process = Get-Process -Name pwsh, powershell
    $process | Select-Object -Property @(
        @{ Name = 'Option'; Expression = { ($counter.index++) }}
        'ProcessName'
        'ID'
        'StartTime'
    ) | Out-Host
    [int]$picked = Read-Host 'Please select an item'
```

```
    Write-Host 'Thank you, you picked:'
    $process[$picked - 1] | Out-Host
}
```

Or `Select-Object` in this case can be substituted with Format-Table, which will also immediately write to the console using `Out-Host`:

```
& {
    $counter = @{ index = 0 }

    Write-Host 'Item picker'
    Write-Host '==========='
    $process = Get-Process -Name pwsh, powershell
    $process | Format-Table -Property @(
        @{ Name = 'Option'; Expression = { ($counter.index++) }}
        'ProcessName'
        'ID'
        'StartTime'
    ) | Out-Host
    [int]$picked = Read-Host 'Please select an item'

    Write-Host 'Thank you, you picked:'
    $process[$picked - 1] | Out-Host
}
```

With either change, the output from the script displays content in the right order:

```
Item picker
===========

Option ProcessName    Id StartTime
------ -----------    -- ---------
     1 powershell  27572 10/03/2024 11:22:08
     2 pwsh         2296 10/03/2024 08:43:21
     3 pwsh         5600 10/03/2024 08:43:04

Please select an item: 1
Thank you, you picked:

 NPM(K)    PM(M)      WS(M)     CPU(s)      Id  SI ProcessName
```

```
------    -----     -----    ------       --  -- -----------
    38   142.37    159.36      0.47    27572   1 powershell
```

This feature of formatted output is a relatively common problem for those writing menus and other interactive prompts.

Formats can be used to present a human friendly view of something that is often a lot more complicated. As a by-product of this, what is shown by a format may differ from what is available.

Format-only properties

One of the more frustrating features of PowerShell is that authors can create properties that exist for the purposes of a formatted view only.

The ability to do this is useful, but where it hides the origin of a value it is detrimental to discovery and an unfriendly practice.

The `Get-Process` command has been used in many of the examples in this chapter. The `Get-Process` command outputs `Process` objects; the `Process` objects are subject to a format as shown below:

```
PS> Get-Process -Id $PID

 NPM(K)    PM(M)      WS(M)     CPU(s)      Id  SI ProcessName
 ------    -----      -----     ------      --  -- -----------
     92    75.65     114.28       1.41    5512   1 pwsh
```

Looking at the output above, it is reasonable to expect that it should be possible to select two of those columns:

```
Get-Process -Id $PID | Select-Object ProcessName, 'NPM(K)'
```

However, while `ProcessName` will show, `NPM(K)` will not. The `NPM(K)` column is added by a format and the value is derived from the value in the `NPM` property.

In this case, it does not take much to figure out that the "(K)" is just a divisor, a unit (KB) applied to the value. `Get-Process` is not the only command that exhibits this behavior. Modules such as `UpdateServices` use this feature extensively and the link between the displayed field and actual data is much less obvious.

Unfortunately, format-only values are not shown by `Get-Member` and it is therefore not possible to use this as a tool to explore the origin of a value.

> **Note**
>
> **Advanced examples**
>
> The examples that follow are the most complex in this chapter. They follow the nested objects which are derived from `PSControl`: `https://learn.microsoft.com/en-us/dotnet/api/system.management.automation.pscontrol`
>
> It is possible to explore these fully using tools like `Get-Member`, but doing so is a multi-stage process. Properties at every level must be expanded and explored. These examples are left without that deep explanation but may be used as-is.

The formats used can be found using the `Get-FormatData` command, along with the type of the object being formatted. The easiest way to access the `Type` name is by using the hidden `PSTypeNames` property of all objects in PS:

```
$process = Get-Process -Id $PID
$format = Get-FormatData -TypeName $process.PSTypeNames
```

In this case, multiple formats are available, but only the Table and List formats will be explored in the code that follows.

The format definitions are nested under a `FormatViewDefinition` property. Then the `Control` property is used to describe each format.

To make this more complicated, a `Process` object (returned by `Get-Process`) has more than one table format. These are the values used with the `View` parameter of `Format-Table`.

For example, the command below shows the table formats:

```
$format.FormatViewDefinition | Where-Object {
    $_.Control.GetType().Name -eq 'TableControl'
}
```

One of those definitions is called Priority, this may be used with `Format-Table`:

```
Get-Process | Format-Table -View Priority
```

Only the `process` view definition is of interest. This is the default view displayed when looking at the output from `Get-Process`:

```
$tableFormat = $format.FormatViewDefinition | Where-Object {
    $_.Control.GetType().Name -eq 'TableControl' -and
    $_.Name -eq 'process'
}
```

Because this is a table format, the `Control` property defines Headers and Rows, which describe how the table is formed.

A header is associated with a specific entry in a row by position in an array. A `loop with` a counter can be used to link these together:

```
$tableFormat | ForEach-Object {
    $viewName = $_.Name
    $viewType = $_.Control.GetType().Name

    $index = 0
    $columns = $_.Control.Rows.Columns

    $_.Control.Headers | ForEach-Object {
        [PSCustomObject]@{
            ViewName = $viewName
            ViewType = $viewType
            Label    = $_.Label
            Entry    = $columns[$index].DisplayEntry
        }
        $index++
    }
}
```

The output from this process is shown below:

```
ViewName ViewType     Label  Entry
-------- --------     -----  -----
process  TableControl NPM(K) script: [long]($_.NPM / 1024)
process  TableControl PM(M)  script: "{0:N2}" -f [float]($_.PM / 1MB)
process  TableControl WS(M)  script: "{0:N2}" -f [float]($_.WS / 1MB)
process  TableControl CPU(s) script: "{0:N2}" -f [float]($_.CPU)
process  TableControl        property: Id
```

```
process  TableControl        property: SI
process  TableControl        property: ProcessName
```

And this shows that the `NPM(K)` property is created by taking the `NPM` property, dividing it by 1,024 and casting it to `[long]` (a 64-bit number).

A `Process` object does not have a List view defined, but a Module returned by the `Get-Module` command does.

List views are slightly simpler and require slightly less work to extract. List views are described as a list of entries; there is no need to try and link up an array of headers to an array of values in rows.

The example below finds the format data for a `PSModuleInfo` object, the object type returned by the `Get-Module` command. It filters and expands the format data to create a short set of objects describing the composition of that format. This example combines several of the commands used in this chapter to dig into the output from `Get-FormatData`:

```
$module = Get-Module | Select-Object -First 1
Get-FormatData -TypeName $module.PSTypeNames |
    ForEach-Object FormatViewDefinition |
    Where-Object {
        $_.Control.GetType().Name -eq 'ListControl'
    } |
    ForEach-Object {
        $viewName = $_.Name
        $viewType = $_.Control.GetType().Name

        $_.Control.Entries.Items | Select-Object -Property @(
            @{ Name = 'ViewName'; Expression = { $viewName }}
            @{ Name = 'ViewType'; Expression = { $viewType }}
            'Label'
            @{ Name = 'Entry'; Expression = 'DisplayEntry' }
        )
    }
```

Formatting is a relatively small but complex and critical part of PowerShell. Like much of PowerShell, there is an opportunity to delve into the details, often without ever leaving the console.

Formatting is itself a small part of this much broader topic, which explores many of the capabilities of these generic commands for working in pipelines in PowerShell.

Summary

The pipeline is a key component of PowerShell. It allows data, complex objects, to be sent from one command to another. Each command can act on the data it has received and, in many cases, return more data.

PowerShell includes a variety of commands for working with objects in a pipeline.

The `Get-Member` command allows the members (properties, methods, and so on) to be explored, which can be used to understand what an object is capable of.

`[PSCustomObject]` and `[Ordered]` can be used to create new custom objects. Historically, `New-Object` and `Add-Member` have had a significant part to play in creating custom objects but their usage has been deprecated.

`ForEach-Object` is a common command used to run arbitrary code against objects in a pipeline. `Where-Object` may be used to filter a pipeline, returning only relevant objects.

The `Select-Object` command is used to define what properties should be returned. `Select-Object` can be used to include or remove objects from a pipeline, for example, by selecting the first few objects from a pipeline. The `Sort-Object` command takes pipeline input and allows it to be sorted based on property names, or more complex criteria described by a script block.

Comparisons of collections of objects are made possible using the `Compare-Object` command.

Content in PowerShell can be exported to and imported from files in a variety of different ways. This chapter explored exporting and importing content using the `Export-Csv` and `Import-Csv` commands, as well as the more complex output created by `Export-CliXml`.

Finally, formatting in PowerShell was briefly explored, as well as common issues with integrating commands into interactive sequences.

The next chapter, *Chapter 5, Operators*, explores the wide variety of operators available in PowerShell, ranging from arithmetic and comparison operators to binary and redirection operators.

5

Operators

In programming, an operator is a keyword that is used to manipulate an item of data. An operator might be used to compare values, add or subtract, perform replacements, split or join values, and so on. An operator is a fundamental part of any programming language, and PowerShell is no exception.

PowerShell has a wide variety of operators; each is explored within this chapter.

Many of the operators in PowerShell are binary, requiring two arguments (operands), such as `-eq`, `-like`, and so on.

Unary operators require a single argument (on the right-hand side), such as the `-not` and `-bnot` operators.

Ternary operators, which are new in PowerShell 7, require three arguments.

A small number of operators can be used as both unary and binary, including `-join` and `-split`.

This chapter covers the following topics:

- Precedence, grouping, and sub-expressions
- Unary, Binary, and Ternary operators
- Arithmetic operators
- Comparison operators
- Regular expression-based operators
- Logical operators
- Bitwise operators
- Assignment operators

- Type operators
- Redirection operators
- Other operators
- Precedence and grouping are topics that apply to all operators.

Let's get started!

Precedence, grouping, and sub-expressions

Each operator in PowerShell is given a precedence, an order in which it will be evaluated.

The operators used in this section are explored during this chapter.

Operator precedence

Operations are executed in a specific order depending on the operator used. For example, consider the following two simple calculations:

```
3 + 2 * 2
2 * 2 + 3
```

The result of both preceding expressions is 7 (2 multiplied by 2 and then 3 added) because the multiplication operator has higher precedence than the addition operator.

Where operator precedence is equal, the expression is evaluated from left to right.

PowerShell includes a help document describing the precedence for each operator. The precedence list is long and not duplicated in this chapter:

```
Get-Help about_Operator_Precedence
```

The online version of the same document is available at Microsoft Learn: `https://learn.microsoft.com/en-us/powershell/module/microsoft.powershell.core/about/about_operator_precedence`.

The `help` topic lists the operators in the order they are evaluated. The multiplication operator, *, has higher precedence (is higher in the list) than addition, +; therefore, in an operation using both operators, * is calculated first.

The grouping operator can be used to affect the order in which terms in an expression are evaluated.

Grouping

Expressions in parentheses have the highest precedence and are, therefore, always calculated before any other.

Parentheses may, therefore, be used to group expressions together in cases where the default operator precedence would give an incorrect result.

For example, if the intent of the expression below were to add together 3 and 2, then multiply that by 2, the default operator precedence would cause an incorrect result:

```
3 + 2 * 2
```

Because the multiplication operator has a higher precedence, `2 * 2` is executed first, then 3 is added to the result.

Adding parentheses around the expression will make it match the intent stated above:

```
(3 + 2) * 2
```

The result of the preceding calculation is 10; the expression in parentheses is calculated first, giving 5, and the result of that is multiplied by 2.

Sub-expression operator

Sub-expressions in PowerShell are somewhat like grouping operators in appearance.

PowerShell includes two sub-expression operators:

- Sub-expression: `$( )`
- Array sub-expression: `@( )`

The sub-expression operator is almost exclusively used in double-quoted strings to expand the properties of objects for inclusion in the string. For example, the `Length` property of a string is included in the double-quoted string below:

```
$word = 'one'
"Length: $($word.Length)"
```

The sub-expression is evaluated before the value is inserted into the string. If the sub-expression is omitted, PowerShell will expand `$word`; "`.Length`" is a literal value:

```
PS> $word = 'one'
PS> "Length: $word.Length"
Length: one.Length
```

The sub-expression operator can also be used when calling executables that use `/Name:Value` style parameters.

For example, if an object has a `Path` property containing a path to search, a sub-expression is required to pass that value to the `/D` parameter of `FindStr`:

```
$dir = [PSCustomObject]@{ Path = (Get-Item ~).FullName }
FindStr /D:$($dir.Path) SomeValue *.txt
```

The sub-expression is used here because PowerShell expands values in arguments as if they were double-quoted strings. If the sub-expression is omitted, `FindStr` will be handed the value of `$dir` converted to a string followed by the literal value "`.Path`".

While `FindStr` is Windows-specific, this problem applies for any command argument which is expected to expand a property in a string.

The array sub-expression operator is not used inside strings, except perhaps inside a sub-expression.

Array sub-expression operator

The array sub-expression operator will always create an array regardless of the number of items enclosed by the operator.

It can, therefore, be used to create an array out of a single object:

```
$processes = @(Get-Process -ID $PID)
```

Piping the array to `Get-Member` will not show that it is an array because the pipeline enumerates array values. `Get-Member`, therefore, would show information about the `Process` object element inside the array.

If the value is directly used with the `InputObject` parameter, it can be shown to be an array, denoted by the `TypeName`:

```
PS> $processes = @(Get-Process -ID $PID)
PS> Get-Member -InputObject $Processes

   TypeName: System.Object[]
...
```

The array sub-expression operator can include any number of commands or elements, and even complex statements such as other commands:

```
$myArray = @(
    Get-Process | Where-Object ProcessName -in @(
        'pwsh'
        'powershell'
    )
    Get-Process notepad
)
```

Or expressions based on keywords:

```
$shouldAddMore = $true
$myArray = @(
    1, 2, 3
    if ($shouldAddMore) {
        4, 5, 6
    }
)
```

Statements within the array sub-expression are enumerated (flattened or expanded) unless the comma operator is explicitly used to separate all elements. The array created by the example above will have 6 elements.

The comma operator was used in *Chapter 3, Variables, Arrays, and Hashtables* to create a multi-dimensional array like the example below:

```
$myArray = @(
    @(1, 2, 3),
    @(4, 5, 6)
)
```

In general, PowerShell prefers to enumerate output, expanding nested collections.

It can be useful to take advantage of this desire to expand or flatten arrays. It occurs with the array sub-expression when each element is a separate statement. For example:

```
$one = 1, 2, 3
$two = 4, 5, 6
$myArray = @(
    $one   # This is statement 1
    $two   # This is statement 2
)
```

If it were desirable to write two elements on the same line, it is tempting to use the comma operator between each element:

```
$myArray = @($one, $two)
```

However, this will create an array of two elements, each element being an array.

The statement separator operator can be used instead to cause each statement to be independently evaluated:

```
$myArray = @($one; $two)
```

The result this time will contain 6 elements, joining the arrays in each variable together.

The examples above have already made some simple use of the arithmetic operators.

Unary, Binary, and Ternary operators

As mentioned at the start of this chapter, operators can expect different numbers of arguments.

A unary operator requires a single argument (acting on a single item), and in PowerShell, this argument is normally placed on the right-hand side of the operator. For example, the `-not` operator is a unary operator used as shown below:

```
-not $false
```

Several operators can be used as either unary or binary. The addition operator, +, and subtraction operators can be used as unary operators:

```
+1
-1
```

Addition and subtraction operators may also be used as binary operators (acting on two items), i.e., an operator that expects two arguments, one of the left and one on the right:

```
1 + 1
1 - 1
```

A third type of operator is one that expects three arguments, a ternary operator (acting on three items).

PowerShell only has one operator that is strictly classed as ternary. It is used to express a logical condition.

About the ternary operator

The ternary operator is a conditional operator that performs a comparison and returns one of two values.

The ternary operator can be used to replace the following statement:

```
$result = if ($value) {
    1
} else {
    2
}
```

When the ternary operator is used, the statement can be simplified to the following:

```
$result = $value ? 1 : 2
```

If `$value` is true, PowerShell sets `$result` to `1`. If `$value` is false, PowerShell sets `$result` to `2`.

As the ternary operator acts on a Boolean value, the values 0, null, empty strings, and empty arrays are all considered to be false.

Complex expressions that might affect precedence, or commands, can be used with the ternary operator if the expression is enclosed in parentheses. For example:

```
(Get-Process notepad -ErrorAction Ignore) ? 'Running' : 'Not running'
```

The ternary operator is very concise and a useful addition for code targeting PowerShell 7 and above.

Arithmetic operators

Arithmetic operators are used to perform numeric calculations. The arithmetic operators in PowerShell are as follows:

- Addition: +
- Subtraction: -
- Multiplication: *
- Division: /
- Remainder: %

As well as its use in numeric calculations, the addition operator may also be used with strings, arrays, and hashtables. The multiplication operator may also be used with strings and arrays.

The addition operator attempts to add two values together.

Addition operator

The addition operator may be used to add values together or to add objects of any type that supports addition.

For example, the following simple addition operation will result in the value `5.14159`:

```
2.71828 + 3.14159
```

The addition operator may also be used to concatenate strings:

```
'good' + 'bye'
```

This style of concatenation can be applied to the example used with a sub-expression:

```
$word = 'one'
"Length: " + $word.Length
```

If an attempt is made to concatenate a string with a number, the number will be converted into a string:

```
'hello number ' + 1
```

The addition operator can be used as a unary operator, for example:

```
+1
```

Practically, this value is the same as writing 1 alone. The utility of + as a unary operator comes when converting string values to numeric:

```
# Read-Host will read a string
$number = Read-Host 'Please enter a number'
# + can be used to convert this to a number
$number = +$number
```

The result of the operation can be demonstrated by using `Get-Member` to view the type name:

```
PS> $number | Get-Member

   TypeName: System.Int32
...
```

This approach will work even if the user responds to the prompt with a negative number. However, if the user responds with a string, an error will be shown. The same error as would be seen when running:

```
PS> +'string'
InvalidArgument: Cannot convert value "string" to type "System.Int32". Error: "The
input string 'string' was not in a correct format."
```

The same error is seen when an explicit attempt is made to add a string to a number.

PowerShell expects the entire expression to be numeric if the left-hand side of the expression is numeric:

```
PS> 1 + ' is the number I like to use'
InvalidArgument: Cannot convert value "is the number I like to use" to type
"System.Int32". Error: "Input string was not in a correct format."
```

PowerShell will try and coerce the value on the right-hand side into a number; therefore, a string containing a number is acceptable and will complete without error:

```
1 + '4'
```

The addition operator may be used to add single elements to an existing array. As arrays are of fixed size, a new array will be created containing 1, 2, and 3:

```
@(1, 2) + 3
```

Joining arrays with the addition operator is simple. Each of the following three examples creates an array, and each array contains the values 1, 2, 3, and 4:

```
@(1, 2) + @(3, 4)
(1, 2) + (3, 4)
1, 2 + 3, 4
```

The last example is an array containing 1, 2, 3, and 4 because the array operator has higher precedence than addition. Therefore, two arrays are added together.

The attempt to add like this will fail if the left of + is a scalar, a single value:

```
PS> 1 + 3, 4
InvalidOperation: Method invocation failed because [System.Object[]] does not
contain a method named 'op_Addition'.
```

Hashtables may be joined in a similar manner:

```
@{key1 = 1} + @{key2 = 2}
```

The addition operation fails if keys are duplicated as part of the addition operation:

```
PS> @{key1 = 1} + @{key1 = 2}
OperationStopped: Item has already been added. Key in dictionary: 'key1'  Key
being added: 'key1'
```

Like the addition operator, the subtraction operator can be used as both a binary and unary operator.

Subtraction operator

The subtraction operator may only be used for numeric expressions. The results of the following expressions are 3 and -18, respectively:

```
5 - 2
2 - 20
```

Used as a unary operator, - is often used to represent negative numbers (numbers below 0):

```
-5
```

Subtraction is a simple but important operation used in everyday calculations. The following sections explore the multiplication, division, and remainder operators.

Multiplication operator

The multiplication operator can perform simple numeric operations. For example, the result of the following expression is 5:

```
2.5 * 2
```

The multiplication operator can be used to duplicate strings, as shown in the following example that results in `hellohellohello`:

```
'hello' * 3
```

As with the addition operator, the multiplication operator will throw an error if a number is on the left of the expression. PowerShell will expect the entire expression to be numeric if the value on the left-hand side is numeric:

```
PS> 3 * 'hello'
InvalidArgument: Cannot convert value "hello" to type "System.Int32". Error:
"Input string was not in a correct format."
```

The multiplication operator may also be used to duplicate arrays. Each of the following examples creates an array containing one, two, one, and two:

```
@('one', 'two') * 2
('one', 'two') * 2
'one', 'two' * 2
```

The division operator complements the multiplication operator.

Division operator

The division operator performs numeric division:

```
PS> 20 / 5
4
```

Division by any non-zero numeric value is permitted as shown in the simple example above.

An error will be thrown if an attempt to divide by 0 is made:

```
PS> 1 / 0
RuntimeException: Attempted to divide by zero.
```

Division using negative numbers is permitted in PowerShell. When a positive number is divided by a negative number, the result is negative.

Remainder operator

The remainder operator returns the remainder of the whole-number (integer) division. For example, the result of the following operation is 1:

```
3 % 2
```

One possible use of the remainder operator is alternating, that is, swapping between two values repeatedly. This can be used to perform an action on every second, third, fourth, and nth increment in an iteration. For example:

```
1..20 | ForEach-Object {
    if ($_ % 2 -eq 0) {
        $foregroundColor = 'Cyan'
    } else {
        $foregroundColor = 'White'
    }
    Write-Host $_ -ForegroundColor $foregroundColor
}
```

The preceding example alternates the color of the text.

Increment and decrement operators

The ++ and -- operators are used to increment and decrement numeric values. The increment and decrement operators are split into pre-increment and post-increment versions.

Post-increment and decrement operators are written after a value, for example:

```
$i = 0
$i++    # Post-increment
$i--    # Post-decrement
```

The pre-increment operators are written before a value, for example:

```
$i = 0
++$i    # Pre-increment
--$i    # Pre-decrement
```

In the examples above, nothing is shown in the console when these values run. Extra lines can be added to show the value after each operation:

```
$i = 0
Write-Host "i starts at $i"
$i++
Write-Host "i is now $i"
$i--
Write-Host "i is now $i"
```

The output of the example above is identical whether the pre- or post-versions of the operators are used.

These operators have output if they are enclosed in parentheses or used as an argument for another operator. The post-increment operator is shown below; the values are only changed after the current value is displayed.

```
$i = 0
($i++)    # Post-increment
($i--)    # Post-decrement
```

And here is the pre-increment version that shows that the values change before display:

```
$i = 0
(++$i)    # Pre-increment
(--$i)    # Pre-decrement
```

The post-increment operators are frequently seen in `for` loops, which are explored in more detail in *Chapter 6, Conditional Statements and Loops*. The value for `$i` is used and then incremented by one after use. In the case of the `for` loop, the value is incremented after the statements inside the loop block have executed:

```
for ($i = 1; $i -le 15; $i++) {
    Write-Host $i -ForegroundColor $i
}
```

The post-decrement reduces the value by one after use:

```
for ($i = 15; $i -ge 0; $i--) {
    Write-Host $i -ForegroundColor $i
}
```

Post-increment and post-decrement operators are often seen when iterating through an array, in this case, a while loop, which is also explored in more detail in *Chapter 6, Conditional Statements and Loops.*

```
$array = 1..15
$i = 0
while ($i -lt $array.Count) {
    # $i will increment after this statement has completed.
    Write-Host $array[$i++] -ForegroundColor $i
}
```

Pre-increment and pre-decrement are rarely seen. Instead of incrementing or decrementing a value after use, the change happens before the value is used. For example:

```
$array = 1..5
$i = 0
while ($i -lt $array.Count - 1) {
    # $i is incremented before use, 2 will be the first printed.
    Write-Host $array[++$i]
}
```

The post-increment operator, ++, is common and is typically used in looping scenarios like those above.

Comparison operators

Comparison operators can be used to compare two values. PowerShell has a wide variety of comparison operators, which are as follows:

- Equal to and not equal to: `-eq` and `-ne`
- Like and not like: `-like` and `-notlike`
- Greater than and greater than or equal to: `-gt` and `-ge`
- Less than and less than or equal to: `-lt` and `-le`

- Contains and not contains: `-contains` and `-notcontains`
- In and not in: `-in` and `-notin`

Values can be directly compared to one another in PowerShell using the equality operators.

eq and ne

The `-eq` (equal to) and `-ne` (not equal to) operators perform exact (and, by default, case-insensitive) comparisons. In the following example, `true` is returned for each of the comparisons:

```
1 -eq 1
'string' -eq 'string'
```

Similarly, `-ne` (not equal) will return `true` for each of the following:

```
20 -ne 100
'this' -ne 'that'
```

When working with comparison expressions, it is important to consider the left-hand side of the expression.

PowerShell will always attempt to convert the value on the right-hand side to match the type on the left. For example, in the following statement, the value on the right is converted to match the left (an `int`):

```
1 -eq '1'
```

Reversing the statement will return the same result:

```
'1' -eq 1
```

If PowerShell cannot convert the value, it will try a direct comparison. For example, PowerShell cannot convert the value on the right below to an integer:

```
1 -eq 'one'
```

Because PowerShell will always attempt to coerce values, a comparison of a Boolean value to a string is possible:

```
$true -eq 'True'
```

However, this style of comparison should be discouraged, as it suggests that the following is also possible:

```
$false -eq 'False'
```

In both cases, PowerShell takes the value on the right-hand side of the expression and coerces it directly to a Boolean value. As neither string is empty, the result of the conversion is always true:

```
[bool]'True'
[bool]'False'
```

The comparison of the Boolean value `$false` with the not-empty string `'False'`, therefore, will always show that the values differ.

Not all comparisons can be exact; a different operator is required for a wildcard-based comparison.

like and notlike

The `-like` and `-notlike` operators support wildcard terms on the right-hand side of the expression. The most obvious of these wildcards is the * character. * matches a string of any length, zero or more characters long:

```
'The cow jumped over the moon' -like '*moon*'
'' -like '*'
```

Individual characters may be represented by the ? character. This wildcard is exactly one character long:

```
'Hello world' -like '?ello ?orld'
'Hello world' -like '??llo w*'

'' -notlike '?*'
```

Extending this, a string containing one or more characters can be matched:

```
'Hello world' -like '?*'
'Hello world' -like '*?'
```

If the string is empty, the result of the comparison will be false:

```
'' -like '?*'
```

In addition to * and ?, a range of characters can be defined using square brackets:

```
'Hello world' -like '[f-k]*'
```

If a wildcard expression should be literal, then the wildcard must be escaped, for example:

```
'*.txt' -like '`*.txt'
'*.txt' -like '`*.*'
```

The ` character escapes the special meaning of *. PowerShell can help provide a pattern with wildcard characters escaped. The command below escapes all the wildcard expressions in the string:

```
[WildcardPattern]::Escape('* [a-z] ?')
```

This will escape each character used to express a wildcard with a grave accent character:

```
`* `[a-z`] `?
```

When comparing numbers, or ordering values, the greater than and less than operators are used.

Greater than and less than

When comparing numbers, each of the operators `-ge` (greater than or equal to), `-gt` (greater than), `-le` (less than or equal to), and `-lt` (less than) is simple to use:

```
1 -ge 1         # Returns true
2 -gt 1         # Returns true
1.4 -lt 1.9     # Returns true
1.1 -le 1.1     # Returns true
```

String comparisons using operators follow invariant-culture rules. By default, they are case-insensitive. It is also important to note the following:

- **Cultural variants of characters**: For example, the character å falls between A and b in the list.
- **Other alphabets**: For example, Cyrillic and Greek come after the Roman alphabet (after Z).

Comparisons can be made in a specific culture when using commands such as `Sort-Object` with the `Culture` parameter. Comparisons are always based on en-US when using the operators:

```
'apples' -lt 'pears'    # Returns true
'Apples' -lt 'pears'    # Returns true
'bears' -gt 'Apples'    # Returns true
'å' -gt 'a'             # Returns true
```

When a case-sensitive operator, such as `-clt`, is used, B can be seen to fall between b and c:

```
'bat' -clt 'Bat'   # True, b before B
'Bat' -clt 'cat'   # True, B before c
```

The use of greater than and less than with strings may often be difficult to apply. Careful testing is recommended.

Case sensitivity

The comparison operators are not case-sensitive by default. Each of the comparison operators has two additional variants, one that explicitly states it is case-sensitive and another that explicitly states it is case-insensitive.

For example, the following statement returns true:

```
'Trees' -eq 'trees'
```

Adding a c prefix in front of the name of the operator forces PowerShell to make a case-sensitive comparison. The following statement returns false:

```
'Trees' -ceq 'trees'
```

In addition to the case-sensitive prefix, PowerShell also has an explicit case-insensitive modifier. In the following example, the statement returns true:

```
'Trees' -ieq 'trees'
```

However, as case-insensitive comparison is the default, it is extremely rare to see examples of the `i` prefix.

These behavior prefixes can be applied to all the comparison operators.

The behavior of comparison operators used changes again when the left-hand side of the comparison is an array.

Comparison operators and arrays

When comparison operators are used with scalar values (a single item as opposed to an array), the comparison results in true or false.

When a comparison operator is used with an array or collection, the result of the comparison is all matching elements, that is, the array is enumerated, and all successfully compared values are returned. For example:

```
1, $null -ne $null                    # Returns 1
1, 2, 3, 4 -ge 3                      # Returns 3, 4
'one', 'two', 'three' -like '*e*'     # Returns one, three
```

This array comparison behavior does not apply when using `-contains`, `-notcontains`, `-in`, or `-notin`.

A little care is required when using comparisons with arrays as conditional expressions. For example, take the condition below in an `if` statement:

```
$value = 'one'
if ($value -notlike 't*') {
    'two or three not found'
}
```

In this example, the left is a scalar; `-notlike` will return a true or false value.

The condition can be removed to explore the output from -like and `-notlike`:

```
$value = 'one'
$value -like 't*' # Will be false
$value -notlike 't*' # Will be true
```

When the value on the left is an array, the outcome can yield a less obvious result:

```
$value = 'one', 'two', 'three'
If ($value -notlike 't*') {
    'two or three not found'
}
```

This happens because the comparison no longer returns a true or false value; instead, it returns the values that satisfy the condition:

```
$value = 'one', 'two', 'three'
$value -notlike 't*'   # Returns the value "one"
```

To establish the absence of a thing in an array when using a wildcard comparison, the `-not` operator and a positive comparison must be used instead:

```
$value = 'one', 'two', 'three'
If (-not ($value -like 't*')) {
    'two and three not found'
}
```

The variable `$value` is tested to see if it contains any value matching the wildcard expression `t*`. Extra parentheses are required to stop `-not` acting only on `$value`. Then, the whole expression returns true if none of those values are found.

These steps are broken down below:

```
$value = 'one', 'two', 'three'

# Will find the values two and three
$value -like 't*'

# True because the array of results is not empty
[bool]($value -like 't*')
```

```
# Negates the result above, simulating -notlike on a single value
-not ($value -like 't*')
```

The ability to compare against an array is why it is suggested that `$null` is placed on the left of a comparison expression.

Comparisons to null

Returning each matching value from an array can be problematic if a comparison is used to test whether a variable holding an array exists.

In the following example, `-eq` is successfully used to test that a value has been assigned to a variable called array:

```
$array = 1, 2
if ($array -eq $null) { Write-Host 'Variable not set' }
```

This test is valid if the array does not hold two or more null values. When two or more values are present, the condition unexpectedly returns true:

```
PS> $array = 1, 2, $null, $null
PS> if ($array -eq $null) { Write-Host 'No values in array' }
No values in array
```

This happens because the result of the comparison is an array with two null values. PowerShell returns matching values from the array, not just true or false.

If the value of `$array` were a single null value, PowerShell would flatten the array for the comparison. With two values, PowerShell cannot do that. The effect of two null values can be seen when casting each to Boolean:

```
[bool]@($null)            # Returns false
[bool]@($null, $null)     # Returns true
```

To avoid this problem, `$null` must be on the left-hand side of the expression. For example, the following `Write-Host` statement does not execute; the array variable is not null:

```
$array = 1, 2, $null, $null
if ($null -eq $array) { Write-Host 'Variable not set' }
```

In this case, the array is not enumerated; null is compared with the entire array. The result will be false; the array variable is set.

contains and in

The `-contains`, `-notcontains`, `-in`, and `-notin` operators are used to test the content of arrays. Each comparison is exact; wildcards cannot be used on the right-hand side of the operator.

When using `-contains` or `-notcontains`, the array must be on the left-hand side of the operator:

```
1, 2 -contains 2        # Returns true
1, 2, 3 -contains 4     # Returns false
```

When using `-in` or `-notin`, the array must be on the right-hand side of the operator:

```
1 -in 1, 2, 3    # Returns true
4 -in 1, 2, 3    # Returns false
```

Note

-contains or -in?

When using comparison operators, I tend to write the subject (the item I want to compare) on the left and the object on the right.

Comparisons to null are an exception to this rule: null is placed on the left.

The subject is the variable or property I am testing; the object is the thing I am testing against. For example, I might set the subject to a user in Active Directory:

```
$subject = Get-ADUser -Identity $env:USERNAME -Properties @(
    'department'
    'memberOf'
)
```

I use `-contains` where the subject is an array, and the object is a single value:

```
$subject.MemberOf -contains 'CN=Group,DC=domain,DC=example'
```

I use `-in` where the subject is a single value, and the object is an array:

```
$subject.Department -in 'Department1', 'Department2'
```

The `-contains` and `-in` operators are used for literal comparisons against arrays. For partial or wildcard matching, `-like` or a regular expression operator might be used.

Regular expression-based operators

Regular expressions are an advanced form of pattern matching. In PowerShell, some operators have direct support for regular expressions.

The following operators use regular expressions:

- **match**: `-match`
- **not match**: `-notmatch`
- **replace**: `-replace`
- **split**: `-split`

The split and replace operators should not be confused with the .NET `Split` and `Replace` methods of the `System.String` type.

The match operator tests a string, or array of strings, against a pattern.

match and notmatch

The `-match` and `-notmatch` operators test whether a string matches a regular expression. If so, the operators will return `$true` or `$false`:

```
'The cow jumped over the moon' -match 'cow'  # Returns true
'The       cow' -match 'The +cow'            # Returns true
```

In the preceding example, the + symbol is reserved; it indicates that "`The`" is followed by one or more spaces before cow.

> Note
>
> **Match is a comparison operator**
>
> Like the other comparison operators, if `-match` (or `-notmatch`) is used against an array, it returns each matching element instead of true or false. The following comparison returns the values one and three:
>
> ```
> "one", "two", "three" -match 'e'
> ```
>
> When `-match` is used against an array, the `$matches` variable is not set.

In addition to returning a true or false value about the state of the match, a successful match adds values to a reserved variable, `$matches`. For example, the following regular expression uses a character class (a set of values enclosed in square brackets) to indicate that it should match any character from 0 to 4, repeated 0 or more times:

```
'1234567689' -match '[0-4]*'
```

Once the match has been executed, the `$matches` variable (a hashtable) is populated with the part of the string that matched the expression:

```
PS> $matches

Name                           Value
----                           -----
0                              1234
```

Regular expressions use parentheses to denote groups. Groups may be used to capture interesting elements of a string:

```
PS> 'Group one, Group two' -match 'Group (.*), Group (.*)'
True
PS> $matches

Name                           Value
----                           -----
2                              two
1                              one
0                              Group one, Group two
```

The captured value one is held in the group named 1, and it is accessible using either of the following statements:

```
$matches[1]
$matches.1
```

The `$matches` variable is an automatically filled hashtable. The `$matches` variable shown above is not cleared when a match is unsuccessful.

```
PS> 'Group one, Group two' -match 'Group (.*), Group (.*)'
True
```

```
PS> $matches[1]
one
PS> 'Other text' -match 'Group (.*), Group (.*)'
False
PS> $matches[1]
one
```

In the preceding examples, value `1` is used as a key to access a capture group; this might be used with the `-replace` operator.

replace

The `-replace` operator performs string replacement based on a regular expression. For example, it can be used to replace several instances of the same thing:

```
PS> 'abababab' -replace 'a', 'c'
cbcbcbcb
```

In the example, `a` is the regular expression that dictates what must be replaced and `c` is the value any matching values should be replaced with.

The syntax for the `-replace` operator can be generalized, as follows:

```
<Value> -replace <Match>, <Replace-With>
```

If the `Replace-With` value is omitted, the matches are replaced with nothing (that is, they are removed):

```
PS> 'abababab' -replace 'a'
bbbb
```

Regular expressions use parentheses to capture groups (a substring of the original). The `-replace` operator can use those groups. Each group may be used in the `Replace-With` argument. For example, a set of values can be reversed:

```
'value1,value2,value3' -replace '(.*),(.*),(.*)', '$3,$2,$1'
```

In the preceding regular expression, `.*` matches zero or more of any character. Each capture group is expected to be separated by a comma.

The values $1, $2, and $3 are references to each of the capture groups in the order they appear in the expression. These tokens or references are only substituted if the match includes a group to replace them with. For example:

```
'1' -replace '.', 'No groups, $1 is not substituted'
```

If a literal value of $1 is required in the Replace-With text, the value can be escaped using an additional $ character:

```
'1' -replace '(1)', 'The value of group $$1 is $1'
```

The extra $ will be removed by -replace regardless of whether the pattern contains the group.

When performing the operations above, the Replace-With argument uses single quotes to prevent PowerShell from evaluating the group references as if they were variables. This problem is shown in the following example. The first attempt works as expected; the second shows an expanded PowerShell variable instead:

```
PS> 'value1,value2,value3' -replace '(.*),(.*),(.*)', '$3,$2,$1'
value3,value2,value1
PS> $1 = $2 = $3 = 'Oops'
PS> 'value1,value2,value3' -replace '(.*),(.*),(.*)', "$3,$2,$1"
Oops,Oops,Oops
```

Finally, the -replace operator can use a script block as the Replace-With argument. In the example below, -replace is used on an array of strings. Each string contains a ProcessID. The Get-Process command is used on each value to replace the ID with a process name. The example below uses Windows-specific process IDs and is not expected to work on other platforms:

```
'0', '4', $PID -replace '.+', { (Get-Process -Id $_.Value).Name }
```

The script block, enclosed in { }, uses the variable $_ which holds a System.Text.RegularExpressions.Match object. This object in turn has a Value, which includes the matched value:

```
@(
    'Process: 0'
    'Process: 4'
    "Process: $PID"
```

```
) -replace '\d+', {
    (Get-Process -ID $_.Value).Name
}
```

The output from this example is:

```
Process: Idle
Process: System
Process: pwsh
```

The `-replace` operator is incredibly useful and widely used.

split

The `-split` operator splits a string into an array based on a regular expression.

The following example splits a string into an array containing a, b, c, and d, based on each of the numbers in the string:

```
PS> 'a1b2c3d4' -split '[0-9]'
a
b
c
d
```

The `-split` operator can be used as a unary operator to split up a string based on contiguous whitespace. The example below will return an array of a, b, and c:

```
-split "a`tb     c"
```

The syntax for the `-split` operator can be generalized, as follows; only the `Match` argument is mandatory:

```
<Value> -split <Match>, <Max-substrings>, <Options>
```

The results of a split can be assigned to one or more variables. For example:

```
$first, $second, $third = '1,2,3,4,5' -split ','
```

The string 1 will be assigned to `$first` and 2 to `$second`. The variable `$third` will contain the strings 3, 4, and 5 as an array. Using `$null` instead would discard 3, 4, and 5:

```
$first, $second, $null = '1,2,3,4,5' -split ','
```

`Max-substrings` can be used to limit the number of substrings returned from the string on the left-hand side.

The default value of `Max-substrings` is 0, meaning that all substrings are returned. The following example will result in an array containing two elements: the first element will be the string 1, and the second element will be "2,3,4,5":

```
PS> $split = '1,2,3,4,5' -split ',', 2
1
2,3,4,5
```

A negative Max-substrings value changes the expression to split from right to left (instead of the default left to right). For example, the first element in this example will be "1,2,3,4", and the second will be 5:

```
PS> $split = '1,2,3,4,5' -split ',', -2
1,2,3,4
5
```

If `-3` is used instead, three elements will be created, splitting from the end of the string:

```
PS> $split = '1,2,3,4,5' -split ',', -3
1,2,3
4
5
```

The `Options` field is used to change how the match is performed. It includes several options:

- `SimpleMatch`
- `RegexMatch`
- `CultureInvariant`
- `IgnorePatternWhitespace`
- `Multiline`
- `Singleline`

- `IgnoreCase`
- `ExplicitCapture`

The .NET reference has descriptions of each of these possible values: `https://learn.microsoft.com/en-gb/dotnet/api/system.management.automation.splitoptions`

For example, the `SimpleMatch` option changes `-split` to perform a literal match instead of using a regular expression, as shown in the following example:

```
'a?b?c?d?' -split 'b?', 0, 'SimpleMatch'
```

The preceding example splits the string in two; the first value will be `a?`, and the second `c?d?`. If `SimpleMatch` is taken away, the result will be very different. In a regular expression, the `?` character makes the preceding character optional.

Multiple options can be used as a comma-separated list. For example:

```
'axbxcxd' -csplit ' X ', 0, 'IgnoreCase, IgnorePatternWhiteSpace'
```

The `-csplit` variant of the `-split` operator makes the match case-sensitive; setting the `IgnoreCase` option switches back to case-insensitive.

Logical operators

Logical operators evaluate two or more comparisons or other operations that produce a `Boolean` (true or false) result.

The following logic operators are available:

- **And**: `-and`
- **Or**: `-or`
- **Exclusive or**: `-xor`
- **Not**: `-not` and `!`

and

The `-and` operator returns true if the values on the left-hand and right-hand sides are both true.

For example, each of the following returns `$true`:

```
$true -and $true
1 -lt 2 -and "string" -like 's*'
1 -eq 1 -and 2 -eq 2 -and 3 -eq 3
(Test-Path C:\Windows) -and (Test-Path 'C:\Program Files')
```

The `-and` operator is often combined with the `-or` operator.

or

The `-or` operator returns true if the value on the left, the value on the right, or both are true.

For example, each of the following returns `$true`:

```
$true -or $true
2 -gt 1 -or "something" -ne "nothing"
1 -eq 1 -or 2 -eq 1
(Test-Path C:\Windows) -or (Test-Path D:\Windows)
```

The `-and` and `-or` operators are very frequently used, and often in combination with the `-not` operator.

not

The `-not` (or `!`) operator, a unary operator, is used to negate the expression that follows it.

For example, each of the following returns true:

```
-not $false
-not (Test-Path X:\)
-not ($true -and $false)
!($true -and $false)
```

The `-not` operator will always coerce the value on the right-hand side to a Boolean value. The result of the two examples below is false because the string has a value:

```
-not 'string'
!'string'
```

It is rare but entirely possible to use a `-not` operator next to another `-not` operator. For example, the expression below returns true:

```
$string = 'string'
-not -not $string
```

This is slightly contrary, and is more often used with the `!` variant of the operator:

```
$string
!!$string
```

The result is always a Boolean value: `true` if the string is not empty and `false` if the string is empty.

The `-xor` operator is perhaps the least common of the logic operators.

xor (eXclusive OR)

The `-xor` operator will return true if either the value on the left or the value on the right is true, but not both.

For example, each of the following returns `$true`:

```
$true -xor $false
1 -le 2 -xor 1 -eq 2
(Test-Path C:\Windows) -xor (Test-Path D:\Windows)
```

The `-xor` operator is perhaps one of the least frequently used operators in PowerShell.

Bitwise operators

Bitwise operators are used to perform operations based around the bits that make up a numeric value. Each operator returns the numeric result of a bitwise operation.

The available operators are:

- **Binary and**: `-band`
- **Binary or**: `-bor`
- **Binary exclusive or**: `-bxor`
- **Binary not**: `-bnot`

- **Shift left**: `-shl`
- **Shift right**: `-shr`

All numeric values can be broken down into bytes and, in turn, bits, a base 2 value.

A byte is made up of 8 bits. Each bit in the byte has a value based on its position, with the highest value (or most significant) first. These bits can be combined to make up any number between 0 and 255.

The possible bit values for a byte in base 10 can be represented as a table:

Bit position	1	2	3	4	5	6	7	8
Bit value	128	64	32	16	8	4	2	1

Table 5.1: Bit (base 2) values of a base 10 byte

This is not to say that the bitwise operators only work on byte values. The examples in this section use a single byte as the easiest to describe as a table.

The bitwise operators demonstrated here will often return a 32-bit integer (`int` or `System.Int32`) value. When both values are numerically smaller (in maximum absolute value) than a 32-bit integer, the result will be a 32-bit integer.

A 32-bit integer can have a minimum value of `-2147483648` and a maximum of `2147483647`. It comprises one sign bit and 31 bits that can be used to define the number.

`Get-Member` can be used to show this in action:

```
# Both sides are int, result is System.Int32
1 -band 1 | Get-Member
```

In this case, both sides of the expression are an `int`, so the result will also be `int`.

Similarly, if the input value is a `byte`, the result will be an `int`. A byte has a minimum value of `0` and a maximum of `255`:

```
# Both sides are byte, result is Int32
[byte]1 -band [byte]1 | Get-Member
```

The output type only changes when the value type on either side can possibly exceed the capacity of a 32-bit integer. At that point, the largest of the types is used.

A 64-bit integer (System.Int64) is made up of 8 bytes and has a maximum value of 9223372036854775807. This value therefore cannot possibly be represented as a 32-bit integer. If the value used on either side is a 64-bit integer, the result will be a 64-bit integer.

Both statements below show that the operator creates a System.Int64 value:

```
[Int64]1 -band 1 | Get-Member
1 -band [Int64]1 | Get-Member
```

Each of the examples above has made use of the bitwise AND operator.

band (Bitwise AND)

The result of -band is a number in which each bit that is set in both the value on the left and the value on the right is set.

In the following example, the result is 2:

```
11 -band 6
```

This bitwise AND operation can be shown in a table. Each value is shown in binary:

Bit value		8	4	2	1
Left-hand side	11	1	0	1	1
Right-hand side	6	0	1	1	0
-band	2	0	0	1	0

Table 5.2: 11 -band 6

The result of -band is a number where both the value on the left-hand side and the value on the right-hand side include the bit.

bor (Bitwise OR)

The result of -bor is a number where the bits are set in either the value on the left or right.

In the following example, the result is 15:

```
11 -bor 12
```

This operation can be shown in a table:

Bit value		8	4	2	1
Left-hand side	11	1	0	1	1
Right-hand side	12	1	1	0	0
-bor	15	1	1	1	1

Table 5.3: 11 -bor 12

The result is a number made up of the bits from each number where either number has the bit set.

bxor (Bitwise eXclusive OR)

The result of `-bxor` is a number where the bits are set in either the value on the left or the value on the right, but not both.

In the following example, the result is 11:

```
6 -bxor 13
```

This operation can be shown in a table:

Bit value		8	4	2	1
Left-hand side	6	0	1	1	0
Right-hand side	13	1	1	0	1
-bxor	11	1	0	1	1

Table 5.4: 6 -bxor 13

The `-bxor` operator is useful for toggling bit values. For example, `-bxor` might be used to toggle the `AccountDisable` bit of `UserAccountControl` in Active Directory:

```
512 -bxor 2 # Result is 514 (Disabled, 2 is set)
514 -bxor 2 # Result is 512 (Enabled, 2 is not set)
```

The exclusive `OR` operator is useful to toggle bits in a value; to reverse the bits in a value, `-bnot` must be used.

bnot (Bitwise NOT)

The -bnot operator is applied before a numeric value; it does not use a value on the left-hand side. The result is a value that's composed of all bits that are not set.

The -bnot operator works with signed and unsigned 32-bit and 64-bit integers (Int32, UInt32, Int64, and UInt64). When working with 8-bit or 16-bit integers (SByte, Byte, Int16, and UInt16), the result is always a signed 32-bit integer (Int32).

In the following example, the result is -123:

```
-bnot 122
```

As the preceding result is a 32-bit integer (Int32), it is difficult to show the effect in a small table. If this value were an SByte, the operation could be expressed in a table as follows:

Bit value		Signing	64	32	16	8	4	2	1
Before -bnot	122	0	1	1	1	1	0	1	0
After -bnot	-123	1	0	0	0	0	1	0	1

Table 5.5: -bnot 122

As shown in the preceding table, the -bnot operator reverses the value for each bit. The signing bit is not treated any differently.

shl and shr (Shift left and right operators)

The -shl and -shr operators were introduced with PowerShell 3.0. These operators perform bit-shifting.

The -shl and -shr operators have the lowest precedence and are only executed after all other operators. For example, the result of the following calculation is 128; the multiplication and addition operators are evaluated before -shl:

```
2 * 4 -shl 2 + 2
```

The effect of shift operators is best demonstrated by representing numeric values in binary. For the value of 78, the following bits must be set:

Bit value	128	64	32	16	8	4	2	1
On or off	0	1	0	0	1	1	1	0

Table 5.6: Bit values

When a left-shift operation is performed, every bit is moved a defined number of places to the left; in the following example, it is one bit to the left:

```
78 -shl 1
```

The result is 156, which is expressed in this bit table:

Bit value	128	64	32	16	8	4	2	1
Before shift	0	1	0	0	1	1	1	0
After shift	1	0	0	1	1	1	0	0

Table 5.7: Shift left

Shifting one bit to the right reverses the operation:

```
PS> 156 -shr 1
78
```

When the shift right (`-shr`) operator shifts values, bits that are set and shifted past the rightmost bit (bit value 1) become `0`. For example:

```
PS> 3 -shr 1
1
```

This is expressed in the following table. Bits that end up in the rightmost column are discarded; they are outside of the range of bits used by the numeric value:

Bit value	128	64	32	16	8	4	2	1	Out of range
Before shift	0	0	0	0	0	0	1	1	

After shift	0	0	0	0	0	0	0	1	1

Table 5.8: Shift right – discarded bits

If the numeric value is of a specific numeric type, the resulting number cannot exceed the maximum value for that type. For example, a byte has a maximum value of 255; if the value of 255 is shifted one bit to the left, the resulting value will be 254:

```
PS> [byte]255 -shl 1
254
```

Shifting out of range is shown in this table:

Bit value	Out of range	128	64	32	16	8	4	2	1
Before shift		1	1	1	1	1	1	1	1
After shift	1	1	1	1	1	1	1	1	0

Table 5.9: Shift left – discarded bits

If the value were capable of being larger, such as a 16- or 32-bit integer, the value would be allowed to increase, as it no longer falls out of range:

```
PS> [Int16]255 -shl 1
510
```

Bit shifting like this is easiest to demonstrate with unsigned types such as `Byte`, `UInt16`, `UInt32`, and `UInt64`. Unsigned types cannot support values lower than 0 (negative numbers), as they have no way of describing a negative value.

Signed types, such as `SByte`, `Int16`, `Int32`, and `Int64`, use the highest-order bit to indicate whether the value is positive or negative. For example, this table shows the bit positions for a signed byte (`SByte`):

Bit position	1	2	3	4	5	6	7	8
Bit value	Signing	64	32	16	8	4	2	1

Table 5.10: Signed byte

The preceding bit values may be used to express numbers between 127 and -128. The binary forms of 1 and -1 are shown as an example in the following table:

Bit value	Signing	64	32	16	8	4	2	1
1	0	0	0	0	0	0	0	1
-1	1	1	1	1	1	1	1	1

Table 5.11: Positive and negative in bits

For a signed type, each bit (except for signing) adds to a minimum value:

- When the signing bit is not set, add each value to 0
- When the signing bit is set, add each value to -128

When applying this to left shift, if the value of `64` is shifted one bit to the left, it becomes -128:

```
PS> ([SByte]64) -shl 1
-128
```

The shift left into the signing bit is expressed in the following table:

Bit value	Signing	64	32	16	8	4	2	1
Before shift	0	1	0	0	0	0	0	0
After shift	1	0	0	0	0	0	0	0

Table 5.12: Shift into signing bit

Shift operations such as these are common in the networking world. For example, the IP address `192.168.4.32` may be represented in several different ways:

- In hexadecimal: `C0A80420`
- As an unsigned 32-bit integer: `3232236576`
- As a signed 32-bit integer: `-1062730720`

The signed and unsigned versions of an IP address are calculated using left shift. For example, the IP address `192.168.4.32` may be written as a signed 32-bit integer (`Int32`):

```
(192 -shl 24) + (168 -shl 16) + (4 -shl 8) + 32
```

Shift operations such as these can be useful but are not common. The next section explores the assignment operator.

Assignment operators

Assignment operators are used to give values to variables. The assignment operators that are available are as follows:

- **Assign**: =
- **Add and assign**: +=
- **Subtract and assign**: -=
- **Multiply and assign**: *=
- **Divide and assign**: /=
- **Remainder and assign**: %=

As with the arithmetic operators, add and assign may be used with strings, arrays, hashtables, and many more. Multiply and assign may be used with strings and arrays.

Assign, add and assign, and subtract and assign

The assignment operator (=) is used to assign values to variables and properties; for example, it may be used to assign a value to a variable:

```
$variable = 'some value'
```

Alternatively, the PowerShell console window title (or Windows Terminal tab title) might be changed by assigning a new value to the `WindowTitle` property:

```
$host.UI.RawUI.WindowTitle = 'PowerShell window'
```

The add and assign operator (+=) operates in a similar manner to the addition operator. The following example assigns the value 1 to a variable, and then += is used to add 20 to that value:

```
$i = 1
$i += 20
```

The preceding example is equivalent to writing the following:

```
$i = 1
$i = $i + 20
```

The add-and-assign operator, +=, can be used to concatenate strings:

```
$string = 'one'
$string += 'one'
```

As with the addition operator, attempting to add a numeric value to an existing string is acceptable. Attempting to add a string to a variable containing a numeric value is not:

```
PS> $variable = 1
PS> $variable += 'one'
InvalidArgument: Cannot convert value "one" to type "System.Int32". Error: "Input
string was not in a correct format."
```

The += operator may be used to add elements to an existing array:

```
$array = 1, 2
$array += 3
```

The += operator can be used to add another array:

```
$array = 1, 2
$array += 3, 4
```

The += operator may be used to join two hashtables:

```
$hashtable = @{key1 = 1}
$hashtable += @{key2 = 2}
```

As seen when using the addition operator, the operation fails if one of the keys already exists.

The subtract and assign operator (-=) is intended for numeric operations, as shown in the following examples:

```
$i = 20
$i -= 2
```

After this operation has been completed, `$i` has a value of 18.

Multiply and assign, divide and assign, and modulus and assign

Numeric assignments using the multiply and assign operator may be performed using `*=`. The value held by the variable `$i` is 4:

```
$i = 2
$i *= 2
```

The multiply and assign operator may be used to duplicate a string held in a variable:

```
$string = 'one'
$string *= 2
```

The value on the right-hand side of the `*=` operator must be numeric or able to convert to a number. For example, a string containing the number 2 is acceptable:

```
$string = 'one'
$string *= '2'
```

Using a string that PowerShell cannot convert to a number will result in an error, as follows:

```
PS> $variable = 'one'
PS> $variable *= 'one'
InvalidArgument: Cannot convert value "one" to type "System.Int32". Error: "Input
string was not in a correct format."
```

The multiply and assign operator may be used to duplicate an array held in a variable. In the following example, the variable holds the value 1, 2, 1, 2 after this operation:

```
$variable = 1, 2
$variable *= 2
```

The divide-and-assign operator is used to perform numeric operations. The variable holds a value of 1 after the following operation:

```
$variable = 2
$variable /= 2
```

The remainder-and-assign operator will assign the result of the remainder operation to a variable:

```
$variable = 10
$variable %= 3
```

After the preceding operation, the variable holds a value of 1, which is the remainder when dividing 10 by 3.

Statements can be assigned to a variable

In PowerShell, statements can be assigned to variables. All output from that statement will be captured in the variable.

The most common use for this is capturing arrays of results. The following example creates a custom object that includes output from both the `Win32_Service` CIM class and the `Get-Process` command. All the generated objects are assigned to the `$serviceInfo` variable:

```
$services = Get-CimInstance Win32_Service -Filter 'State="Running"'
$serviceInfo = foreach ($service in $services) {
    $process = Get-Process -ID $service.ProcessID
    [PSCustomObject]@{
        Name        = $service.Name
        ProcessName = $process.Name
        ProcessID   = $service.ProcessID
        Path        = $process.Path
        MemoryUsed  = $process.WorkingSet64 / 1MB
    }
}
```

Assigning statements such as loops in PowerShell is the most efficient way of gathering a set of results into a variable.

The assignment of statements such as loops in PowerShell will be discussed in *Chapter 6, Conditional Statements and Loops*.

Assignment and other operators

Assigning a value to a variable is a useful step in simplifying a piece of code. It can be used to break up a complex statement into multiple parts, and it acts as a point that can be inspected if debugging code.

For example, the `if` statement below might be considered unclear and too complex:

```
$value = 1, 2, 3
if ($value -and $value.Count -eq 3 -and $value -contains 2 -and -not ($value -gt
4)) {
    <# Script statements #>
}
```

Assigning a value before the if condition can make it easier to read the condition:

```
$value = 1, 2, 3
$isValidValue = $value -and $value.Count -eq 3 -and $value -contains 2 -and -not
($value -gt 4)
if ($isValidValue) {
    <# Script statements #>
}
```

Adding line breaks to the comparison might improve how readable the expression is:

```
$isValidValue = $value -and
    $value.Count -eq 3 -and
    $value -contains 2 -and
    -not ($value -gt 4)

if ($isValidValue) {
    <# Script statements #>
}
```

Combining operators and assigning the result is a useful technique that can be used to simplify code without sacrificing readability.

Type operators

Type operators are designed to work with and test .NET types. The following operators are available:

- **As**: `-as`
- **Is**: `-is`
- **Is not**: `-isnot`

These operators may be used to convert an object of one type into another, or to test whether an object is of a given type.

as

The `-as` operator is used to attempt to convert a value into an object of a specified type. The operator returns null (without throwing an error) if the conversion cannot be completed.

For example, the operator may be used to perform the following conversions:

```
"1" -as [Int32]
'String' -as [Type]
```

If the attempt to convert the value fails, nothing is returned, and no error is raised:

```
$true -as [DateTime]
```

The `-as` operator can be useful for testing whether a value can be cast to a specific type, or whether a specific type exists.

For example, the `System.Windows.Forms` assembly is not imported by default, and the `System.Windows.Forms.Form` type does not exist in the current PowerShell session.

The `-as` operator may be used to test if it is possible to find the `System.Windows.Forms.Form` type:

```
if (-not ('System.Windows.Forms.Form' -as [Type])) {
    Write-Host 'Adding assembly' -ForegroundColor Green
    Add-Type -Assembly System.Windows.Forms
}
```

If the `System.Windows.Forms` assembly has not been imported, attempting to turn the string, `System.Windows.Forms.Form`, into a type will fail. The failure to convert will not generate an error.

is and isnot

The `-is` and `-isnot` operators test whether a value is of a specified type.

For example, each of the following returns true:

```
'string' -is [String]
1 -is [Int32]
[String] -is [Type]
123 -isnot [String]
```

The `-is` and `-isnot` operators are especially useful for testing the exact type of a value, often in an if statement when the action taken depends on the value type.

Redirection operators

Chapter 4, Working with Objects in PowerShell, started exploring the different output streams that PowerShell utilizes.

Information from a command may be redirected using the redirection operator, >. Information may be sent to another stream or a file.

For example, the output from a command can be directed to a file. The file contains the output as it would have been displayed in the console:

```
PS> Get-Process -Id $pid > process.txt
PS> Get-Content process.txt

NPM(K)    PM(M)      WS(M)     CPU(s)      Id  SI ProcessName
 ------    -----      -----     ------      --  -- -----------
     78   144.69     186.91      12.69   15284   1 pwsh
```

Each of the streams (except for Progress) in PowerShell has a number associated with it. These are shown in the following table:

Stream name	Stream number
Success	1
Error	2
Warning	3
Verbose	4
Debug	5
Information	6

Table 5.13: PowerShell streams

Each of the preceding streams can be redirected. In most cases, PowerShell provides parameters for commands that can be used to capture the streams. Examples include the `ErrorVariable`, `InformationVariable`, and `WarningVariable` parameters.

About Write-Host

Before PowerShell 5, the output written using the `Write-Host` command could not be captured, redirected, or assigned to a variable. In PowerShell 5, `Write-Host` became a wrapper for `Write-Information`; the message is sent to the information stream.

Information written using `Write-Host` is unaffected by the `InformationPreference` variable and the `InformationAction` parameter, except when either is set to `Ignore`.

When `InformationAction` for the `Write-Host` command is set to Ignore, the output will be suppressed. When `Ignore` is set for the `InformationPreference` variable, an error is displayed, stating that it is not supported.

Redirection to a file

Output from a specific stream may be directed by placing the stream number on the left of the redirect operator.

For example, the output written by `Write-Warning` can be directed to a file:

```
function Test-Redirect {
    'This is success'
    Write-Warning 'This is a warning'
```

```
}
$output = Test-Redirect 3> 'warnings.txt'
```

The `$output` variable will contain the string "This is success". The warning message from stream 3 is redirected to the `warnings.txt` file.

When using the redirect operator, any file of the same name is overwritten. If data is to be appended to a file, the operator is changed to >>:

```
function Test-Redirect {
    Write-Warning "Warning $i"
}
$i = 1
Test-Redirect 3> 'warnings.txt'    # Overwrite

$i++
Test-Redirect 3>> 'warnings.txt'  # Append
```

It is possible to redirect additional streams, for example, `warning` and `error`, by adding more redirect statements. The following example redirects the error and warning streams to separate files:

```
function Test-Redirect {
    'This is standard out'

    Write-Error 'This is an error'
    Write-Warning 'This is a warning'
}
Test-Redirect 3> 'warnings.txt' 2> 'errors.txt'
```

The wildcard character * may be used to represent all streams if all content was to be sent to a single file:

```
function Test-Redirect {
    'This is standard out'

    Write-Information 'This is information'
    Write-Host 'This is information as well'
    Write-Error 'This is an error'
    Write-Verbose 'This is verbose'
    Write-Warning 'This is a warning'
```

```
}

$VerbosePreference = 'Continue'
Test-Redirect *> 'alloutput.txt'
```

The preceding example sets the `$VerbosePreference` variable. Without this, or the addition of the -Verbose parameter to the `Write-Verbose` command, the output from Write-Verbose will not be shown at all.

PowerShell and default file encoding

The encoding of a file, including text files, can be optionally described using a **BOM** or **byte-order mark**. The BOM is written to the first few bytes of a file and describes the encoding used by the content that follows, that is, how to interpret the bytes in the file to represent characters to display. The BOM is not normally displayed as text by editors.

The different BOM values are described on Wikipedia: `https://wikipedia.org/wiki/Byte_order_mark`.

The BOM is optional; files without a BOM that are opened in a text editor are generally assumed to be UTF-8 (depending on the editor).

In Windows PowerShell, files written using redirection are encoded using UTF-16LE. In PowerShell 6 and later, files are written using UTF8NoBOM.

If PowerShell 6 or later uses >> to append to a file created using > in Windows PowerShell, the result will be a file with mixed encoding. The presence of the Unicode BOM renders the content unreadable in most cases.

Streams can be redirected to other streams rather than a file.

Redirecting streams to the Success stream

Streams can be redirected to the Success stream in PowerShell. The destination stream is written on the right-hand side of the redirect operator (without a space). Stream numbers on the right-hand side are prefixed with an ampersand (&) to distinguish the stream from a filename.

Only Success stream

Each of the following examples shows redirection to the Success stream, `&1`. It is not possible to redirect to streams other than Success.

For example, the output from `Write-Information`, stream 6, is redirected to the Success stream:

```
PS> function Test-Redirect {
>>     'This is standard out'
>>     Write-Information 'This is information'
>> }
PS> $success = Test-Redirect 6>&1
PS> $success
This is standard out
This is information
```

It is possible to redirect from additional streams, for example, error and warning, by adding more redirect statements. The following example redirects the error and warning streams to the Success stream:

```
function Test-Redirect {
    'This is standard out'
    Write-Error 'This is an error'
    Write-Warning 'This is a warning'
}
$stdOut = Test-Redirect 2>&13>&1
```

The wildcard character * may be used to represent all streams if all streams were to be sent to another stream:

```
function Test-Redirect {
    'This is standard out'
    Write-Information 'This is information'
    Write-Host 'This is information as well'
    Write-Error 'This is an error'
    Write-Verbose 'This is verbose'
    Write-Warning 'This is a warning'
}

$VerbosePreference = 'Continue'
$success = Test-Redirect *>&1
```

The preceding example sets the `$VerbosePreference` variable. Without this, the output from `Write-Verbose` will not be shown at all.

Redirection to null

Redirecting output to null can be used as a technique to drop unwanted output. The `$null` variable takes the place of the filename:

```
Get-Process > $null
```

The stream number or * may be included to the left of the redirect operator. For example, warnings and errors might be redirected to null:

```
.\somecommand.exe 2> $null 3> $null
.\somecommand.exe *> $null
```

Redirection like this is often used with native executables; redirection is rarely necessary with PowerShell commands.

Other operators

PowerShell has a wide variety of operators, a few of which do not easily fall into a specific category:

- Comma: `,`
- Index: `[ ]`
- Range: `..`
- Call: `&` (at the start of a command)
- Format: `-f`
- Increment and decrement: `++` and `--`
- Join: `-join`
- Null coalescing: `??` and `??=`
- Null conditional: `${object}?.PropertyOrMethod`
- Pipeline chain: `&&` and `||`
- Background: `&` (at the end of a command)

Each of these operators is in common use. The range operator is often used with the index operator and arrays. The call operator can run a command based on a string. The format operator can be used to build up complex strings, and so on.

Comma

The comma operator may be used to separate elements in an array. For example:

```
$array = 1, 2, 3, 4
```

If the comma operator is used before a single value (as a unary operator), it creates an array containing one element:

```
$array = ,1
```

The index operator can be used to access the elements of an array.

Index

The index operator is used to access elements in an array by position, numbering from 0. For example, the following accesses the first element in the array:

```
$array = 1, 2, 3, 4, 5
$array[0]
```

More than one index can be accessed using the comma operator:

```
$array = 1, 2, 3, 4, 5
$array[0, 1]
```

Using negative values accesses values in an array from the end. The example below will return the values 5 (-1) and 4 (-2):

```
$array = 1, 2, 3, 4, 5
$array[-1, -2]
```

The index operator can be used with any value that is indexable. For example, the index operator can be used with a string:

```
$name = 'Andrew'
$firstLetter = $name[0]
```

The index operator can be combined with the range operator.

Range

The range operator, as the name suggests, can be used to create a range of values. For example, the statement below creates an array of numbers from 1 to 10:

```
1..10
```

The start and end values are arbitrary and do not have to be written in ascending order. For example, a descending array of numbers can be created:

```
90..75
```

In PowerShell 6 and later (but not in Windows PowerShell), the same notation can be used to create an array of characters:

```
'a'..'f'
```

The range operator can be used with the index operator to select a range of values from an array.

```
$array = 1, 2, 3, 4, 5
$array[2..4]
```

The range operator might be quickly used to loop a fixed number of times. In the example below, we make use of the `ForEach-Object` command in a pipeline:

```
1..10 | ForEach-Object { Start-Sleep -Seconds 1 }
```

The range operator is widely used both to create ranges of numbers and as a simple means of iterating a fixed number of times.

Call

The call operator (&) is used to execute a string or script block. The call operator is particularly useful when running commands (executables or scripts) that have spaces in the path.

The following example runs `pwsh.exe` using a full path held in a string:

```
& 'C:\Program Files\PowerShell\7\pwsh.exe'
```

The path to `pwsh.exe` is normally in the PATH environment variable, so using the full path as in the example above should not be necessary.

The call operator is also useful if the command name changes based on circumstances, for example, the operating system running a command. For example, if a command is described by a variable, we use the call operator as follows:

```
$pwsh = 'C:\Program Files\PowerShell\7\pwsh.exe'
& $pwsh
```

This technique can be applied to any command, including PowerShell commands, scripts, and other Windows executables.

Any arguments required by the command can be written in-line, as if the call operator were not present. For example:

```
$pwsh = 'C:\Program Files\PowerShell\7\pwsh.exe'
& $pwsh -NoProfile -NoLogo -Command "Write-Host 'Hello world'"
```

Alternatively, arguments can be supplied as an array, a technique that is useful for commands expecting many arguments:

```
$pwsh = 'C:\Program Files\PowerShell\7\pwsh.exe'
$argumentList = @(
    '-NoProfile'
    '-NoLogo'
    '-Command'
    'Write-Host "Hello world"'
)
& $pwsh $argumentList
```

The call operator may also be used to execute script blocks:

```
$scriptBlock = { Write-Host 'Hello world' }
& $scriptBlock
```

Parameters and arguments can be passed to the script block either in-line, as shown in the previous examples, or by using splatting. Splatting was introduced in *Chapter 1, Introduction to PowerShell*.

Format

The `-f` operator can be used to create complex formatted strings.

The format operator is often used as an alternative to including variables in strings or using sub-expressions.

The string format is known as a composite format. Microsoft maintains detailed examples and format references for numeric, DateTime, and Timespan types: `https://learn.microsoft.com/en-us/dotnet/standard/base-types/composite-formatting`.

The `-f` operator uses a placeholder, a number in curly braces (`{<number>}`) in a string on the left of the operator. The number is the index of a value in an array on the right. For example:

```
PS> '1: {0}, 2: {1}, 3: {2}' -f 'one', 'two', 'three'
1: one, 2: two, 3: three
```

At the start of this chapter, the following example was used:

```
$word = 'one'
"Length: $($word.Length)"
```

If the format operator were used instead, the example would become:

```
$word = 'one'
'Length: {0}' -f $word.Length
```

The format operator is one possible way to assemble complex strings in PowerShell. In addition, `-f` may be used to simplify some string operations. For example, a decimal may be formatted as a percentage:

```
'The pass mark is {0:P}' -f 0.8
```

An integer may be formatted as a hexadecimal string:

```
'244 in Hexadecimal is {0:X2}' -f 244
```

A number may be written as a culture-specific currency; in the UK, it will use the £ symbol, in the US, $, and so on:

```
'The price is {0:C2}' -f 199
```

A date may be formatted as a string, which is useful if parts of the date are used in several places in the string:

```
'Today is {0:dddd} the {0:dd} of {0:MMMM}' -f (Get-Date)
```

When using the `-f` operator, curly braces are considered reserved characters. If a curly brace is to be included in a string as a literal value, it can be escaped:

```
'The value in {{0}} is {0}' -f 1
```

The array sub-expression operator may be used on the right-hand side of `-f` for longer or more complex lists of values. For example, to set up a window title for PowerShell:

```
$host.UI.RawUI.WindowTitle = '{0}{1} - PowerShell {2}' -f @(
    [Environment]::UserName
    [IntPtr]::Size -eq 4 ? ' (32-bit)' : ''
    $PSVersionTable.PSVersion
)
```

The example above also makes use of the ternary operator, demonstrated earlier in this chapter.

Any array on the right-hand side of `-f` must at least have as many elements as there are placeholders. However, PowerShell will also accept arrays that contain more elements:

```
'{0}, {1}' -f 'one', 'two', 'three', 'four'
```

This means that a common set of values can be used with different format strings:

```
$errorDetails = @(
    'Error!'
    'My error message'
    'At line 1, character 30'
)
$shortFormat = '{0} {1}'
$longFormat = '{0} {1}: {2}'
```

Then, each format string can be used with the `$errorDetails` variable:

```
$shortFormat -f $errorDetails
$longFormat -f $errorDetails
```

The format operator is a potential alternative to embedding variables and sub-expressions into strings or using the + operator to concatenate.

join

The `-join` operator joins arrays using a string. In the following example, the string is split based on a comma, and then it is joined based on a tab (`` `t ``):

```
PS> 'a', 'b', 'c', 'd' -join "`t"
a       b       c       d
```

The `-join` operator may also be used in front of an array (used as a unary operator) when there is no need for a separator. For example:

```
PS> -join ('hello', 'world')
helloworld
```

If the parentheses are excluded from the example, the statement will be considered incomplete and will not execute.

Null coalescing

The null coalescing operator in PowerShell 7 may be used to define a default for a value when the subject is null.

For example, null coalescing is useful if the value for a variable is dependent on another. This operation might be performed using an if statement:

```
$valueA = $null
if ($null -eq $valueA) {
    $valueB = 'Default value'
} else {
    $valueB = $valueA
}
```

The null coalescing operator can simplify this expression:

```
$valueA = $null
$valueB = $valueA ?? 'Default value'
```

If `$valueA` is given a non-null value, it will be returned as the result of the expression:

```
$valueA = 'Supplied value'
$valueA ?? 'Default value'
```

Null coalescing operators can be chained to build up a more complex expression. In the following example, the value of the variable will be set to the first of the functions that returns a non-null value:

```
function first { }
function second { 'second' }
function third { 'third' }

(first) ?? (second) ?? (third)
```

The preceding expression will return the value `second`, as the function `first` does not return a value. The function `third` will not be called in this case.

If the value were removed from the second function, the result of the expression would be `third` as the only non-null value in the expression:

```
function first { }
function second { }
function third { 'third' }

(first) ?? (second) ?? (third)
```

A default value might be added to the end to always ensure the result is never null:

```
(first) ?? (second) ?? (third) ?? 'default'
```

The null coalescing operator allows a complex conditional expression to be defined with a very concise statement. The operator may also be used in an assignment operation.

Null coalescing assignment

The null coalescing assignment operator can be used to simplify the use of the null coalescing operator when assigning values.

In the following example, `$value` will only become 1 if it is null:

```
$value = $null
if ($null -eq $value) {
    $value = 1
}
```

The expression can be simplified by using the null coalescing assignment operator:

```
$value = $null
$value ??= 1
```

In the preceding example, because `$value` is already set, it will not be changed by the second assignment:

```
$value = 1
$value ??= 2
```

The value must be explicitly null (not false, 0, or an empty string) for the assignment to complete.

This approach might be used to ensure a variable has a reference to a specific folder:

```
$dev = Get-Item ~/dev -ErrorAction Ignore
$dev ??= New-Item ~/dev -ItemType Directory
```

In the preceding example, Notepad will only start if the process does not exist.

Null conditional

The null conditional operator can be used to avoid errors when a property or method is used on an object, and the object itself is null.

The behavior of the operator is best described by an example. The following command will raise an error if the variable has not been set or the value is null:

```
PS> $someObject.ToString()
InvalidOperation: You cannot call a method on a null-valued expression.
```

The null conditional operator can be used so the method is only run if the object is not null:

```
${someObject}?.ToString()
```

As the ? character can be part of a normal variable name, curly braces must be used to separate the variable name from the null conditional operator.

The same technique can be used for properties of objects that may not be set. As the ? character is not normally part of a property name, curly braces are not required:

```
$someOtherObject = [PSCustomObject]@{
    Value = $null
}
$someOtherObject.Value?.ToString()
```

If a value for the `Value` property is set, the method executes and returns as normal. This operator avoids the need for conditional statements to test the property value:

```
$someOtherObject = [PSCustomObject]@{
    Value = $null
}
if ($someOtherObject.Value) {
    $someOtherObject.Value.ToString()
}
```

If the value were created in a way that meant it included a ? character, the curly braces can again be used to describe the extent of the property name:

```
$someOtherObject = [PSCustomObject]@{
    'Value?' = $null
}
$someOtherObject.{Value?}?.ToString()
```

This operator cannot be used to avoid errors accessing non-existent properties when strict mode is enabled.

For example, because the `Value` property does not exist in `$someOtherObject` below, an error will be displayed when strict mode is enabled.

```
& {
    Set-StrictMode -Version Latest
    $someOtherObject = [PSCustomObject]@{}
    $someOtherObject.Value?.ToString()
}
```

See `Get-Help Set-StrictMode` to explore the features and functionality of strict mode in PowerShell.

Pipeline chain

The pipeline chain operators allow conditional execution of commands based on the success (or failure) of another command. Two operators are available, `&&` and `||`.

These operators are present in `cmd.exe` and are also implemented in Bash on Linux.

Evaluating success or failure is based on the value of the `$?` variable.

To demonstrate these operators, two commands are used. The following command gets the current directory and should therefore always succeed:

```
Get-Item .
```

`Write-Host` is used to show when the right-hand side runs.

When the `&&` operator is used, the command on the right-hand side only runs if the command on the left-hand side is successful:

```
PS> Get-Item . && Write-Host 'Exists'

        Directory: C:\

Mode                 LastWriteTime         Length Name
----                 -------------         ------ ----
d----          21/01/2024     12:53               workspace
Exists
```

The statement above is, therefore, the equivalent of the example below, which will have the same output:

```
Get-Item .
if ($?) {
    Write-Host 'Exists'
}
```

If the left-hand side command were to fail, the right-hand side command would not run. The `ErrorAction` parameter is added to the example below to hide the error and demonstrate that the right-hand side does not run:

```
Get-Item DoesNotExist -ErrorAction Ignore &&
    Write-Host 'Exists'
```

In this example, there will be no output.

The `||` operator causes the right-hand side to run only when the left-hand side fails. As before, failure is determined by the value of the `$?` variable.

```
Get-Item DoesNotExist -ErrorAction Ignore ||
    Write-Host 'Does not exist'
```

This time, the command will show the `Does not exist` message and no other output.

This is equivalent to the example below:

```
Get-Item DoesNotExist -ErrorAction Ignore
if (-not $?) {
    Write-Host 'Does not exist'
}
```

Fixing the path will cause the directory object to display and not the message.

```
PS> Get-Item . -ErrorAction Ignore || Write-Host 'Does not exist'

        Directory: C:\

Mode                 LastWriteTime         Length Name
----                 -------------         ------ ----
d----          21/01/2024     12:53                workspace
```

These pipeline chain operators may be useful if installing and then running an application, for example, using the made-up commands shown here:

```
installApplication.exe && application.exe
```

These operators are a small addition to PowerShell and may help users approaching PowerShell from other languages or shells.

Background

The background operator may be used to send the command preceding the operator into a job. For example, running the following command creates a background job:

```
$job = Get-Process &
```

The background job is visible using the `Get-Job` command as shown in the following example:

```
PS> Get-Job

Id  Name  PSJobTypeName  State    HasMoreData  Location   Command
--  ----  -------------  -----    -----------  --------   -------
1   Job1  BackgroundJob  Running  True         localhost  Micro...
```

Any output from the job may be retrieved using the `Receive-Job` command:

```
$job = Get-Process &
$job | Receive-Job
```

Summary

This chapter covered many of the operators PowerShell has to offer, including operators for performing arithmetic, assignment, and comparison.

Several specialized operators that use regular expressions were introduced for matching, replacing, and splitting. Binary, logical, and type operators were demonstrated.

Finally, several other significant operators were introduced, including the call, format, increment, decrement, and join operators, along with the new ternary, null-coalescing, pipeline chain, and background operators.

Chapter 6, Conditional Statements and Loops, explores how to test and react to values and how to make use of loops in PowerShell.

6

Conditional Statements and Loops

Conditional statements and loops are the backbone of any programming or scripting language. Being able to react to a state and choose a path to take or to repeat instructions is vital.

Each conditional statement or loop creates a branch in a script or piece of code. The branch represents a split in the instruction set. Branches can be conditional, such as one created by an `if` statement, or unconditional, such as a `foreach` loop. As the number of branches increases, so does the complexity. The paths through the script spread out in the same manner as the limbs of a tree.

Statements or lines of code may be executed when certain conditions are met. PowerShell provides `if` and `switch` statements for this purpose. Loops allow code to be repeated for a set of elements or until a specific condition is met.

Loops can be combined with components such as collections like queues and stacks to perform even more advanced operations – for example, to perform recursion-like operations on filesystems.

In this chapter, the following topics are covered:

- if, else, and elseif
- Implicit Boolean
- switch statements
- switch, break, and continue
- Loops
- Loops, break, and continue

- Loops and labels
- Loops, queues, and stacks

The `if` statement is a vital keyword and is likely used in most scripts.

if, else, and elseif

An `if` statement is used to execute an action when a condition is met. The following shows the syntax for an `if` statement; the statements enclosed by the `if` statement execute if the condition evaluates to true:

```
if (<condition>) {
    <statements>
}
```

The `else` statement is optional and runs if all previous conditions evaluate as false:

```
if (<first-condition>) {
    <first-statements>
} else {
    <second-statements>
}
```

The `elseif` statement allows several conditions to be tested in order:

```
if (<first-condition>) {
    <first-statements>
} elseif (<second-condition>) {
    <second-statements>
} elseif (<last-condition>) {
    <last-statements>
}
```

The `else` statement may be added after any number of `elseif` statements.

Execution of a block of conditions stops as soon as a single condition is true. For example, both the first and second condition would evaluate to true, but only the first executes:

```
$value = 1
if ($value -eq 1) {
    Write-Host 'value is 1'
```

```
} elseif ($value -lt 10) {
    Write-Host 'value is less than 10'
} else {
    Write-Host 'value is not equal to 1'
}
```

When the example above runs, and because the value is 1, the first `Write-Host` statement runs. The output from the example is shown below:

```
value is 1
```

If the `if` statement structure becomes too complicated, a `switch` statement might be used instead. This is explored later in this chapter.

Assignment within if statements

Values may be assigned to variables inside `if` statements, as shown here:

```
if ($i = 5) {
    Write-Host "The variable i is $i"
}
```

The condition will be true if the value of the variable evaluates to true; that is, it is true because 5 is greater than 0.

This is most used when testing for the existence of a value in a variable, for example:

```
if ($interface = Get-NetAdapter | Where-Object Status -eq 'Up') {
    Write-Host "$($interface.Name) is up"
}
```

In the previous example, the statement to the right of the assignment operator (=) is executed, assigned to the `$interface` variable, and then the value in the variable is treated as an implicit Boolean.

Supporting this type of assignment means PowerShell does not alert the author of a script if an assignment operation is used instead of a comparison. This is most often a problem when the assignment was intended instead to be a comparison.

Implicit Boolean

Implicit Boolean is a feature that allows conditions to be simplified. A value that is not Boolean but is tested as if it were true or false is an implicit Boolean. For example, the following `if` statement tests the output from a command:

```
if (Get-ChildItem c:\users\a*) {
    # If statement body
}
```

The condition evaluates as true when the `Get-ChildItem` command finds one or more files or folders. The condition evaluates as false when no files or folders are found.

An explicit version of the same comparison is shown here:

```
if ($null -ne (Get-ChildItem c:\users\c*)) {
    # If statement body
}
```

The explicit statement above is more complex and arguably more difficult to read.

A condition with no comparison operator implicitly evaluates to false if it is any of the following:

- `$null`
- An empty string
- An empty array
- The numeric value 0

A variable containing a single object evaluates according to that object's value. A single-element array evaluates according to the Boolean value of its element; an array containing more than one element evaluates to true.

`switch` is a common alternative to if, elseif, and else statements.

switch statements

A `switch` statement executes statements where a case evaluates as true. The case can be written as a number, a string, or any other value. However, `switch` will always compare literal values as strings. This facet of `switch` is explored in more detail later in this section.

A `switch` statement is similar in some respects to an `if`, `elseif`, and `else` statement. The key difference is that in `switch`, more than one condition can run for the value being tested.

A `switch` statement uses the following generalized notation:

```
switch [-Regex | -Wildcard | -Exact] [-CaseSensitive] (<value>) {
    <case>    { <statements> }
    <case>    { <statements> }
    default   { <statements> }
}
```

The value is the "subject" of the `switch` statement; it is compared to each of the cases in turn.

The `CaseSensitive` parameter applies when the subject is a string. The `Regex` and `Wildcard` parameters are explored later in this section.

Within a `switch` statement, the variables `$_` and `$PSItem` are set to the value of the subject:

```
[PSCustomObject]@{ Name = 'Bill' } | ForEach-Object {
    switch ($_.Name) {
        'Bill' { "Subject is $_" }
    }
}
```

This is an important consideration if `switch` is nested inside another command which uses `$_`, and if the original variable is needed inside switch, an additional variable assignment might be required.

Each case in a `switch` statement is evaluated in turn and, by default, all matching cases will execute.

switch statement cases

A `switch` statement is typically made up of one or more explicit cases which can be followed by an optional default case.

The default case will only be executed if no other case matches as shown here:

```
$value = 2
switch ($value) {
    1       { Write-Host 'value is 1' }
    default { Write-Host 'No conditions matched' }
}
```

Cases are often explicit values as used in the example above. Where the case is a string, quotes are not required unless the case value contains a space:

```
$value = 'One'
switch ($value) {
    One { Write-Host 'value is One' }
}
```

Variables may also be used as a case:

```
$value  = 2
$caseA = 1
$caseB = 2
switch ($value) {
    $caseA { Write-Host "value is $caseA" }
    $caseB { Write-Host "value is $caseB" }
}
```

Unquoted cases are permitted as they are evaluated as if they were double-quoted strings. Variables within unquoted string values will therefore also expand:

```
$caseA = ' world'
switch ('Hello world') {
    Hello$caseA { $true }
}
```

A more complex comparison might make use of an enum to express the case.

enum cases

An enum, or enumeration, is a list of constant values where each value is given a name.

The `DayOfWeek` enumeration, as the name suggests, describes the names of each day in the week and gives each day a numeric value. This enumeration is used with the `DateTime` type. An instance of `DateTime` is returned by the `Get-Date` command.

A single value in the enumeration can be accessed as follows:

```
[DayOfWeek]::Monday
```

If a `switch` statement uses an enumeration value as a case, it is tempting to write the case as shown below:

```
switch ((Get-Date).DayOfWeek) {
    [DayOfWeek]::Monday    { 'Monday' }
    [DayOfWeek]::Tuesday   { 'Tuesday' }
    [DayOfWeek]::Wednesday { 'Wednesday' }
    [DayOfWeek]::Thursday  { 'Thursday' }
    [DayOfWeek]::Friday    { 'Friday' }
    [DayOfWeek]::Saturday  { 'Saturday' }
    [DayOfWeek]::Sunday    { 'Sunday' }
    default { 'It is not a week day at all' }
}
```

However, this will not act as might be expected because the case is parsed as a double-quoted string. Using `Monday` as an example, the first case will only match if the subject is the same string (not the enumeration value):

```
switch ('[DayOfWeek]::Monday') {
    [DayOfWeek]::Monday { 'This case matched' }
}
```

Where the value is an enumeration, there are two possible solutions. The name of the enumeration value can be used, with the first two days shown below:

```
switch ((Get-Date).DayOfWeek) {
    'Monday'  { 'Monday' }
    'Tuesday' { 'Tuesday' }
}
```

Or each case can be enclosed in parentheses; the first two days are shown below:

```
switch ((Get-Date).DayOfWeek) {
    ([DayOfWeek]::Monday)  { 'Monday' }
    ([DayOfWeek]::Tuesday) { 'Tuesday' }
}
```

The same applies if the case is a static property. Static properties are accessed using the same notation as was used with the enumeration. For example, the `DateTime` type has a `Today` static property. In this case, the only option is to use parentheses around the case:

```
switch ((Get-Date).Date) {
    ([DateTime]::Today) { 'It is still today' }
}
```

Irrespective of how it is written, the comparison still treats the subject and case as a string. This is important if the subject is of a different type and an explicit conversion is expected.

switch case comparisons

For example, in the `if` statements below, PowerShell will implicitly coerce the right-hand side of the comparison to match the left-hand side. That means that all the comparisons below will succeed:

```
$day = [DayOfWeek]::Monday
if ($day -eq [DayOfWeek]::Monday) { 'Success: No coercion' }
if ($day -eq 'Monday') { 'Success: String to enum' }
if ($day -eq 1) { 'Success: Int to enum value' }
```

The last case was successful because the numeric constant behind the Monday enum name is 1:

```
PS> [int][DayOfWeek]::Monday
1
```

Considering the above, it is reasonable to expect the same behavior from a `switch` statement. However, `switch` will not implicitly convert the case to the type of the subject; it instead converts both subject and case to a string.

```
$day = [DayOfWeek]::Monday
switch ($day) {
    ([DayOfWeek]::Monday) { 'Success: Explicit enum name' }
    'Monday'              { 'Success: String' }
    1                     { 'Int to enum value' }
}
```

When this runs, the first two cases will match but the third will not.

The limitation of `switch` for more complex case expressions can be overcome by using a script block case.

Script block cases

The `switch` statement allows a script block to be used in place of simpler direct comparisons. As mentioned at the start of this section, inside the script block, the variable `$_` or `$PSItem` is set to the value of the subject. This variable may be used in any script block expressions.

The script block is executed, and the result determines whether the case is matched. For example:

```
switch (Get-Date) {
    { $_ -is [DateTime] } { Write-Host 'This is a DateTime type' }
    { $_.Year -ge 2020 }  { Write-Host 'It is 2020 or later' }
}
```

Script block cases like those used above may be mixed with other values. The following example uses a single `ScriptBlock` expression as well as a comparison with 5:

```
$Value = 5
switch ($Value) {
    { $_ -is [int] } { Write-Host 'This is an Int32 type' }
    5                { Write-Host 'The value is five' }
}
```

Expressions like the example above might replace a more complex if-elseif statement or may be used to perform more complex comparison combinations.

For example, shared code might be established to use with more than one case:

```
function Set-FileState {
    param (
        [Parameter(Mandatory)]
        [ValidateSet('Update', 'Create', 'Delete')]
        [string]$Action
    )
    $params = @{
        Path = '~\test.txt'
    }
    switch ($Action) {
        { $_ -in 'Update', 'Create' } {
            $params['Value'] = 'File content'
        }
        'Update' { Set-Content @params }
```

```
        'Create' { New-Item @params -ItemType File }
        'Delete' { Remove-Item @params }
    }
}
Set-FileState -Action Update
```

Inside a `switch` statement, `$_` is the value that is being tested. It is possible to re-assign the value of `$_` in one case, allowing a second case (or any other cases) to be applied:

```
function Set-FileState {
    param (
        [Parameter(Mandatory)]
        [ValidateSet('Update', 'Create', 'Delete')]
        [string]$Action
    )
    $params = @{
        Path = '~\test.txt'
        ItemType = 'File'
        Value    = 'File content'
    }
    switch ($Action) {
        { $_ -in 'Delete', 'Update' } {
            if (Test-Path -Path $params.Path) {
                Remove-Item -Path $params.Path
            }
            if ($_ -eq 'Update') {
                $_ = 'Create'
            }
        }
        'Create' {
            New-Item @params
        }
    }
}
Set-FileState -Action Update
```

The use of the pipeline variable, `$_` or `$PSItem`, to refer to the subject is important when switch is acting on an array of values.

switch statements and arrays

The `switch` statement can be used on both scalar (single) values and arrays of values. If the value is an array, then each case will be tested against each element of the array:

```
$arrayOfValues = 1..3
switch ($arrayOfValues) {
    1 { 'One' }
    2 { 'Two' }
    3 { 'Three' }
}
```

The pipeline variable can be used to refer to the current value of the subject in the statement:

```
$arrayOfValues = 1..3
switch ($arrayOfValues) {
    1 { "One: $_" }
    2 { "Two: $_" }
    3 { "Three: $_" }
}
```

The `switch` statement executes once for each item in an array of items. The statement does not execute at all if given an empty array (such as `@()`). In the following example, an empty array is the value. As `switch` has no values to compare, it does not execute any cases:

```
switch (@()) {
    default { 'this default case will not run' }
}
```

The `switch` statement will be executed if an explicit `$null` value is used. For example:

```
switch ($null) {
    default { 'this default case will run' }
}
```

The ability to act on an array allows `switch` to act on file content.

switch statements and files

The `switch` statement can be used to work on the content of a file using the following notation:

```
switch [-Regex | -Wildcard] [-CaseSensitive] -File <Name> {
    <condition> { <statements> }
    <condition> { <statements> }
}
```

The `File` parameter can be used to select from a text file (line by line); the content of the file is read as an array.

Wildcard and Regex parameters

The `Wildcard` and `Regex` parameters are used when matching strings.

The `Wildcard` parameter allows the use of the characters "?" (any single character) and "*" (any string of zero or more characters) in a condition, and ranges defined in square brackets. For example:

```
switch -Wildcard ('cat') {
    'c*'          { Write-Host 'The word begins with c' }
    '???'         { Write-Host 'The word is 3 characters long' }
    '*t'          { Write-Host 'The word ends with t' }
    '*[aeiou]*'   { Write-Host 'The word contains a vowel' }
}
```

In the example above, the wildcards used will cause each of the four cases to display as shown below:

```
The word begins with c
The word is 3 characters long
The word ends with t
The word contains a vowel
```

The `Regex` parameter allows for the use of regular expressions to match patterns. For example:

```
switch -Regex ('cat') {
 '^c'      { Write-Host 'The word begins with c' }
  '^.{3}$' { Write-Host 'The word is 3 characters long' }
  't$'     { Write-Host 'The word ends with t' }
}
```

When the example above runs, all three of the cases match. The output is shown below:

```
The word begins with c
The word is 3 characters long
The word ends with t
```

The `switch` statement also allows the cases to be defined as a script block.

The `switch` statement will run every case that matches the value in turn until the last is reached. The `break` and `continue` keywords may be used to affect how a `switch` statement ends.

switch, break, and continue

By default, `switch` executes every case where the case evaluates as true when compared with the value.

The `break` and `continue` keywords may be used within the `switch` statement to control when testing should stop:

- When `break` is used in a case, the `switch` statement ends.
- When `continue` is used and the value is a scalar, the switch statement ends.
- When `continue` is used and the value is an array, it moves to the next element.

`break` is often most appropriate if the value is a scalar, and `continue` when the value is an array. However, either may be used as needed.

The `switch` statement will not stop testing conditions unless the `break` keyword is used. In the example below, all conditions are tested:

```
$value = 1
switch ($value) {
    1 { Write-Host 'value is 1' }
    1 { Write-Host 'value is still 1' }
}
```

The example above will show the following output:

```
value is 1
value is still 1
```

In the following example, where switch is acting on an array, both statements will execute:

```
switch (1, 2) {
    1 { Write-Host 'Equals 1' }
    2 { Write-Host 'Equals 2' }
}
```

In the example above, both statements will be displayed as shown here:

```
Equals 1
Equals 2
```

If the `break` keyword is included, as shown here, only the first executes and then the `switch` statement stops:

```
switch (1, 2) {
    1 { Write-Host 'Equals 1'; break }
    2 { Write-Host 'Equals 2' }
}
```

The output from the example above is shown below:

```
Equals 1
```

The first example in this section has two cases that match the value 1. If `continue` is used, the second matching statement is skipped, and `switch` continues to the next element in the array:

```
switch (1, 2) {
    1 { Write-Host 'Equals 1'; continue }
    1 { Write-Host 'value is still 1' }
    2 { Write-Host 'Equals 2' }
}
```

The second condition in the example above is skipped; the result is shown below:

```
Equals 1
Equals 2
```

Finally, `break` and `continue` can be mixed if necessary. In the following example, the condition for the value 3 will never be reached if the array contains the value 2:

```
switch (1, 2, 3) {
    1 { Write-Host 'One'; continue }
    1 { Write-Host 'One again' }
    2 { Write-Host 'Two'; break }
    3 { Write-Host 'Three' }
}
```

The output from the example above is shown below:

```
One
Two
```

The `switch` statement is incredibly flexible and allows relatively complex condition structures to be described in a concise manner.

PowerShell has several other loop keywords that may be used to repeat statements.

Loops

Loops may be used to iterate through collections, perform an operation against each element in the collection, or repeat an operation (or series of operations) until a condition is met.

The following loops will be demonstrated in this section:

- `foreach`
- `for`
- `do`
- `while`

Keyword loops like those above are the fastest means of iterating over a collection of items. Conversely, commands like `ForEach-Object` are typically a lot slower, in part because they are commands, and in part because of the flexibility they provide.

A pipeline might be more beneficial than a keyword loop where a trade-off between speed and memory use is required, or where it forms part of a more extensive pipeline.

The `ForEach-Object` command also offers the `Parallel` parameter which should be considered in some cases.

The `foreach` loop is perhaps the most common of these loops.

foreach loop

The `foreach` loop executes against each element of a collection using the following notation:

```
foreach (<element> in <collection>) {
    <statements>
}
```

For example, the foreach loop may be used to iterate through each of the processes returned by `Get-Process`:

```
foreach ($process in Get-Process) {
    Write-Host $process.Name
}
```

If the collection is empty, the body of the loop will not execute.

foreach keyword and foreach alias

PowerShell comes with the alias `foreach` for the `ForEach-Object` command. How this alias acts depends on context.

If `foreach` is first in a statement, then the loop keyword is used:

```
$array = 1..3
foreach ($value in $array) {
    'Will repeat three times!'
}
```

If `foreach` is placed after a pipe, the alias is used instead of the keyword; that is, the `ForEach-Object` command is used:

```
$array = 1..3
$array | foreach {
    'Will repeat three times!'
}
```

Because this can cause confusion, it is rarely a good idea to use the `foreach` alias.

for loop

The `for` loop is typically used to step through a collection using the following notation:

```
for (<initial>; <condition>; <repeat>) {
    <body-statements>
}
```

Each of the three blocks can include arbitrary code and each of the three is optional, which makes the `for` loop one of the most complex available.

`<initial>` runs before the loop starts and is normally used to set the initial state; this normally consists of variables used within the loop, typically a counter of some kind.

The loop continues to run if `<condition>` evaluates to true.

The `<repeat>` block is executed after each iteration of the loop. This is most often used to increment a value set in the initial block.

Much like the `foreach` loop, the `for` loop can be used to loop over the content of a variable:

```
$processes = Get-Process
for ($i = 0; $i -lt $processes.Count; $i++) {
    Write-Host $processes[$i].Name
}
```

The `for` loop provides a significant degree of control over the loop. It is useful where the increment, or the actions inside the loop, need to be completed in an order other than a simple ascending order. The examples that follow show some of the possible ways in which the `for` loop can be used.

For example, the `<repeat>` expression can increment the counter by three so that the body executes for every third element:

```
for ($i = 0; $i -lt $processes.Count; $i += 3) {
    Write-Host $processes[$i].Name
}
```

Or the <initial> parameter can be set to start at the end and work toward the beginning of an array:

```
for ($i = $processes.Count - 1; $i -ge 0; $i--) {
    Write-Host $processes[$i].Name
}
```

As the body of the loop in the preceding example has access to the index, it can easily access elements adjacent or relative to the current element. The following example reads two characters at a time from `$encodedString`:

```
$encodedString = '68656C6C6F20776F726C64'
[char[]]$characters = for ($i = 0; $i -lt $encodedString.Length; $i += 2) {
    $hex = '0x{0}{1}' -f @(
        $encodedString[$i]
        $encodedString[$i + 1]
    )
    +$hex
}
[string]::new($characters)
```

The example above will show the decoded string content. The output from this loop is shown below:

```
hello world
```

Running the preceding example will allow PowerShell to convert each pair of characters into a hexadecimal number based on `$i` incrementing two at a time. The result is a single string.

This technique can be used to parse any string containing hexadecimal character pairs (nibbles). The loop acts to convert each pair of nibbles into an integer value between 0 and 255. Common cases might include some certificate formats or other values commonly written as strings such as RGB colors.

Each element in the `for` loop is optional; the following loop only ends because the body contains break:

```
for (;;) {
    break
}
```

Any of the three elements, `initial`, `condition`, and `repeat`, may be included individually or in any combination to describe how the loop should act.

The `for` loop can also act on more than one variable at a time, although it is incredibly rare to find this used in practice.

In the following example, two variables are given an initial state, and two variables are incremented after each iteration of the loop:

```
for (($i = 0), ($j = 0); $i -le 10 ; $i++, ($j += 2)) {
    Write-Host "$i :: $j"
}
```

The preceding condition only tests the state of one variable in the preceding example, but a more complex expression might have been used, for example:

```
$i -le 10 -and $j -le 20
```

The preceding example works because the different elements of the `for` loop, initial, condition, and repeat, are arbitrary blocks of code.

`do` and `while` loops are more commonly used than the `for` loop.

do-until and do-while loops

`do-until` and `do-while` each execute the body of the loop at least once. The condition to see if the loop should continue is at the end of the statement. Loops based on `do-until` will exit when the condition evaluates as true; loops based on `do-while` will exit when the condition evaluates as false.

`do` loops are written using the following notation:

```
do {
    <body-statements>
} <until | while> (<condition>)
```

A `do-until` loop is suited to exit conditions that are expected to be positive. Using until avoids the need to test for a false value in the condition. For example, a script might wait for a computer to respond to a ping:

```
do {
    Write-Host "Waiting for boot"
```

```
    Start-Sleep -Seconds 5
} until (Test-Connection 'SomeComputer' -Quiet -Count 1)
```

A do-until loop can also be a good choice when validating user input via the Read-Host command:

```
do {
    $yesOrNo = Read-Host 'Continue?'
} until ($yesOrNo -in 'y', 'n')

if ($yesOrNo -eq 'n') {
    return
}
Write-Host "Continuing"
```

The do-while loop is more suitable for exit conditions that are negative. For example, a loop might wait for a remote computer to stop responding to WSMan:

```
do {
    Write-Host "Waiting for shutdown"
    Start-Sleep -Seconds 5
} while (Test-WSMan -ComputerName 'SomeComputer')
```

Or a do-while loop might be used to work on paged responses from a web service. The example below will not run as the URI is not valid, but the pattern used is common:

```
$uri = 'https://somewebservice'
do {
    $response = Invoke-WebRequest -Uri $uri
    $response.Value
    $uri = $response.Next
} while ($uri)
```

As noted above, the do loop will execute at least once before testing the condition at the end. The while loop, on the other hand, places the condition first.

while loop

As the condition for a while loop comes first, the body of the loop will only execute if the condition evaluates to true:

```
while (<condition>) {
    <body-statements>
}
```

A while loop may be used to wait for something to happen. In the following example, the loop continues until a file exists:

```
while (-not (Test-Path $env:TEMP\test.txt -PathType Leaf)) {
    Start-Sleep -Seconds 10
}
```

A `while` loop is a good choice for operations like generating usernames:

```
$baseUsername = $username = 'chris'
$i = 1
while (Get-ADUser -Filter "SamAccountName -eq '$username'") {
    $username = '{0}{1:D2}' -f $baseUsername, $i
    $i++
}
```

The first time the loop runs, it tests the original value of `$username`. Then, each iteration of the loop changes a number at the end. The following values are tested:

- `chris`
- `chris01`
- `chris02`
- `chris03`

And so on, until a name that does not exist in Active Directory (in this case) is found.

It is often desirable to stop a loop earlier than a condition at the start or end of the loop might allow, or to stop a loop that does not have an explicit exit condition, such as `foreach`. Loops can make use of the `break` and `continue` keywords to achieve this.

Loops, break, and continue

The `break` and `continue` keywords can be used to control flow within a loop, typically to exit earlier than a condition at the start or end of the loop would normally permit.

In the example below, a set of random numbers is created, then the foreach loop is used to find the first instance of any number greater than 10:

```
$randomNumbers = Get-Random -Count 30 -Minimum 1 -Maximum 30
foreach ($number in $randomNumbers) {
    if ($number -gt 10) {
        break
    }
}
$number
```

The loop in the following example would continue until the value of `$i` is 20. `break` is used to stop the loop when `$i` reaches 10:

```
for ($i = 0; $i -lt 20; $i += 2) {
    Write-Host $i
    if ($i -eq 10) {
        break    # Stop this loop
    }
}
```

The `break` keyword acts on the loop it is nested inside. In the following example, the `inner while` loop breaks early when the variable `$i` is less than or equal to 2 and the variable `$k` is greater than or equal to 3:

```
$i = 1 # Initial state for i
do {
    Write-Host "i: $i"
    $k = 1 # Reset k
    while ($k -lt 5) {
        Write-Host "    k: $k"
        $k++ # Increment k
        if ($i -le 2 -and $k -ge 3) {
            break
        }
```

```
    }
    $i++ # Increment i
} while ($i -le 3)
```

The output from the loop in the example above is shown below:

```
i: 1
  k: 1
  k: 2
i: 2
  k: 1
  k: 2
i: 3
  k: 1
  k: 2
  k: 3
  k: 4
```

The `continue` keyword may be used to move on to the next iteration of a loop immediately. For example, the following loop executes a subset of the loop body when the value of the `$i` variable is less than 2:

```
for ($i = 0; $i -le 5; $i++) {
    Write-Host $i
    if ($i -lt 2) {
        continue    # Continue to the next iteration
    }
    Write-Host "Remainder when $i is divided by 2 is $($i % 2)"
}
```

The output from the example above is shown below:

```
0
1
2
Remainder when 2 is divided by 2 is 0
3
Remainder when 3 is divided by 2 is 1
4
Remainder when 4 is divided by 2 is 0
```

```
5
Remainder when 5 is divided by 2 is 1
```

The `break` and `continue` keywords are meant to be used inside loops (or within the `switch` statement).

break and continue outside loops

If `break` is used outside a loop, switch statement, or trap statement, PowerShell will look up the call stack until it finds an enclosing construct to stop or runs out of calls to search.

In the following example, `break` **is erroneously** used to end a function early:

```
function Test-Value {
    [CmdletBinding()]
    param (
        [int]$Value
    )
    if ($Value -eq 7) {
        break
    }
    $true
}
```

A casual test may suggest that break is only stopping the function, and everything is working as it should. However, if the function is used within a loop, `break` will affect that loop. This happens no matter how many function calls there are between the loop below and the function:

```
foreach ($value in 1..10) {
    Write-Verbose "Working on $value" -Verbose
    if ($value -gt 5) {
        if (Test-Value $value) {
            Write-Host "$value is OK"
        }
    }
}
```

The script should repeat the `Write-Host` statement for 6, 8, 9, and 10. However, because `break` is used in the function, the foreach loop stops as soon as it reaches 7.

The `continue` keyword has the same problem, although it will `continue` to the next iteration of the enclosing loop instead of terminating the loop.

`break` and `continue` in loops can make use of labels to identify a specific loop.

Loops and labels

In PowerShell, a loop can be given a label. The label may be used with `break` and `continue` to define a specific loop to act on.

The label is written before the loop keyword (`for`, `while`, `do`, or `foreach`) and is preceded by a colon character. For example:

```
:ThisIsALabel foreach ($value in 1..10) {
    $value
}
```

The label may be placed directly before the loop keyword or on the line above. For example:

```
:ThisIsALabel
foreach ($value in 1..10) {
    $value
}
```

The example above will work when saved as a script, but if it is pasted into the console, the label will be split from the loop. Pressing *Shift+Enter* between the label and loop is required when typing the example into the console.

White space may appear between the label and the loop keyword.

The label is used with `break` or `continue` and can be useful when one loop is nested inside another. The label name is written after the `break` or `continue` keyword without the colon:

```
:outerLoop for ($i = 1; $i -le 5; $i++) {
    :innerLoop foreach ($value in 1..5) {
        Write-Host "$i :: $value"
        if ($value -eq $i) {
            continue outerLoop
        }
    }
}
```

The `break` statement may be used in a similar manner to end a labeled loop.

Loops, especially `do` or `while`, can be combined with queues (a First In, First Out collection) or stacks (a First In, Last Out collection) to perform operations that behave like recursion.

Loops, queues, and stacks

The file system is an example of a tree-like structure that can be traversed by making use of a loop and a queue or stack.

Consider the following directory tree:

```
Project
  | - A
  |   | - B
  |       | - C
  |       | - Large
  |           | - Tree
  | - D
      | - Large
          | - Tree
```

The `Get-ChildItem -Recurse` command may be used to find items in this path and all child paths.

However, if there was a requirement to avoid looking inside folders named `Large`, then the `Recurse` parameter is not particularly efficient. Any filtering would have to happen after the command had run, and the command would still visit those directories.

The snippet below may be used to create this directory tree, allowing the loop below to be tested. The folders are created in the current working directory:

```
New-Item Project\A\B\C -ItemType Directory
New-Item Project\A\B\Large\Tree -ItemType Directory
New-Item Project\D\Large\Tree -ItemType Directory
```

To achieve this, the functionality provided by the `Recurse` parameter of `Get-ChildItem` must be replaced.

It is possible to write recursive functions in PowerShell; that is, functions that call themselves repeatedly.

Using a loop with a queue or stack is generally more efficient than implementing a recursive function. The loop is required to visit directories. The loop will continue if there are items to visit.

Both `Stack` and `Queue` can be used for this. The choice affects the order of items in the output from this code. This first variant uses `Queue`. The queue is created before the loop starts, and the Project directory, the starting point, is enqueued:

```
$path = Get-Item Project
$queue = [System.Collections.Generic.Queue[object]]$path
```

A loop is created to process items in the queue. The loop will end when there are no more items to process. The `Count` property can be used to see if the queue is empty, and a `while` loop can be used to check the state before the iteration starts.

Each time the loop finds a child directory, the child directory gets added to the queue.

The version below does not have assignable output and just shows how items are added and removed from the queue. This version does not avoid the `Large` folder:

```
$path = Get-Item Project
$queue = [System.Collections.Generic.Queue[object]]$path
while ($queue.Count) {
    $current = $queue.Dequeue()
    Write-Host "Taking $current from the queue"
    foreach ($child in Get-ChildItem -Path $current -Directory) {
        Write-Host "Adding $child to the queue"
        $queue.Enqueue($child)
    }
}
```

To make this loop have output, the value of `$current` may be emitted. The loop is assigned to a variable to capture that output:

```
$path = Get-Item Project
$queue = [System.Collections.Generic.Queue[object]]$path
$output = while ($queue.Count) {
    $current = $queue.Dequeue()
    $current
    foreach ($child in Get-ChildItem -Path $current -Directory) {
        $queue.Enqueue($child)
    }
```

```
}
$output.Name
```

The example above will show each of the directories it visits. The names of those are shown below:

```
Project
A
D
B
Large
C
Large
Tree
Tree
```

To make this ignore the content of the `Large` folder, an if statement is needed within the `foreach` loop:

```
$path = Get-Item Project
$queue = [System.Collections.Generic.Queue[object]]$path
$output = while ($queue.Count) {
    $current = $queue.Dequeue()
    $current
    foreach ($child in Get-ChildItem -Path $current -Directory) {
        if ($current.Name -eq 'Large') {
            continue
        }
        $queue.Enqueue($child)
    }
}
$output.Name
```

With the change in the example above, the folders nested under each Large folder are no longer included in the output, as shown below:

```
Project
A
D
B
Large
```

```
C
Large
```

Using a `Stack` instead of a `Queue` is a very small change:

```
$path = Get-Item Project
$stack = [System.Collections.Generic.Stack[object]]$path
$output = while ($stack.Count) {
    $current = $stack.Pop()
    $current
    foreach ($child in Get-ChildItem -Path $current -Directory) {
        if ($current.Name -eq 'Large') {
            continue
        }
        $stack.Push($child)
    }
}
$output.Name
```

The only effective difference is the order in which folders in the tree are visited. The output from the example above is shown below:

```
Project
D
Large
A
B
Large
C
```

The loop demonstrated here may be enhanced to allow it to return files in the folder, or it may make use of faster methods to enumerate folder content than `Get-ChildItem`. It might allow control of search depth, and so on.

Summary

This chapter explored the different conditional and looping statements available in PowerShell.

The `if` statement allows statements to be run when a condition is met and may be extended to test several conditions with elseif.

The `switch` statement has similarities with if: both compare one value against another. However, `switch` can test many individual cases expressed in a concise manner, allows more than one case to apply to a value, and can operate on an array.

Looping is a vital part of any programming language and PowerShell is no exception. The `foreach` loop is perhaps the most used, allowing repeated code to be enclosed and executed against several objects. The `foreach` loop keyword can often be replaced with the `ForEach-Object` command (or vice versa) depending on circumstances, but the two should not be confused.

The `for` loop is more complex but offers a great deal of flexibility for any operation based on a numeric sequence. The while and do loops can be used to carry on working until a condition is met, for example, until a timeout occurs or an item is created.

PowerShell is a deep and complex language. This introductory book has just started to scratch the surface.

Mastering PowerShell Scripting continues the exploration, diving into more complex topics.

PowerShell is supported by a fantastic, friendly community, willing to help and chat regardless of experience level. User groups exist in many parts of the world, and the virtual PowerShell user group is always available: `https://poshcode.org/`.

7

Unlock Your Exclusive Benefits

Your copy of this book includes the following exclusive benefits:

DRM-Free PDF Version

Download DRM-free PDF and ePub copies of this book.

7-Day Packt Library Access

Get 7-day unlimited access to 8,000+ books and videos. No credit card required.

Available for first-time Packt+ trial users only.

Next-Gen Reader Access

Read this book on Packt Reader with progress sync, dark mode and note-taking.

Follow the guide below to unlock them. The process takes only a few minutes and needs to be completed once.

Unlock this Book's Free Benefits in 3 Easy Steps

Step 1

Keep your purchase invoice ready for *Step 3*. If you have a physical copy, scan it using your phone and save it as a PDF, JPG, or PNG.

For more help on finding your invoice, visit `https://www.packtpub.com/en-us/unlock?step=1`.

> **Note**
>
> **Note:** If you bought this book directly from Packt, no invoice is required. After *Step 2*, you can access your exclusive content right away.

Step 2

Scan the QR code or go to `packtpub.com/unlock`.

On the page that opens (similar to *Figure 7.1* on desktop), search for this book by name and select the correct edition.

Figure 7.1: Packt unlock landing page on desktop

Step 3

After selecting your book, sign in to your Packt account or create one for free. Then upload your invoice (PDF, PNG, or JPG, up to 10 MB). Follow the on-screen instructions to finish the process.

Need Help

If you get stuck and need help, visit `https://www.packtpub.com/unlock-benefits/help` for a detailed FAQ on how to find your invoices and more. This QR code will take you to the help page.

> Note
>
> **Note**: If you are still facing issues, reach out to `customercare@packt.com`.

Other Books You May Enjoy

If you enjoyed this book, you may be interested in these other books by Packt:

Mastering Windows Server 2025, Fifth Edition

Jordan Krause

ISBN: 978-1-83702-991-4

- Create an entire lab of new servers and configure multiple roles
- Manage servers using Server Manager, PowerShell, and Windows Admin Center
- Close knowledge gaps in core infrastructure technologies such as Active Directory, DNS, DHCP, and Group Policy
- Virtualize your datacenter with Hyper-V
- Create redundancy through Failover Clustering services
- Deploy Remote Desktop Services
- Design and implement Distributed File System with Replication (DFSR) and Storage Replica
- Don the DevOps cap as you explore containers and Nano Server

Mastering PowerShell Scripting, Fifth Edition

Chris Dent

ISBN: 978-1-80512-027-8

- Create scripts that run across systems for automation
- Extend PowerShell by integrating it with other languages
- Use PowerShell's command-line interface for efficient operations
- Develop reusable scripts and functions to streamline tasks
- Apply PowerShell for administration, automation, and data processing
- Integrate with .NET, COM, and WMI for advanced functionality
- Work with XML, JSON, and CSV for structured data handling
- Build custom modules and cmdlets to enhance scripting

Packt is searching for authors like you

If you're interested in becoming an author for Packt, please visit `authors.packtpub.com` and apply today. We have worked with thousands of developers and tech professionals, just like you, to help them share their insight with the global tech community. You can make a general application, apply for a specific hot topic that we are recruiting an author for, or submit your own idea.

Share your thoughts

Now you've finished *PowerShell Fundamentals,* we'd love to hear your thoughts! Scan the QR code below to go straight to the Amazon review page for this book and share your feedback or leave a review on the site that you purchased it from.

`https://packt.link/r/1808761391`

Your review is important to us and the tech community and will help us make sure we're delivering excellent quality content.

Index

W

X

Made in the USA
Monee, IL
05 November 2026

67845289R00175